Current
Directions
in
GENDER
PSYCHOLOGY

READINGS FROM THE ASSOCIATION FOR PSYCHOLOGICAL SCIENCE

Current Directions in

GENDER PSYCHOLOGY

EDITED BY

Wendy A. Goldberg

University of California, Irvine

Allyn & Bacon

Boston • New York • San Francisco

Mexico City • Montreal • Toronto • London • Madrid • Munich • Paris

Hong Kong • Singapore • Tokyo • Cape Town • Sydney

Acquisitions Editor: Michelle Limoges
Series Editorial Assistant: Lisa Dotson
Marketing Manager: Kate Mitchell
Production Supervisor: Patty Bergin
Editorial Production Service: TexTech International
Manufacturing Buyer: JoAnne Sweeney
Electronic Composition: TexTech International
Cover Designer: Kristina Mose-Libon

Library of Congress Cataloging-in-Publication Data

Current directions in gender psychology / edited by Wendy A. Goldberg.
     p. cm.
Includes bibliographical references.
  ISBN-13: 978-0-205-68012-2
  ISBN-10: 0-205-68012-7
 1. Sex differences (Psychology) 2. Sex differences. 3. Sex factors in disease.
4. Mental illness—Sex factors. I. Goldberg, Wendy A.
  BF692.2.C87 2010
  155.3—dc22

2009016958

10 9 8 7 6 5 4 3 2 1   13 12 11 10 09

Allyn & Bacon
is an imprint of

ISBN-10: 0-205-68012-7
www.pearsonhighered.com ISBN-13: 978-0-205-68012-2

Contents

Current Directions in GENDER PSYCHOLOGY

Introduction

In 1974, Eleanor Maccoby and Carol Nagy Jacklin published the seminal volume, *The Psychology of Sex Differences*. There was more than enough research conducted by that time in domains such as intelligence, achievement, aggression, prosocial behavior, temperament, socialization to fill more than 600 pages! The interest in gender has hardly waned in the decades since then. Indeed, new directions have been forged as advances have taken place in fields such as neuroscience. New, too, are some of the theories for understanding the origins of gender differences and similarities, the methodologies for examining human psychology and physiology, the techniques for analyzing data and summarizing findings across studies, and the sophistication of the conceptualization of gender vis-à-vis other factors. A noteworthy change since the 1970s has been in terminology. "Gender" rather than "sex" is the preferred term in most contemporary psychological research. Sex is often reserved for biological origins and applications, and gender is used more expansively to represent social and cultural influences on males and females.

This collection of articles from *Current Directions* brings the reader up to date on research and theory concerning gender. The first section addresses gender and health. A fascinating paradox is that women have higher rates of illness but men have higher death rates at every age period in the life span. Three of the articles in the health section focus on the role of stressors and stress responses to explain the gender gap in mortality and morbidity. The fourth article in this section takes an existential approach to men's and women's concerns about their physical bodies and eventual mortality.

Whereas the first section deals with gender and physical health, the second section shifts the focus to psychological health and well-being. Here again we encounter a large gender difference, this time in rates of depression. The first article in this section makes it clear that biopsychosocial factors need to be considered to understand this gender gap. Two of the other articles address topics that are important to well-being (relational victimization and self-esteem) and that might also impinge on which sex is most vulnerable to depression. Also included in this section is research that examines children's well-being in relation to whether their parents are gay or lesbian. The final article in this section takes a life course event, retirement, and looks at its consequences for men's and women's marital quality and well-being.

The themes in the third section concern gender and cognitive functioning at different points in the life span. All of the articles show that differential experiences with the genders as well as biological factors affect what information is processed and how it is processed. In the second article, theories are discussed to explain how gendered cognitions influence children's behavior. In the fourth article, a hypothesis is advanced to explain contradictory findings about the protective role of certain hormones for women's cognitive functioning later in life.

Evolutionary theory concerns the survival of our species and often draws upon findings from other species in the application of the principles of evolution to the study of human cognition, emotion, and behavior. Different evolutionary pressures on the mating and sexual behaviors of males and females are thought by some, but not all, psychologists to be responsible for some gendered roles and behaviors. Evidence for gender differences in mating behaviors and sexuality and the explanations for those differences are the major themes of section four.

The final section encompasses contextual influences on gender. The first two empirical articles concern, respectively, social/cultural influences on peer exclusion based on gender and race and differences in language processing based on the gender of the speaker and listener. The last two articles in section six tackle the complex questions of not only how best to study gender but also how to frame the essential question about gender. The conclusions reached by these authors should help guide further theory development and research about gender.

Section 1: Physical Health

In industrialized nations, women outlive men by an average of 5-10 years. However, women report more health symptoms and spend more days in bed. What makes gender such a good predictor of health status and accounts for the large gender differences in mortality and morbidity? To answer this question, Kajantie focuses on the role of estrogen and the functioning of the hypothalamic-pituitary-adrenal axis to understand gender differences in physiological responses to acute stress. The review of animal and human studies points to the effects of estrogen on stress responsiveness, starting as early as pregnancy, as a mediator of gender differences in morbidity and mortality.

Coronary artery disease (CAD) is the leading cause of death, disease, and economic loss in industrialized countries. Although cardiovascular disease is the leading cause of death for both men and women, marked gender differences exist in rates of CAD. Stoney explains the gender differences in terms of risk factors, clinical symptoms and diagnosis, and treatment and outcome. Attention is given to factors that bridge psychological and physiological domains in the explication of persistent gender differences in risk factors, diagnosis, and treatment.

Daily stressors, sometimes called daily hassles, include regularly occurring events such as family arguments, commuter traffic jams, and work deadlines. Although minor compared to job loss or death of a loved one, these disruptions in daily living can take a toll on individual health and well-being. Almeida makes a case for how improvements in daily diary methods have deepened our understanding of intra-individual fluctuations in stress. National data are presented that reveal gender differences in the content of the stressors, the subjective assessment of the severity of the stressors, and the domain of life potentially disrupted by the stressor. Almeida discusses the implications of these stress-related gender differences for gender difference in psychological distress and physiological well-being.

Why do cultures have so many prescriptions and constraints over the human body? Goldenberg takes the position that existential concerns about mortality and discomfort with the body underlie the drive to conform to cultural standards for bodily appearance, even to the point of causing themselves harm and denying themselves pleasure. Goldenberg also applies this existential approach to explain gender differences in views of sex, sexuality and physical appearance.

Physiological Stress Response, Estrogen, and the Male–Female Mortality Gap

Eero Kajantie[1]

*The National Public Health Institute, Helsinki, Finland,
and Hospital for Children and Adolescents, Helsinki University
Central Hospital, Helsinki, Finland*

Abstract

Whether one is male or female is one of the most important predictors of how long one is likely to live and what diseases one is likely to encounter. Researchers have long been puzzled by the mechanisms that could underlie such profound sex differences. Recent findings suggest a key role is played by physiological stress responses—how men and women respond differently to psychosocial stressors in everyday life. This review focuses on two important physiological stress systems: the hypothalamic-pituitary-adrenal axis (which regulates the stress hormone cortisol) and the autonomic nervous system. The general pattern is that between puberty and menopause, the responses of these systems to experimental psychosocial stress are lower in females, and their changes with menopause, estrogen administration, and pregnancy have suggested that estrogen plays a key role in regulating stress responsiveness. This review presents a hypothesis that mechanisms that regulate these sex differences have been driven by evolutionary pressures to transform information about prevailing environmental conditions to the fetus, through maternal stress, to adjust its development to circumstances it will encounter in extrauterine life.

Keywords

sex; gender; estrogen; stress; cortisol

Whether you are male or female is one of the most important predictors of your health. Women outlive men by approximately 5 to 10 years in industrialized countries. Cardiovascular and many infectious diseases are more frequent in men than in women of the same age, whereas diseases more common in women include many, although not all, autoimmune disorders and many psychiatric and psychosomatic disorders such as depression, posttraumatic stress disorder, fibromyalgia, and chronic pain. Considerable effort has been devoted to understanding the mechanisms of these profound sex differences.

Physiological responses to stress are important determinants of health. A stressful stimulus results in the activation of several physiological pathways including the hypothalamic-pituitary-adrenal axis (HPAA, with its effector hormone cortisol, see Fig. 1) and the autonomic nervous system. Overactivity of either or both of these systems is implicated in the origins of several common disorders including depression, cognitive impairments, coronary heart disease, and type-2 diabetes. Reduced activity of the HPAA is an important feature of posttraumatic stress disorder, fibromyalgia, and chronic pain (reviewed in Kajantie & Phillips, 2006). Importantly, the HPAA and autonomic nervous system both show a clear sex-specific pattern of response to stress.

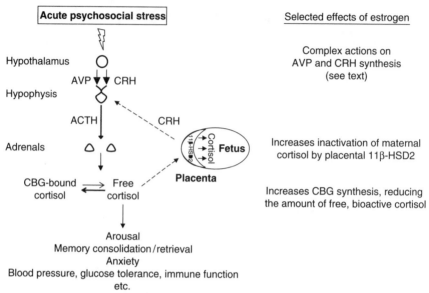

Fig. 1. Key components of the hypothalamic-pituitary-adrenal axis (HPAA) and selected actions of estrogen on the function of the axis during the nonpregnant and pregnant (dashed arrows) state. Stressors cause the hypothalamus to release arginine vasopressin (AVP) and corticotropin-releasing hormone (CRH), which stimulate the hypophysis (pituitary gland) to release adrenocorticotropin (ACTH). ACTH stimulates the adrenal glands to release cortisol, which has a wide array of effects that enable the organism to adapt to, or recover from, a stressful situation. The activity of cortisol is regulated by corticosteroid-binding globulin (CBG)—only unbound cortisol is biologically active. Cortisol also regulates its own secretion by inhibiting upper levels of the axis (not shown in the figure). During pregnancy, there are major changes: Most of the circulating CRH is produced by the placenta, a process stimulated by cortisol. This is accompanied by an increase in cortisol concentrations in a nonstressed state but a decrease in cortisol responses to stress. The fetus is protected from the high maternal cortisol concentrations by the placental enzyme 11β–hydroxysteroid dehydroxenase-2 (11β–HSD2), which converts cortisol to inactive cortisone. The considerable variation in the activity of this enzyme and the exposure of the fetus to cortisol is thought to convey to the fetus a message about prevailing environmental conditions, allowing optimal adaptation of its development. Selected effects of estrogen on multiple levels of the HPAA are listed on the right.

The aim of this review is to describe key patterns in how physiological response to acute psychosocial stress differs according to sex and hormonal status, with a focus on the role of estrogen. More technical details are available from other recent reviews (Kajantie & Phillips, 2006; Kudielka & Kirschbaum, 2005; Otte et al., 2005).

This review focuses on studies performed in a standardized setting in a psychophysiological laboratory. Other important tools in studying HPAA and autonomic nervous system function include physical stressors (exercise; changing posture; immersion of arm in cold water, or the "cold pressor test"; a single breath of 35% CO_2; or nutritional challenges such as high-protein meals) and biochemical challenges that, however, remain outside the scope of this review.

DIFFERENCES IN STRESS RESPONSIVENESS
ACCORDING TO SEX AND HORMONAL STATUS

In 1987, an editorial in the journal *Psychophysiology* (Stoney, Davis, & Matthews, 1987) highlighted the importance of sex differences in physiological stress responsiveness as a potential mechanism in explaining sex differences in rates of cardiovascular disease. At that time, however, evidence was scanty. Since then, increased interest in this possibility has produced methodological improvements, particularly psychological stress tests such as the Trier Social Stress Test (TSST) that are able to generate HPAA responses like those occurring in stressful situations in everyday life (reviewed in Dickerson & Kemeny, 2004). These improvements have greatly increased our understanding. In the TSST, the participant performs demanding speaking and arithmetic tasks in front of an impassive two- or three-member committee. Key elements creating HPAA response in this test include ego involvement, social-evaluative judgment by others, and uncontrollability of the situation. The test is considered to have high ecological validity—in other words, it resembles stressful conditions encountered in everyday life. Although some studies have suggested that women are more physiologically reactive to social-rejection challenges and men to achievement challenges (Stroud, Salovey, & Epel, 2002), the TSST is considered a valid tool in both sexes. Other commonly used tasks such as video games, mental arithmetic, driving simulations, line tracing, and so on are thought to produce a predominantly sympatho-adrenal stimulation rather than an HPAA response (Dickerson & Kemeny, 2004; Kajantie & Phillips, 2006; Kudielka & Kirschbaum, 2005).

There is now an extensive literature on sex differences in physiological stress responsiveness (Kajantie & Phillips, 2006; Kudielka & Kirschbaum, 2005). Although the details vary, the overall conclusion of these studies is that sex differences in the basal, unstressed state are subtle but become pronounced following a psychological stressor. The responses are lower in women, at least from puberty to menopause. These differences are clearly associated with hormonal status.

Menstrual Status and Oral Contraceptive Use

During the early menstrual cycle (calculated from the first day of menstruation), estrogen and progesterone concentrations are low. Around days 5 to 7 of the menstrual cycle, estrogen concentrations start to rise, peaking before ovulation and remaining at high levels thereafter during the luteal phase (the latter half of the menstrual cycle). Progesterone concentrations rise after ovulation and, together with estrogen, concentrations decrease abruptly before menstruation. The HPAA response to stress shows considerable variation across the menstrual cycle (reviewed in Kajantie & Phillips, 2006; Kudielka & Kirschbaum, 2005). Although few studies have assessed psychosocial stress responsiveness around ovulation, when estrogen concentrations are high and progesterone concentrations are low, the effects of estrogen in young adult women have been studied in the context of estrogen-containing oral contraceptives. These contraceptives are associated with lower salivary free cortisol responses to the TSST (Kirschbaum, Kudielka, Gaab, Schommer, & Hellhammer, 1999). Cortisol responses increase again in the luteal phase (Kirschbaum et al., 1999), which may be due to the combined effect of estrogen and progesterone. Data on the effects on menstrual phase on autonomic nervous system responsiveness are more sparse.

Pregnancy

Estrogen concentrations increase approximately 100-fold toward the end of pregnancy. This is accompanied by major changes in the physiology of the HPAA (reviewed in de Weerth & Buitelaar, 2005; see Fig. 1). Cortisol stimulates the synthesis of corticotropin-releasing hormone (CRH) by the placenta. CRH stimulates ACTH and, consequently, cortisol synthesis in the fetus and mother. This creates a positive feedback loop that ultimately leads to delivery. Pregnancy is also characterized by increased activity of the sympathetic nervous system and probably also reduced activity of the parasympathetic nervous system.

At least the second and third trimesters of pregnancy are associated with reduced stress responsiveness to psychological and physical stressors. This has been shown consistently in a large number of studies for blood pressure and sympathetic nervous system responses to a range of physical and psychological stressors (mostly achievement-related, such as mental arithmetic; de Weerth & Buitelaar, 2005; Kajantie & Phillips, 2006). Although less data are available regarding HPAA axis responsiveness, these also point to a reduced response toward the end of pregnancy (Kajantie & Phillips, 2006; Kammerer, Adams, von Castelberg, & Glover, 2002). Stress during pregnancy is associated with a shorter duration of gestation, which has been suggested to be mediated through increased HPAA activity (Talge, Neal, & Glover, 2007). A buffering effect of late pregnancy is illustrated by an intriguing observation during the Northridge, California 1994 earthquake: Women exposed to the earthquake in first trimester gave birth on average at 38.1 weeks of gestation, compared with 39.0 weeks for those exposed during the third trimester (Glynn, Wadhwa, Dunkel-Schetter, Chicz-Demet, & Sandman, 2001).

Menopause

During menopause, estrogen concentrations decrease to levels similar to, and at later ages lower than, those of men the same age. A conclusion from studies comparing postmenopausal women with their premenopausal counterparts is that postmenopausal women usually show enhanced blood pressure and HPAA responses to psychosocial stress and that the difference between men and women fades away after menopause (Kajantie & Phillips, 2006). Moreover, blood pressure, HPAA, and sympathoadrenal responsiveness to a range of physical and psychological stressors is in general reduced after a few weeks' experimental administration of estrogen in postmenopausal women (Kajantie & Phillips, 2006; Lindheim et al., 1992), further arguing for an important role of estrogen in attenuating stress responsiveness.

Estrogen Actions

Most of the differences in stress responsiveness I have described could be nicely explained by physiological differences in estrogen concentrations according to sex and by menstrual or pregnancy status. However, as is frequently the case in human biology, the story appears to be more complex: While many experimental studies of estrogen administration have shown attenuated responses, this has not been the case in all studies; even opposite effects have been described. This discrepancy may give a clue to the complex fine-tuning of estrogen action. Estrogen actions in the brain are largely mediated through either of two different types of estrogen receptor (ER): ER-α or ER-β. A system of two or more types of receptors is by no means unique to estrogen; many hormones have alternative pathways of action that operate in dissimilar proportions in different tissues. Such alternative pathways have developed through evolution to allow distinct regulation of hormone effects in different cell and tissue types. The two types of estrogen receptors regulate the expression of a wide array of target genes; in many cases, when ER-α exerts a stimulatory effect, ER-β is inhibitory. Different brain regions that regulate stress responsiveness have strikingly variable proportions of these receptors. It is therefore possible that estrogen may have varying effects on stress responsiveness, depending on the brain regions that are activated in each specific context (Kajantie & Phillips, 2006). Reasons for such clear differences may have been shaped through complex evolutionary processes that are discussed in the next section.

Estrogen also attenuates HPAA function by stimulating the synthesis of corticosteroid-binding globulin (most cortisol circulates bound to this protein). Higher concentrations of this binding protein result in a reduction of free, bioactive cortisol in circulation and, consequently, reduced glucocorticoid activity. This phenomenon is seen for example in users of estrogen-containing contraceptives (Fig. 1).

Much less is known about the effects of progesterone and testosterone on the autonomic nervous system. It is important to keep in mind that many of the brain effects of the male sex steroid testosterone are actually mediated through estrogen receptors; when testosterone has entered the cell it acts on, it may be converted to estrogen by the intracellular enzyme aromatase.

EVOLUTIONARY BENEFIT—A HYPOTHESIS

Glucocorticoids (cortisol in humans) are important for fetal development, but in excessive amounts they cause reduced fetal growth and may increase the risk of cardiovascular disease and cognitive impairments in the adult life of the offspring. Maternal cortisol concentrations rise with advancing pregnancy and can be further increased during psychosocial stress (reviewed in Kajantie, 2006). To what extent these concentrations are transmitted to the fetus depends on the placental enzyme 11β-hydroxysteroid dehydrogenase 2 (11β–HSD2), which converts cortisol to inactive cortisone and normally keeps concentrations in the fetus several times lower than those in the mother. Sympathetic nervous system overactivity during psychosocial stress can also be harmful by reducing blood flow to the uterus and fetus.

It is obvious that minimizing such harmful effects conveys an evolutionary advantage. However, we hypothesize that the effects may be much more subtle: to facilitate optimal transfer of information about the prevailing environmental conditions, so that the developing fetus can fine-tune its behavioral and metabolic characteristics to match these conditions during later life (reviewed in Kaiser & Sachser, 2005). There is ample evidence from animal studies showing that prenatal social stress and maternal HPAA stimulation are associated with behavioral changes such as overactivity and impaired negative feedback regulation in the offspring (reviewed in Huizink, Mulder, & Buitelaar, 2004). Many of these effects are sex-specific, typically characterized by females showing behaviors that are normally typical for males, and adult males showing behaviors typical for adolescents (Kaiser & Sachser, 2005). The few existing human studies show strikingly similar associations between maternal stress or anxiety and a range of outcomes including hampered adaptation to novelty, altered attention and cognition, increased emotionality, and retarded motor development (Huizink et al., 2004; Talge et al., 2007). While in many circumstances such effects may serve an adaptive purpose—improving coping in situations of increased crowding, for example—in present-day affluent human societies the mismatch between such a prediction and later environment could be potentially harmful to an individual.

It seems therefore likely that there is evolutionary pressure to develop mechanisms to attenuate stress responsiveness during pregnancy. Apart from protecting the offspring from directly harmful consequences, such a mechanism would allow the offspring to "program" its metabolism and behavior to meet the needs of the prevailing environment. Although there are other candidates for such a mechanism, including oxytocin and prolactin, we here focus on estrogen. As stated earlier, estrogen levels rise throughout pregnancy, at term reaching levels 100 times higher than highest concentrations during the menstrual cycle. Estrogen has a well-defined role in increasing the placental 11β–HSD2 activity and thus reducing the transfer of maternal cortisol to the fetus (Pepe & Albrecht, 1995). In the mother, estrogen has a clear effect in attenuating the autonomic nervous system responses, and HPAA activity is accordingly reduced by estrogen in most scenarios. Although this has not been the case in all experiments, we speculate that the striking differences in the distribution of stimulating and inhibitory receptors (ER-α and ER-β) in stress-regulating regions of the brain indicates a complex fine-tuning of stress regulation during states of estrogen abundance, including pregnancy.

These effects may have significant consequences for human health. Estrogen is one of the key candidates to explain the profound sex differences in morbidity and mortality. For example, the 3- to 5-times-lower cardiovascular mortality of women in reproductive age is reduced after menopause to a 1.5- to 2-times difference in women over 65; the role of estrogen is further supported by increased rates of cardiovascular disease in women with premature menopause (European Society of Human Reproduction and Embryology, 2006). It seems likely that the effects of estrogen on stress responsiveness play a key role in mediating these differences.

OPEN QUESTIONS

Although the importance of attenuating stress response during pregnancy is widely supported by findings from animal and human studies, it should be emphasized that most evidence is circumstantial; few studies have tested this hypothesis directly. Moreover, some important areas have been little studied. For example, despite the considerable literature about cortisol responses to different stressors during infancy and childhood, few studies have focused on sex differences. Male infants have very high testosterone concentrations during infancy, but little is known about the possible role of these concentrations in regulating stress responsiveness. There are findings of higher blood pressure responses during later childhood and puberty in boys (Matthews, Woodall, & Stoney, 1990) and higher heart-rate responses during this period in girls. These findings are difficult to interpret, however, because the studies have not included assessments of prevailing hormonal (pubertal) status. The assessment of pubertal status by Tanner criteria (based on assessment of pubic hair and breast or testicle status) provides a simple and useful proxy of the stage of pubertal hormonal status and should be incorporated in the toolkit of psychophysiological research in this age group.

In sum, we propose that during evolution the need to transmit information about the prevailing environment to the maturing fetus has had an important role in developing the effects of sex steroids on stress responsiveness, and that some of the sex differences in stress responsiveness may be by-products of this process. If true, this idea has important practical implications. First, rather obviously, the health consequences of psychosocial stress may be substantially different according to sex and hormonal status. This may explain a substantial proportion of the male–female gap in morbidity and mortality. A second and more tentative hypothesis is that the effects of psychosocial stress during pregnancy and their consequences on the offspring's behavior and health in later life may in part be regulated by variations in sex steroid concentrations during pregnancy. While this hypothesis is supported by some evidence, we still need more data from observational studies to specify the extent and nature of such effects and, ultimately, long follow-ups after randomized trials of interventions to reduce maternal stress during pregnancy.

Recommended Reading

Charmandari, E., Tsigos, C., & Chrousos, G. (2005) Endocrinology of the stress response. *Annual Review of Physiology, 67,* 259–284. A relatively comprehensive yet easy-to-read review, particularly useful for readers who wish to extend their knowledge on stress endocrinology beyond the HPAA.

Jones, A., Godfrey, G.M., Wood, P., Osmond, C., Goulden, P., & Phillips, D.I. (2006). Fetal growth and the adrenocortical response to psychological stress. *Journal of Clinical Endocrinology & Metabolism, 91,* 1868–1871. An original research report showing that normal variation in birth weight predicts HPAA response to psychosocial stress in healthy 7- to-9-year-old children; the article also has methodological importance by describing a psychosocial stress test in children.

Kajantie, E., & Phillips, D.I. (2006). (See References). A comprehensive narrative review summarizing research on the effects of sex and hormonal status on HPAA and sympathoadrenal response to psychosocial stress.

Talge, N.M., Neal, C., & Glover, V (2007). (See References). A review summarizing current evidence on the relationship between maternal antenatal stress and neurodevelopment of the offspring.

Wadhwa, P.D. (2005). Psychoneuroendocrine processes in human pregnancy influence fetal development and health. *Psychoneuroendocrinology, 30,* 724–743. A well-written narrative review introducing the concept of behavioral perinatology, structured around findings from the author's own research program in relation to those from other recent literature.

Note

1. Address correspondence to Eero Kajantie, The National Public Health Institute, Mannerheimintie 166, 00300 Helsinki, Finland; e-mail: eero.kajantie@helsinki.fi.

References

de Weerth, C., & Buitelaar, J.K. (2005). Physiological stress reactivity in human pregnancy—A review. *Neuroscience and Biobehavioral Reviews, 29,* 295–312.

Dickerson, S.S., & Kemeny, M.E. (2004). Acute stressors and cortisol responses: A theoretical integration and synthesis of laboratory research. *Psychological Bulletin, 130,* 355–391.

European Society of Human Reproduction and Embryology. (2006). Hormones and cardiovascular health in women. *Human Reproduction Update, 12,* 483–497.

Glynn, L.M., Wadhwa, P.D., Dunkel-Schetter, C., Chicz-Demet, A., & Sandman, C.A. (2001). When stress happens matters: Effects of earthquake timing on stress responsivity in pregnancy. *American Journal of Obstetrics and Gynecology, 184,* 637–642.

Huizink, A.C., Mulder, E.J., & Buitelaar, J.K. (2004). Prenatal stress and risk for psychopathology: Specific effects or induction of general susceptibility? *Psychological Bulletin, 130,* 115–142.

Kaiser, S., & Sachser, N. (2005). The effects of prenatal social stress on behaviour: Mechanisms and function. *Neuroscience and Biobehavioral Reviews, 29,* 283–294.

Kajantie, E. (2006). Fetal origins of stress-related adult disease. *Annals of the New York Academy of Sciences, 1083,* 11–27.

Kajantie, E., & Phillips, D.I. (2006). The effects of sex and hormonal status on the physiological response to acute psychosocial stress. *Psychoneuroendocrinology, 31,* 151–178.

Kammerer, M., Adams, D., von Castelberg, B., & Glover, V. (2002). Pregnant women become insensitive to cold stress. *BMC Pregnancy and Childbirth, 2,* 8.

Kirschbaum, C., Kudielka, B.M., Gaab, J., Schommer, N.C., & Hellhammer, D.H. (1999). Impact of gender, menstrual cycle phase, and oral contraceptives on the activity of the hypothalamus-pituitary-adrenal axis. *Psychosomatic Medicine, 61,* 154–162.

Kudielka, B.M., & Kirschbaum, C. (2005). Sex differences in HPA axis responses to stress: A review. *Biological Psychology, 69,* 113–132.

Lindheim, S.R., Legro, R.S., Bernstein, L., Stanczyk, F.Z., Vijod, M.A., Presser, S.C., et al. (1992). Behavioral stress responses in premenopausal and postmenopausal women and the effects of estrogen. *American Journal of Obstetrics and Gynecology, 167,* 1831–1836.

Matthews, K.A., Woodall, K.L., & Stoney, C.M. (1990). Changes in and stability of cardiovascular responses to behavioral stress: Results from a four-year longitudinal study of children. *Child Development, 61,* 1134–1144.

Otte, C., Hart, S., Neylan, T.C., Marmar, C.R., Yaffe, K., & Mohr, D.C. (2005). A meta-analysis of cortisol response to challenge in human aging: Importance of gender. *Psychoneuroendocrinology, 30,* 80–91.

Pepe, G.J., & Albrecht, E.D. (1995). Actions of placental and fetal adrenal steroid hormones in primate pregnancy. *Endocrine Reviews, 16*(5), 608–648.

Stoney, C.M., Davis, M.C., & Matthews, K.A. (1987). Sex differences in physiological responses to stress and in coronary heart disease: A causal link? *Psychophysiology, 24,* 127–131.

Stroud, L.R., Salovey, P., & Epel, E.S. (2002). Sex differences in stress responses: Social rejection versus achievement stress. *Biological Psychiatry, 52,* 318–327.

Talge, N.M., Neal, C., & Glover, V. (2007). Antenatal maternal stress and long-term effects on child neurodevelopment: How and why? *Journal of Child Psychology and Psychiatry and Allied Disciplines, 48,* 245–261.

This article has been reprinted as it originally appeared in *Current Directions in Psychological Science*. Citation information for this article as originally published appears above.

Gender and Cardiovascular Disease:
A Psychobiological and Integrative Approach

Catherine M. Stoney[1]

Department of Psychology, Ohio State University,
Columbus, Ohio

Abstract

Coronary artery disease is the most common cause of morbidity, mortality, and economic loss in all industrialized countries. Although there are gender differences in the prevalence, causes, symptoms, treatment, and outcome of heart disease, the differences are complex and often misunderstood. These gender differences are a function of psychological influences, physiological influences, and an interaction of the two. Understanding these complex interactions and how they differentially influence the development and progression of heart disease will ultimately contribute to a greater understanding of how to integrate information from medicine and epidemiology with that from psychology and behavioral medicine. Ultimately, it is this integrated approach that will allow us to better understand heart disease in both men and women.

Keywords

coronary artery disease; gender differences; stress reactivity

Coronary artery disease (CAD) is the number-one cause of death, disability, and economic loss for people in all industrialized countries. CAD is most commonly due to obstruction of the arteries of the heart by atherosclerosis (the accumulation of cholesterol, other fats, and other cells in the arteries), which causes a decreased blood flow to the heart. In the United States, CAD is responsible for about 25% of all deaths per year. The incidence of CAD increases with age among men and women, but the rate of increase is greatest among women after the age of menopause. Although CAD mortality in the United States has declined by more than 50% in the past 40 years, the decline has been greater in men than women. Gender differences in many aspects of the disease are striking. Understanding the contribution of both physiological and psychological factors to these gender differences can be informative.

There are still misconceptions about the gender disparity in the rate of CAD. Although heart disease is the leading cause of death for men, it is also the leading cause of death for women in all industrialized nations. Cardiovascular disease accounts for twice as many deaths among women as do all cancers combined. One of every two women will die of a heart attack, stroke, or other cardiovascular illness, but the diagnosis of the disease occurs 10 years later, on average, in women than in men. Thus, among young and middle-aged individuals, far greater numbers of men than women die of CAD. However, across all ages, CAD kills more women than men every year because of the greater proportion of women among the elderly population. For both men and women, understanding

13

factors leading to the initiation, progression, diagnosis, and treatment of heart disease is therefore critically important.

The gender differences associated with CAD fall into at least three important categories: risk factors, clinical symptoms and diagnosis, and treatment and outcome. For each category of gender differences, it is valuable to differentiate relevant physiological and psychological factors, and clarify how and at what point in the disease process they interact.

RISK FACTORS

The traditional cardiovascular risk factors are similar for men and women, and include nonmodifiable factors (gender, family history) and modifiable factors (obesity, smoking). However, the prevalence of risk factors has changed differently for men and women over the past 40 years. Men have experienced a decline in the presence of risk factors, while women have had less reduction. These population-based changes (i.e., changes that have been noted in the population as a whole) are due almost entirely to changes in the modifiable risk factors, which, by definition, have a primarily psychological (behavioral) component.

The prevalence of risk factors throughout the life span is different among men and women as well. Many risk factors, such as high cholesterol, smoking, and hypertension, are more prevalent among men than women at younger ages; however, at older ages, it is women who have the higher prevalence of risk factors. These patterns are due to a combination of psychological and physiological differences. For example, behavioral factors such as diet can influence the expression of both high blood pressure and high cholesterol and can also change throughout the life span. However, these behaviors have greater physiological impact at older ages than at younger ages.

The impact of risk factors on disease incidence is, in some cases, different for men and women. Both hypertension and obesity confer about the same level of risk to men and women, although hypertension is more common among older women than among older men. Diabetes imparts much greater risk to women than to men, such that the relative protection from CAD that premenopausal women enjoy is entirely abolished among women with diabetes. Smoking is somewhat riskier for women than men. Although the number of smokers has generally declined in the United States over the past several decades, the rate of smoking is on the rise among young women. In addition, women who smoke and use oral contraceptives have a higher risk of cardiovascular disease than do women who engage in just one of these behaviors. Although these risk factors are primarily psychologically determined, they interact with biological predispositions, some of which are sex-linked, to affect disease risk.

One risk factor that demonstrates substantial sex differences is estrogen. Natural estrogen has a cardioprotective effect on premenopausal women, which may be due to a direct, physiological effect on blood vessels. Among post-menopausal women, the levels of estrogen circulating in the blood are greatly diminished; some women opt to take hormone replacement therapy (HRT) to decrease risk of both osteoporosis and CAD, as well as to decrease menopausal symptoms like hot flashes, mood disturbances, and vaginal dryness. However, the health benefits of hormone therapy are currently controversial because of new evidence that these hormones may not decrease CAD risk. The largest trial to date investigating the potential beneficial effects of HRT, the Women's Health Initiative, followed women over 5 years to study the health effects of post-menopausal hormones. The study was terminated early, in July 2002, because of the increased risk of breast cancer in the absence of a decreased risk of cardio-vascular disease (Writing Group for the Women's Health Initiative Investigators, 2002). This study, in combination with other recent studies, has seriously called into question the benefits of long-term HRT for the prevention of CAD in women.

Estrogen is responsive to psychological influences, and behavioral factors can influence estrogen levels. Behavioral factors that decrease estrogen include smoking and intensive exercise training. The effects of smoking are so prominent that chronic smoking actually induces an earlier menopause. In addition, factors that influence peri- and postmenopausal women in their decision whether to take HRT are now more important than ever, as are factors that influence practi-tioners to recommend HRT to their patients.

Among the most well-studied, nontraditional putative risk factors in the development of CAD is physiological reactivity, or physiological responses to psy-chological stimuli. Animal studies and indirect human investigations suggest that large-magnitude physiological reactivity is related to higher risk for CAD. Both real-life and laboratory studies have shown that men's and women's responses to stress differ physiologically. Typically, stressors induce changes in cardiac func-tioning, levels of certain hormones, and cholesterol levels and form in both men and women. But during achievement-focused stressors especially, men have larger responses in almost all of these systems than do women. This does not appear to be a function of different perceptions or the gender relevance of the stressors, but is modified by individual differences in aspects of personality like optimism, anger, and hostility (Stoney & Engebretson, 1994). At least part of the gender differences in reactivity to stressors is related to the presence of estrogen; premenopausal women typically show smaller responses to stressors than do postmenopausal women. In fact, women who have their ovaries removed or pharmacologically sup-pressed and therefore have diminished levels of circulating estrogen have larger physiological stress responses than do premenopausal women with intact ovaries (Stoney, Owens, Guzick, & Matthews, 1997). Thus, it is clear that estrogen avail-ability modulates, in part, physiological adjustment to psychological stress.

CLINICAL SYMPTOMS AND DIAGNOSIS OF CAD

Among men, the first clinical symptom of CAD is most frequently myocardial infarction (MI), or heart attack. In women, the first clinical sign is most fre-quently angina (chest pain). The presence of chest pain is a relatively poor diag-nostic predictor of underlying heart disease in women, because only about half the women who seek medical care for pain have radiographic evidence of obstruc-tive disease.

Among both men and women, delay in seeking medical care after symptoms of a cardiac event can significantly affect the outcome, with greater delay leading to worse outcome and higher probability of death. For all symptoms and diseases, including non-cardiac disease, women use the health care system more frequently than do men, a fact that can be due to poorer health among women, their greater awareness of symptoms, greater tendency to seek health care among women, or differences in delivery of health care to women. Nonetheless, with regard to symptoms of MI, women delay seeking health care longer than do men. Even after seeking health care, women experience a significantly greater delay in being diagnosed as having had a heart attack. This can be due to physicians' bias, and may also be due to the fact that women report different symptoms of MI than do men. So-called classic symptoms of MI (i.e., symptoms common among men) include chest pain radiating to the arm and perspiration. Women, however, are less likely to report radiating pain and more likely to report shortness of breath, often resulting in a (mis)diagnosis of anxiety disorder.

Coronary atherosclerosis appears to be grossly similar in form among men and women. However, because there are dramatic sex differences in the clinical symptoms of CAD, effective diagnostic strategies will necessarily be different in men than women. Noninvasive or minimally invasive diagnostic techniques in men with suspected CAD typically include exercise stress testing, echocardiography, thallium scans, and measures of carotid artery intima-media thickness. Each of these techniques allows, either directly or indirectly, the examination of how easily and efficiently blood flows through the vessels of the heart. They involve the use of ultrasound, x-rays, or the placement of sensors on the body that record the electrical signals of the heart. Substantial evidence suggests that such tools are less effective in diagnosing CAD in women, and more efficacious approaches are needed. The Women's Ischemia Syndrome Evaluation (WISE) trial is a longitudinal, multisite study designed to develop and improve the predictive validity and reliability of diagnostic cardiovascular testing for heart disease in women, and to understand the clinical relevance of chest pain in women (Bairey Merz et al., 1999). The WISE study has demonstrated that a significant portion of women with chest pain but no obstructive CAD have coronary microvascular dysfunction (disordered functioning of the smallest blood vessels of the heart) and reduced blood flow to the heart (myocardial ischemia). Both are frequently missed with diagnostic testing that is traditionally effective for men, and both lead to poor clinical outcomes.

The primary invasive diagnostic tool for men with suspected CAD is cardiac catheterization. This procedure, which not only confirms the presence of the disease, but also provides an indication of the severity of disease, allows internal inspection of the blood vessels of the heart using a catheter. Women are referred less frequently for cardiac catheterization, which may indicate an underutilization of the procedure among women or an overutilization among men. Biologically based reasons for underutilization of catheterization in women are likely partially related to the relatively smaller vessel size in women; the smaller vessel size typically results in a prolonged procedure, with a consequently greater number of complications in women than in men. However, there are also potential psychological reasons for underutilization, including the perception of CAD being less likely in women than in men and women being less willing to undergo invasive testing. Greater investigation of these and other behavioral factors resulting in use of different diagnostic procedures for men and women is needed.

TREATMENT AND OUTCOME

At every point in the diagnosis and treatment of CAD, women are less likely than men to receive a referral for diagnostic testing and rehabilitation, to receive a diagnosis of heart disease, to receive adequate care, and to be aggressively treated for heart disease. This is despite the fact that women with heart disease, even when diagnosed and treated aggressively, fare worse than men. In every age group, women with CAD have a higher risk of death from a coronary event than men. For example, 27% of men but 44% of women will die in the first year after an MI. For people who do survive, recurrent MI and cardiac failure are more common among women, and after an MI women have poorer quality of life, less life satisfaction, and more chronic illnesses than men.

After diagnosis of CAD, there is a gender difference in treatment strategies for men and women. For example, women are less likely to be referred to cardiac rehabilitation (Benz Scott, Ben-Or, & Allen, 2002). These programs typically focus on improved nutrition, smoking cessation, improved exercise adherence, and stress reduction. Even among those referred to rehabilitation programs, the dropout rates are higher and the attendance rates lower among women than men. Women who do successfully complete cardiac rehabilitation do as well as or better than men, so identifying the causes of high dropout among women is essential to providing effective post-MI care.

In addition, pharmacological treatment is more common than surgical treatment for women, and surgical treatment (balloon angioplasty and coronary bypass[2]) is more common than pharmacological treatment for men. It is likely that there are both physiological and psychological explanations for the gender difference in treatment. The adult female heart is smaller than the male heart and accounts for a smaller percentage of body weight; the coronary arteries of women are therefore smaller than those of men. Consequently, surgery has traditionally been more difficult and resulted in less positive outcomes for women. However, it is likely that the differences in how men and women with CAD are treated are influenced more by psychological and social factors than by physiological ones. These psychological and social factors include referral bias on the part of practitioners, the fact that women tend to be sicker and more fragile when diagnosed and therefore poorer surgical candidates, health-care-seeking differences between men and women, and economic and health care issues influencing availability of resources. There is evidence supporting the role of all of these factors, but in recent years the extent of referral bias has been diminishing somewhat. This decrease may also be responsible for the improvement in overall outcome among women undergoing surgery for CAD, because women referred earlier in the disease will be younger, relatively healthier, and likely to have better surgical outcomes than those referred later in the disease.

FUTURE DIRECTIONS

Despite several decades of research on causes and treatment of CAD, prevalence of the disease remains high, and gender differences in the development, treatment, and outcome of CAD remain robust and inadequately explained. Several emergent areas that bridge psychological and physiological parameters are key to understanding gender differences in risk factors, diagnosis, and treatment.

One of the most intriguing non-traditional risk factors for recurrent coronary events is depression, and some investigations have also found that this is a risk factor for primary (or first) coronary events. Depression is a putative independent risk factor, and there appears to be a relationship between severity of depression and magnitude of risk. Despite the fact that depression is more common among women than men, most CAD researchers have either enrolled primarily men or failed to design their studies to investigate potential gender differences. Thus, the importance of depression among women with cardiac disease is poorly understood. It will be particularly important in the future to clarify the mechanisms linking depression to CAD, and to identify gender differences in these mechanisms (Wulsin & Singal, 2003).

Diagnosis of CAD remains a difficulty with ramifications for treatment and outcome, and investigations such as the WISE trial have underscored the notion that CAD can be manifested differently in men and women. A challenge for behavioral scientists is changing the behavior of practitioners, so that they utilize different diagnostic tools for men and women. Meeting this challenge will require a more thorough understanding not only of which diagnostic tools are efficacious, but also of the decision-making process that cardiologists use in employing these instruments.

Efficacious treatment strategies for men with high-risk profiles are fairly well established, but similar strategies are not well determined for high-risk women. For example, high cholesterol appears somewhat riskier in men than women, and one major aim of treatment among men with suspected CAD is to aggressively lower cholesterol values with pharmacological therapy and exercise. However, few prevention trials have included women, and the benefits of cholesterol-lowering strategies among women are not known. Future investigations must focus on potential gender differences in treatment, particularly among the most vulnerable patients.

It is apparent that the combined study of psychological (adherence to cardiac rehabilitation programs, referral bias) and physiological (vessel size, estrogen levels) factors can tell us more about the etiology of gender differences in CAD than the study of either set of variables alone. Exploration of these factors and their interaction may well lead us to recognize the role of other, nonpsychological factors, such as environment, education, and social factors, in the progression of CAD. An understanding of these complex interactions will ultimately lead not only to a more integrated picture of the reasons for the gender differences, but also to new ways of identifying and treating heart disease in both men and women.

Recommended Reading

Benz Scott, L.A., Ben-Or, K., & Allen, J.K. (2002). (See References)
Stoney, C.M., & Engebretson, T.O. (1994). (See References)
Wilansky, S., & Willerson, J.T. (2002). *Heart disease in women*. Philadelphia: Elsevier.

Acknowledgments—This work was supported in part by National Institutes of Health Grant HL68956.

Notes

1. Address correspondence to Catherine M. Stoney, Ohio State University, 210 Townshend Hall, Columbus, OH 43210-1222; e-mail: stoney.1@osu.edu.

2. Angioplasty is a surgical procedure designed to enlarge the diameter of an artery that has been narrowed by atherosclerosis. Coronary bypass is a surgical operation that grafts a vein to a diseased artery, in order to shunt blood flow beyond an atherosclerotic obstruction.

References

Bairey Merz, C.N., Kelsey, S.F., Pepine, C.J., Riechek, N., Reis, S.E., Rogers, W.J., Sharaf, B.L., & Sopko, G. (1999). The Women's Ischemia Syndrome Evaluation (WISE) study. *Journal of the American College of Cardiology, 33,* 1453–1461.

Benz Scott, L.A., Ben-Or, K., & Allen, J.K. (2002). Why are women missing from outpatient cardiac rehabilitation programs? *Journal of Women's Health, 11,* 773–790.

Stoney, C.M., & Engebretson, T.O. (1994). Anger and hostility: Potential mediators of the sex differences in coronary heart disease. In T. Smith & A. Siegman (Eds.), *Anger, hostility and the heart* (pp. 215–237). Hillsdale, NJ: Erlbaum.

Stoney, C.M., Owens, J.F., Guzick, D.S., & Matthews, K.A (1997). A natural experiment on the effects of ovarian hormones on cardiovascular risk factors and stress reactivity: Hysterectomy with or without bilateral oophorectomy. *Health Psychology, 16,* 349–358.

Writing Group for the Women's Health Initiative Investigators. (2002). Risks and benefits of estrogen plus progestin in healthy postmenopausal women. *Journal of the American Medical Association, 288,* 321–333.

Wulsin, L.R., & Singal, B.M. (2003). Do depressive symptoms increase the risk for the onset of coronary disease? *Psychosomatic Medicine, 65,* 201–210.

This article has been reprinted as it originally appeared in *Current Directions in Psychological Science*. Citation information for this article as originally published appears above.

Resilience and Vulnerability to Daily Stressors Assessed via Diary Methods

David M. Almeida[1]
The Pennsylvania State University

Abstract

Stressors encountered in daily life, such as family arguments or work deadlines, may play an important role in individual health and well-being. This article presents a framework for understanding how characteristics of individuals and their environments limit or increase exposure and reactivity to daily stressors. Research on daily stressors has benefited from diary methods that obtain repeated measurements from individuals during their daily lives. These methods improve ecological validity, reduce memory distortions, and permit the assessment of within-person processes. Findings from the National Study of Daily Experiences, which used a telephone-diary design, highlight how people's age, gender, and education and the presence or absence of chronic stressors in their lives predict their exposure and reactivity to daily stressors. Finally, future directions for research designs that combine laboratory-based assessment of stress physiology with daily-diary methods are discussed.

Keywords

daily hassles; diary designs; well-being

"Any idiot can handle a crisis—it's this day-to-day living that wears you out"

—Anton Chekhov

Anyone who has recently experienced a crisis such as job loss, marital disruption, or the death of a loved one would certainly disagree with Chekhov's contention. Indeed, these major life stressors require significant adjustment on the part of the individual and adversely affect psychological and physical health (Brown & Harris, 1989). Major life events, however, are relatively rare, and thus their cumulative effect on health and well-being may not be as great as that of minor yet frequent stressors, such as work deadlines and family arguments (Lazarus, 1999; Zautra, 2003). Daily stressors are defined as routine challenges of day-to-day living, such as the everyday concerns of work, caring for other people, and commuting between work and home. They may also refer to more unexpected small occurrences—such as arguments with children, unexpected work deadlines, and malfunctioning computers—that disrupt daily life.

Tangible, albeit minor, interruptions like these may have a more immediate effect on well-being than major life events. Major life events may be associated with prolonged physiological arousal, whereas daily hassles may be associated with spikes in arousal or psychological distress confined to a single day. Yet minor daily stressors affect well-being not only by having separate, immediate, and direct effects on emotional and physical functioning, but also by piling up over a series of days to create persistent irritations, frustrations, and overloads that may result in more serious stress reactions such as anxiety and depression (Lazarus, 1999; Zautra, 2003).

VULNERABILITY AND RESILIENCE
TO DAILY STRESSORS

Some stressors are unhealthier than other stressors, and some individuals are more prone to the effects of stressors than other individuals. Recent improvements in the measurement of daily stressors and in study design have allowed researchers to address (a) how different types of stressors and personal meanings attached to these stressors affect well-being and (b) how sociodemographic factors and personal characteristics account for group and individual differences in daily-stress processes. Figure 1 provides a model for these two areas of inquiry.

The right side of the figure represents daily-stress processes that occur within the individual. To understand these processes, one must consider both the objective characteristics of daily stressors and individuals' subjective appraisal of stressors. Objective characteristics of daily stressors include their frequency, type (e.g., interpersonal tension, being overloaded or overwhelmed at work), focus of involvement (e.g., whether the stressor involves other persons, such as a sick family member), and objective severity (e.g., degree of unpleasantness and disruption for an average person). Individuals appraise stressors in terms of their perceived severity and in terms of how much they are perceived as disrupting daily goals and commitments. Both objective and subjective components of daily stressors affect daily well-being (Cohen, Kessler, & Gordon, 1997). The objective characteristics of a stressor may play an important role in how that stressor is appraised, which in turn may influence how much distress it causes. Integrating the objective characteristics of stressors with their subjective appraisal allows researchers to investigate whether different kinds of daily stressors elicit different appraisal processes and affect well-being differently.

The left side of Figure 1 represents sociodemographic, psychosocial, and health factors that contribute to individuals' resilience or vulnerability to stress. Resilience and vulnerability factors affect individuals' *exposure* and *reactivity* to daily stressors and, thereby, their daily well-being. Exposure is the likelihood that an individual will experience a daily stressor, given his or her resilience or vulnerability factors. Although daily stressors may be unpredictable, more often they arise out of the routine circumstances of everyday life. The stressor-exposure path illustrates that an individual's sociodemo-graphic, psychosocial, and health characteristics are likely to play a role in determining what kinds of stressors that individual experiences and how he or she appraises them (right side of Fig. 1). Reactivity is the likelihood that an individual will react emotionally or physically to daily stressors and depends on the individual's resilience or vulnerability (Bolger & Zuckerman, 1995). The stressor-reactivity path illustrates that sociodemographic, psychosocial, and health factors modify how daily stressors affect daily well-being. Individuals' personal resources (e.g., their education, income, feelings of mastery and control over their environment, and physical health) and environmental resources (e.g., social support) affect how they can cope with daily experiences (Lazarus, 1999). Finally, the feedback-loop path

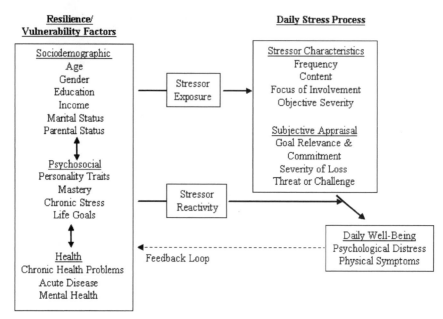

Resilience/
Vulnerability Factors

Daily Stress Process

Sociodemographic
Age
Gender
Education
Income
Marital Status
Parental Status

Psychosocial
Personality Traits
Mastery
Chronic Stress
Life Goals

Health
Chronic Health Problems
Acute Disease
Mental Health

Stressor
Exposure

Stressor
Reactivity

Feedback Loop

Stressor Characteristics
Frequency
Content
Focus of Involvement
Objective Severity

Subjective Appraisal
Goal Relevance &
Commitment
Severity of Loss
Threat or Challenge

Daily Well-Being
Psychological Distress
Physical Symptoms

Fig. 1. Model showing how individual resilience or vulnerability factors affect daily-stress processes and well-being. Such factors include socioeconomic, psychosocial, and health characteristics; these influence the likelihood of being exposed to different kinds of stressors and the way individuals appraise stressors. Objective stressor characteristics and stressors' subjective appraisal by individuals in turn influences individuals' psychological and physical well-being. In addition to influencing stressor exposure, resilience or vulnerability factors influence individuals' reactivity to stressors—that is, their likelihood of reacting emotionally or physically. The feedback loop indicates that aspects of stressors and well-being will have subsequent effects on the vulnerability and resilience factors.

(dotted arrow from the right to the left of the figure) shows how aspects of stressors and well-being will have subsequent effects on the resilience and vulnerability factors.

DAILY-DIARY METHODOLOGY

The understanding of daily stressors has benefited from the development of diary methods that obtain repeated measurements from individuals during their daily lives. In this method, individuals report the stressors they experienced over the course of several days, as well as their behaviors, physical symptoms, and emotional states on these days. The use of paper-and-pencil diaries has been criticized because some participants may not complete their entries at scheduled times (Stone, Shiffman, Schwartz, Broderick, & Hufford, 2002). However, recent diary methods in which participants respond over the telephone, with personal digital assistants, and on Internet Web pages provide more control over compliance and make it possible to obtain more in-depth information by allowing subjects to skip irrelevant questions and go into greater detail on those that are more relevant to them, for instance by describing experiences in their own words. Diary methods have a number of virtues (Bolger, Davis, & Rafaeli, 2003). By obtaining information about individuals' actual daily stressors over short-term intervals, daily diaries circumvent concerns about ecological validity (applicability to real life) that constrain findings from laboratory research. Further, diary methods alleviate memory distortions that can occur in more traditional questionnaire and interview methods that require respondents to recall experiences over longer time frames.

Perhaps the most valuable feature of diary methods is that they allow assessment of within-person processes. This feature entails a shift from assessing mean levels of stressors and well-being in a group of individuals to charting the day-to-day fluctuations in stress and well-being within an individual, as well as to identifying predictors, correlates, and consequences of these fluctuations (Reis & Gamble, 2000).

Stress is a process that occurs within the individual, and research designs need to reflect this fact. For example, instead of asking whether individuals who encounter many stressors at work experience more distress than individuals with less stressful jobs, a researcher can ask whether a worker experiences more distress on days when he or she has too many deadlines (or is reprimanded) than on days when work has been stress free. This within-person approach allows the researcher to rule out personality and environmental variables that are stable over time as explanations for the relationship between stressors and well-being. In addition, the intensive longitudinal aspect of this design permits researchers to examine how stressors are associated with changes in a person's well-being from one day to the next. By establishing within-person, through-time associations between daily stressors and well-being, researchers can more precisely establish the short-term effects of concrete daily experiences (Bolger et al., 2003; Larson & Almeida, 1999).

EMPIRICAL FINDINGS FROM THE NATIONAL STUDY OF DAILY EXPERIENCES

A recent project called the National Study of Daily Experiences (NSDE) is aimed to investigate the sources of vulnerability and resilience to daily stressors. The NSDE is a telephone-diary study of a U.S. national sample of 1,483 adults ranging in age from 25 to 74 years. Interviews occurred over eight consecutive nights, resulting in 11,578 days of information. Although past research advanced the understanding of daily-stress processes, there are important limitations in these studies that are overcome in the NSDE. First, previous diary studies of daily stressors relied on small and often unrepresentative samples that limited the generalizability of findings. In contrast, the NSDE data come from a representative subsample of adults surveyed in a nationwide study on Midlife in the United States (MIDUS). Second, previous studies of individual differences in vulnerability to stress have typically examined only one source of variability, such as neuroticism (i.e., whether a person is dispositionally anxious). The NSDE, in contrast, uses data on a wide array of personality variables and sociodemographic characteristics collected in the MIDUS survey. Third, previous studies typically have relied on self-administered checklists of daily stressors that only indicate whether or not a given stressor has occurred. The NSDE uses a semistructured telephone interview to measure several aspects of daily stressors, including their objective characteristics as rated by expert coders (e.g., content, severity) and their subjective appraisals by study participants.

Prevalence of Daily Stressors

Respondents reported experiencing on average at least one stressor on 40% of the study days and multiple stressors on 10% of the study days (Almeida, Wethington, & Kessler, 2002). Table 1 provides a breakdown by various stressor

Table 1. *Results from the National Study of Daily Experiences: Measures of Stressors*

	Total	Men	Women
	(N = 1,031)	(n = 469)	(n = 562)
Stressor content (% of events)[a]			
Interpersonal tensions	50.0%	49.1%	50.3%
Work or school	13.2	15.7	11.2*
Home	8.2	8.0	8.3
Health care	2.2	1.6	2.7
Network[b]	15.4	12.5	17.8*
Miscellaneous	3.5	4.4	2.7
Type of threat posed by stressor (% of events)			
Loss	29.7	29.9	29.5
Danger	36.2	35.7	36.6
Disappointment	4.2	4.0	4.4
Frustration	27.4	28.3	26.6
Stressor severity (mean)[c]			
Objective assessment	1.8	1.7	1.9
Subjective assessment	2.7	2.5	2.9*
Domain of life potentially disrupted (mean)[d]			
Daily routine	2.3	2.3	2.3
Financial situation	1.3	1.4	1.2*
Way feel about self	1.5	1.4	1.5
Way others feel about you	1.4	1.3	1.4*
Physical health or safety	1.3	1.3	1.3
Health/well-being of someone you care about	1.5	1.5	1.5
Plans for the future	1.4	1.4	1.3

[a]Seven percent of events could not be placed into these content classifications.
[b]Events that happen to other people.
[c]Range: 1–4 (not at all stressful to very stressful).
[d]Range: 1–4 (no risk to a lot of risk).
*Asterisks indicate a significant gender difference, $p < .01$.

categories. The most common stressors for both men and women were inter-personal arguments and tensions, which accounted for half of all the stressors. Gender differences were also evident. Women were more likely than men to report network stressors—stressors involving their network of relatives or close friends—whereas men were more likely than women to report stressors at work or at school. On average, the respondents subjectively rated stressors as having medium severity, whereas objective coders rated the stressors as having low severity. It is interesting that objective and subjective severity were only moderately correlated ($r = .36$). As appraised by respondents, daily stressors more commonly posed a threat to respondents' daily routines than to other domains of their lives (e.g., their finances, health, and safety). The threat dimensions refer to stressful implications for the respondent. Approximately 30% of the reported stressors involved some sort of loss (e.g., of money), nearly 37% posed danger (e.g., potential for future loss), and 27% were frustrations or events over which the respondent felt he or she had no control.

Daily stressors also had implications for well-being. Respondents were more likely to report psychological distress and physical symptoms on days when they experienced stressors than on stress-free days. Certain types of daily stressors, such as interpersonal tensions and network stressors, were more predictive of psychological distress and physical symptoms than other types of stressors. Furthermore, severe stressors that disrupted daily routines or posed a risk to physical health and self-concept were particularly distressing.

Group and Individual Differences in Daily Stressors

As previously mentioned, demographic and psychological characteristics affect how resilient or vulnerable individuals are to daily stressors (see Fig. 1). Horn and I initially investigated this issue by assessing age differences in exposure and reactivity to daily stressors (Almeida & Horn, 2004). Young (25–39 years) and middle-aged (40–59 years) individuals reported a greater daily frequency of stressors than did older individuals (60–74 years). Compared with older adults, younger and midlife adults also perceived their stressors as more severe and as more likely to affect how other people felt about them. Overloads (i.e., having too little time or other resources) and demands (i.e., having too much to do) were a greater source of daily stressors for younger and midlife adults than for older adults, although the focus of the demands tended to differ by gender. Younger men's daily stressors were more likely than those of older men to revolve around demands and overloads as well as interactions with coworkers. Women in midlife reported the same percentage of overloads as younger women but had a greater proportion of network stressors. Although overloads were not a common type of stressor for older adults, these respondents had the greatest proportion of network stressors (stressors that happen to other people) and spouse-related stressors.

Socioeconomic factors may also help or hinder individuals in facing daily stressors. Consistent with research on socio-economic inequalities in health, our analyses indicated that, on any given day, better-educated adults reported fewer physical symptoms and less psychological distress than less-educated adults

(Grzywacz, Almeida, Neupert, & Ettner, 2004). In contrast to studies of life-event stressors, this study found that college-educated individuals reported more daily stressors than those with no more than high-school education. However, college-educated respondents were less reactive to stressors, which indicates that socioeconomic differentials in daily health could be attributed to differential reactivity to stressors rather than to differential exposure to stressors.

Finally, it is important to acknowledge that ongoing difficulties in a person's life (e.g., caring for a sick spouse, poor working conditions) not only may expose him or her to stressors, but also may increase his or her reactivity to daily stressors by depleting resources. Participants who experienced chronic stressors were more likely than those who did not to report psychological distress on days when they experienced daily stressors (Serido, Almeida, & Wethington, 2004). For women, the interaction of home hassles and chronic stressors was significant; for men, it was the interaction of work hassles and chronic stressors that was significant.

FUTURE DIRECTIONS: PHYSIOLOGICAL INDICATORS OF WELL-BEING

Most research on resilience and vulnerability to daily stressors has relied on self-reported well-being. Results have had to be qualified by discussions of possible biases in study participants' responses and questions concerning the validity of self-reported well-being measures. Thus, questions regarding the direct relation between daily stressors and physiological functioning remain. One promising avenue for future research concerns *allostatic load,* the biological cost of adapting to stresssors. Allostatic load is commonly measured by indicators of the body's response to physiological dysregulation—responses such as high cholesterol levels or lowered blood-clotting ability—and has been found to be predictive of decline in physical health (McEwen, 1998). Ironically, researchers have conceptualized allostatic load as physical vulnerability caused by the body having to adjust repeatedly to stressors, yet few studies have examined allostatic load in conjunction with individuals' daily accounts of stressors. The combination of daily-stressor data from diaries and data from laboratory tests of physiological reactivity would provide an opportunity to examine how daily stressors map onto physiological indicators of allostatic load.

In conclusion, the study of daily stress provides a unique window into the ebb and flow of day-to-day frustrations and irritations that are often missed by research on major life events. The focus on naturally occurring minor stressors assessed on a daily basis offers an exciting opportunity to understand how people adapt to the challenges of life. Adaptation occurs within an individual, so understanding adaptation requires consideration both of stressors themselves and of the persons they affect. Because daily stressors are real-life issues that require immediate attention, daily-diary study of stressors can provide the micro-level data needed to understand the immediate relationships between stressors and how individuals respond to and interpret them. It is true that day-to day living can wear you out; however certain days are better than others, and certain people are better equipped to handle stressors than other people are.

Recommended Reading

Affleck, G., Zautra, A., Tennen, H., & Armeli, S. (1999). Multilevel daily process designs for consulting and clinical psychology: A preface for the perplexed. *Journal of Consulting and Clinical Psychology, 67,* 746–754.

Almeida, D.M., Wethington, E., & Kessler, R.C. (2002). (See References)

Bolger, N., Davis, A., & Rafaeli, E. (2003). (See References)

Lazarus, R.S. (1999). (See References)

Zautra, A.J. (2003). (See References)

Acknowledgments—The research reported in this article was supported by the MacArthur Foundation Research Network on Successful Midlife Development and by National Institute on Aging Grants AG19239 and AG0210166.

Note

1. David M. Almeida, Department of Human Development and Family Studies, The Pennsylvania State University, 105 White Building, University Park, PA 16802; e-mail: dalmeida@psu.edu.

References

Almeida, D.M., & Horn, M.C. (2004). Is daily life more stressful during middle adulthood? In O.G. Brim, C.D. Ryff, & R.C. Kessler (Eds.), *How healthy are we? A national study of well-being at midlife* (pp. 425–451). Chicago: University of Chicago Press.

Almeida, D.M., Wethington, E., & Kessler, R.C. (2002). The Daily Inventory of Stressful Experiences (DISE): An interview-based approach for measuring daily stressors. *Assessment, 9,* 41–55.

Bolger, N., Davis, A., & Rafaeli, E. (2003). Diary methods: Capturing life as it is lived. *Annual Review of Psychology, 54,* 579–616.

Bolger, N., & Zuckerman, A. (1995). A framework for studying personality in the stress process. *Journal of Personality and Social Psychology, 69,* 890–902.

Brown, G.W., & Harris, T.O. (1989). *Life events and illness.* New York: Guilford.

Cohen, S., Kessler, R.C., & Gordon, L. (1997). Strategies for measuring stress in studies of psychiatric and physical disorders. In S. Cohen, R.C. Kessler, & L. Gordon (Eds.), *Measuring stress: A guide for health and social scientists* (pp. 3–26). New York: Oxford University Press.

Grzywacz, J.G., Almeida, D.M., Neupert, S.D., & Ettner, S.L. (2004). Stress and socioeconomic differentials in physical and mental health: A daily diary approach. *Journal of Health and Social Behavior, 45,* 1–16.

Larson, R., & Almeida, D.M. (1999). Emotional transmission in the daily lives of families: A new paradigm for studying family processes. *Journal of Marriage and the Family, 61,* 5–20.

Lazarus, R.S. (1999). *Stress and emotion: A new synthesis.* New York: Springer.

McEwen, B.S. (1998). Protective and damaging effects of stress mediators. *New England Journal of Medicine, 338,* 171–179.

Reis, H.T., & Gable, S.L. (2000). Event-sampling and other methods for studying everyday experience. In H.T. Reis & C.M. Judd (Eds.), *Handbook of research methods in social and personality psychology* (pp. 190–222). New York: Cambridge University Press.

Serido, J., Almeida, D.M., & Wethington, E. (2004). Conceptual and empirical distinctions between chronic stressors and daily hassles. *Journal of Health and Social Behavior, 45,* 17–33.

Stone, A.A., Shiffman, S., Schwartz, J.E., Broderick, J.E., & Hufford, M.R. (2002). Patient noncompliance with paper diaries. *British Medical Journal, 324,* 1193–1194.

Zautra, A.J. (2003). *Emotions, stress, and health.* New York: Oxford University Press.

The Body Stripped Down: An Existential Account of the Threat Posed by the Physical Body

Jamie L. Goldenberg[1]
University of South Florida

Abstract

According to terror management theory, cultural beliefs and standards provide protection from fears associated with mortality by convincing individuals that their existence matters more than that of any mere mortal animal. The body threatens the efficacy of such mechanisms by reminding us that we are animals nonetheless, and therefore fated to death. I present research demonstrating that existential concerns contribute to uneasiness with the body, especially regarding sex, and also to pervasive concerns with how the body measures up to cultural standards, most obviously regarding women's appearance. These findings show that in effort to defend against threats associated with the body's physicality, people may deny themselves pleasure and endanger their health.

Keywords

mortality salience; creatureliness; sexuality; appearance; disgust

It is through the physical body that people experience many of life's most basic pleasures, yet individuals go to great lengths to deny or disguise the body's physicality. Around the globe, cultures impose elaborate customs to repress sexuality. Some extreme examples are found in parts of Africa and the Middle East, where every day thousands of girls are forced to have their clitorises surgically removed and some are murdered by their own family for dishonor resulting from unchaste behavior. In the United States, billions of dollars are spent to conceal natural bodily scents and imperfections. As illustration, in 2004 almost three million women willingly injected botox (a form of botulism toxin) into their faces to paralyze muscles and avoid the appearance of wrinkles. Why do cultures so highly control (and individuals so willingly submit to prescriptions for) the body, with taboos surrounding sex, standards for physical attractiveness, and means of concealing the body's more creaturely functions?

Attitudes toward the body are influenced by many factors, but the research I present suggests that uneasiness surrounding the body stems in part from existential concerns associated with human awareness that the physical body is the vehicle through which life passes unto death; consequently, reminders of our physical nature present a threat that humans can defend against by raising themselves above mere animal (and thus mortal) existence.

TERROR MANAGEMENT THEORY

Following a long line of existential thinkers culminating in the work of Ernest Becker (e.g., 1973), terror management theory (Greenberg, Solomon, & Pyszczynski,

1997) suggests that human beings are haunted by unconscious awareness of inevitable death and that they cope with this threat by constructing and conforming to cultural systems of meaning and value. Individual death becomes less traumatic to the extent that an individual conceives of him- or herself as a valuable contributor to something larger, more meaningful, and longer lasting than mere animal existence. Thus, rather than be preoccupied with conscious worries about death, people strive to buttress the validity of culturally specified systems of meaning and to live up to the standards of their own particular anxiety-buffering worldview.

Experiments designed to test terror management theory hypotheses often manipulate the salience of thoughts of death. *Mortality salience* is usually primed with explicit questions about one's own death, which are followed by a distracting task to allow mortality concerns to recede from consciousness (some research has alternatively used a method in which people are subliminally primed with the word *death*). Subsequently, worldview defense or self-esteem striving is measured. For example, compared to a variety of control topics, mortality salience leads people to respond more negatively toward individuals who transgress against cultural norms, to express increased discomfort when they themselves violate cultural mores, and to behaviorally strive to meet culturally endorsed standards of self-esteem. In addition, dispositional or experimentally induced high self-esteem protects individuals from anxiety and reduces defensive reactions associated with mortality concerns. These experiments support the propositions that people are threatened by death and that a sense of meaning and self-esteem may provide a defensive buffer against such concerns.

A BODY OF TERROR

Because death is such a central concern, people are threatened not only by death per se, but by anything that reminds them of their mortal nature. Thus a person's body, which aches, bleeds, and grows old, makes evident their vulnerability and ongoing trajectory toward death. Moreover, bodies exude all sorts of scents and substances that can provide reminders of a person's physical, and thus mortal, nature. If, as terror management theory suggests, humans cope with their mortality through symbolic manifestations of meaning and value, then the physicality of the body threatens the efficacy of these defenses. As Becker (1973) surmised, "[humans] have a symbolic identity that brings [them] sharply out of nature," but the body reminds them that they are "hopelessly in it" (p.26); and it is this paradox that makes the body such a problem. My central thesis is that the body is problematic because it reminds humans of their sheer physicality and their similarity to other animals, which in turn reminds them of their vulnerability to death. My colleagues and I have tested this hypothesis in a number of domains in which individuals appear to protest against their physical and mortal nature.

The Disgusting and Disgusted Animal

The belief that the physical and animal nature of humans is a weakness to be controlled or transcended is a prominent theme cutting across cultures, historical epochs, and philosophical and religious traditions. The soul or spirit is favored over the body, intellectual life over passion, human will over temptation; and the capacity to exert these formers over the latter is viewed as proof of human superiority over animals. Consistent with this view, Haidt, McCauley, and Rozin (e.g., 1994) have suggested that stimuli most likely to elicit disgust are those involving the fundamentals of animal life (i.e., eating, excreting, grooming, reproduction, injury, death, and decay). Interestingly, on their measure of disgust sensitivity, Haidt et al. (1994) found that items assessing contact with death (e.g., "touching a corpse") were most predictive of overall disgust proneness. This finding fits nicely within the current framework, in which people's concerns about mortality underlie their need to distinguish themselves from animals and in which disgust is viewed as an emotional reaction toward whatever threatens this need.

We designed two experiments to test this hypothesis (Goldenberg et al., 2001). In the first, after priming mortality salience, participants were asked to evaluate an essay describing either the biological similarities between humans and animals (creatureliness) or one emphasizing culture as distinguishing humans from animals (cultural distinction). The results showed that death reminders increased preference for the cultural distinction essay over the essay emphasizing human creatureliness. In a second experiment, mortality salience increased disgust reactions to bodily products and animals, providing converging support for the claim that existential factors motivate humans to distance themselves from other animals and cause them to react to reminders of animality with disgust.

The Problem With Sex

These ideas logically extend to the widely observed ambivalence surrounding human sexuality. Sex is clearly a source of pleasure, but also of anxiety, shame, guilt, and inhibition. Although there is tremendous variability across cultures and between individuals, unencumbered acceptance of sex is rare. Acceptance of sex is usually qualified by conditions: e.g., only in love or marriage, with an appropriate opposite-sex partner; not during menstruation; only for procreation; even through a hole in a sheet; or never, if you are a member of the clergy. I posit that, in sharp contrast to its obvious redeeming qualities, sex poses a psychological threat due to its potential to make evident our core animal (and thus mortal) nature.

Goldenberg, Cox, Pyszczynski, Greenberg, and Solomon (2002) manipulated how likely participants were to perceive sex as an animalistic act by randomly assigning individuals to read one of the two aforementioned essays that highlighted either the creatureliness or cultural distinction of humans. In a first study, the essay prime was followed by a mortality salience manipulation, after which we measured the appeal of physical and romantic aspects of sex. Results showed that when the similarities between humans and animals were made salient via the creatureliness essay, reminders of death decreased the appeal of physical, but not romantic (and hence uniquely human), aspects of sex. In the cultural distinction essay condition, mortality salience had no effect on the appeal of sex. Thus when people were led to associate the physical aspects of sex with animalistic behavior, mortality concerns inhibited desire for sex.

In a second study, after reading one of the two essays, thoughts about either physical or romantic aspects of sex were primed and then the likelihood of participants spontaneously generating thoughts about death (referred to as *death-thought accessibility*) was measured by counting up the number of word fragments they completed with death-related words (e.g., COFF _ _ could be *coffee* or *coffin*). Findings revealed that, when participants had been reminded of their creatureliness (but not when cultural distinction was primed), thinking about physical, but not romantic, aspects of sex increased the accessibility of death-related thoughts. These studies provide converging evidence that the association between physical aspects of sex and awareness of one's animal nature is threatening due to existential concerns.

The Body Beautiful

Although the precise features that particular cultures deem beautiful vary, all cultures value physical appearance and reinforce its members who successfully attain its standards of attractiveness. Although some cultural standards may have an evolutionary basis in characteristics associated with reproductive health (e.g., youthful women with a .7 hip-to-waist ratio), some are so exaggerated as to be mostly unattainable or even life-endangering. The culture and its agents (e.g., television, movies, newspapers, magazines, the fashion and cosmetic industries) of course play a significant role in setting standards and motivating individuals to measure up. However, the existential perspective proposed here can shed additional light on why all cultures regulate the body's appearance and why individuals strive so hard to live up to cultural standards. Through the body's appearance, humans can transform the animal body into a symbol through which they can acquire self-esteem and thereby ward off fears of death.

My colleagues and I have examined the hypothesis that mortality concerns underlie individuals' vigorous striving to attain cultural standards of bodily appearance. For example, after being primed with mortality salience, women expressed greater intentions to tan their skin, especially after being primed to associate tanned skin with attractiveness (via an advertisement featuring a tanned attractive woman; Routledge, Arndt, & Goldenberg, 2004). In other research (Goldenberg, Arndt, Hart, & Brown, in press), after a reminder of mortality, women (but not men) restricted their eating of a nutritious, but fattening, snack food. Furthermore, women who were relatively higher in body weight viewed their figures as more discrepant from what they perceived to be a culturally ideal thinness after being primed with mortality salience and this perceived discrepancy mediated the tendency to restrict food consumption. Thus, motivation to attain cultural standards for the body was enhanced by mortality concerns.

As the preceding examples illustrate, often women are evaluated on their appearance, and therefore strive to enhance it, to a greater degree than men. An existential perspective can augment sociocultural and evolutionary explanations of this discrepancy: Women play a more obvious role in reproduction (i.e., women menstruate, lactate, and bear children) and, to the extent that reproductive processes are threatening reminders of creatureliness, objectification of women's bodies may provide a viable defense. Roberts, Goldenberg, Power, and Pyszczynski (2002) provided support for this notion by showing that male and female participants evaluated a woman who revealed her menstrual cycle by "accidentally" dropping a wrapped tampon more negatively than one who dropped a hairclip instead; participants also responded to this event by viewing women in a more objectified light (i.e., placing greater importance on women's appearance). Thus, the greater emphasis on women's beauty may be understood in part as a means of obscuring their threatening creaturely reproductive responsibility.

IMPLICATIONS

Several general implications follow from this program of research. We have already shown evidence of health implications (e.g., tanning, dieting) associated with existentially motivated efforts to attain an ideal body, particularly for women. In addition, threats associated with human creatureliness may pose barriers to certain health-protective behaviors that involve intimate confrontation with the physical body. In recent work, we (Goldenberg, Arndt, Routledge, & Hart, 2005) have begun to uncover a direct negative impact of concerns about the physicality of the body on women's willingness to perform breast self-exams. Reminders of creatureliness led to decreased intentions to conduct breast self-exams when mortality (but not dental pain, primed in the control condition) was salient (Fig. 1).

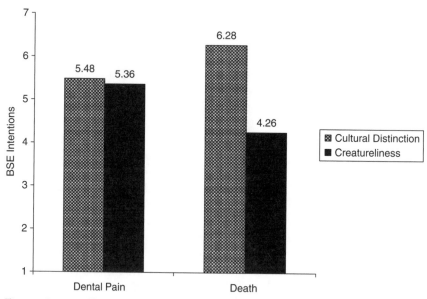

Fig. 1. Breast self-exam (BSE) intentions as a function of creatureliness and mortality salience. After thinking about mortality (but not the control topic of dental pain), an essay emphasizing human creatureliness reduced women's intentions to perform breast self-examinations compared to an essay emphasizing culture as distinguishing humans from animals.

In a subsequent study in which women performed an exam for breast cancer detection on a breast model (an experience that was shown to make thoughts of death salient), a creatureliness prime decreased exam durations in the absence of any explicit mortality salience manipulation. These studies support terror management theory as an explanatory tool for increasing understanding of health consequences associated with behaviors that make salient the physicality and frailty of the human body.

Existential discomfort with the body may have psychological costs in addition to physical health risks. As already shown, concerns about mortality and creatureliness cause individuals to experience disgust and to distance themselves from the physical aspects of sex. These reactions presumably lead to difficulties accepting one's own physical nature, to shame and anxiety about the body, and perhaps to difficulties in romantic relationships. They may also contribute to inhibitions of one's experience of bodily pleasure. Indeed, my colleagues and I (Goldenberg, Hart et al., 2005) recently found that reminders of mortality led some individuals to shorten the duration in which they engaged in an activity that they described as physically pleasurable (i.e., using an electric foot massager) but not another nonphysical activity. Thus, existential threats posed by the body may hinder one's emotional satisfaction and physically fulfillment.

CONCLUSION

Erich Fromm (1955) posed the question, "Why did man not go insane in the face of an existential contradiction between a symbolic self, that seems to give man infinite worth in a timeless scheme of things, and a body that is worth about 98 cents?" (p. 34). In concluding, I suggest that people do often behave as if insane when it comes to their relationship with their bodies: Individuals regulate, adorn, and judge their bodies by the rules and standards of their culture, and in doing so, they sometimes deny themselves pleasure and even willingly cause their bodies harm.

However, such outcomes are by no means unalterable aspects of the human condition. Recognizing factors that create psychological difficulties and understanding the nature of the defenses against such difficulties is a critical first step toward altering negative outcomes. Informed efforts can then be made to intervene. For example, Goldenberg, Pyszczynski, McCoy, Greenberg, and Solomon (1999) showed that thinking about love after thinking about the physical aspects of sex reduced the threatening connotations associated with the latter; and it makes sense that similarly meaningful contexts can be applied to other bodily experiences. For example, by encouraging a sense of empowerment associated with breast self-exams, women may view the behavior not as a mere physical act but as a symbolic reflection of their value. By stripping the body of its illusions and revealing an impact of existential concerns on human motivation, people may be in a better position to uncover more benign ways to view the body and cope with mortality. The body, after all, is not only associated with death, but can be an exhilarating reminder that one is, for the moment, alive.

Recommended Reading

Becker, E. (1973). (See References)

Goldenberg, J.L., Pyszczynski, T., Greenberg, J., & Solomon, S. (2000). Fleeing the body: A terror management perspective on the problem of human corporeality. *Psychology and Social Psychology Review, 4,* 200–218.

Goldenberg, J.L., & Roberts, T.-A. (2004). The beast within the beauty: An existential perspective on the objectification and condemnation of women. In J. Greenberg, S.L., Koole, and T. Pyszczynski (Eds.), *Handbook of Experimental Existential Psychology* (pp.71–85). New York: Guilford.

Greenberg, J., Solomon, S., & Pyszczynski, T. (1997). (See References)

Rozin, P., Haidt, J., & McCauley, C.R. (2000). Disgust. In M. Lewis & J. Haviland (Eds.), *Handbook of emotions* (2nd ed., pp. 637–653). New York: Guilford.

Acknowledgments—This research was supported by National Cancer Institute Grant R01 CA96581-01 and National Science Foundation grants SBR-9729946 and SBR-9731626. The author warmly acknowledges Jeff Greenberg, Tom Pyszczynski, and Jessica Tracy's feedback while preparing this manuscript.

Note

1. Address correspondence to Jamie Goldenberg, Department of Psychology, University of South Florida, 4202 East Fowler Ave, PCD 4118G, Tampa, FL 33620-7200; e-mail: jgoldenb@cas.usf.edu.

References

Becker, E. (1973). *The denial of death*. New York: Free Press.

Fromm, E. (1955). *The sane society*. New York: Fawcett Books.

Goldenberg, J.L., Arndt, J., Hart, J., & Brown, M. (in press). Dying to be thin: The effects of mortality salience and body-mass index on restricted eating among women. *Personality and Social Psychology Bulletin*.

Goldenberg, J.L., Arndt, J., Routledge, C., & Hart, J. (2005). *Uncovering an existential barrier to breast cancer screening behavior*. Manuscript submitted for publication.

Goldenberg, J.L., Cox, C.R., Pyszczynski, T., Greenberg, J., & Solomon, S. (2002). Understanding human ambivalence about sex: The effects of stripping sex of meaning. *Journal of Sex Research, 39,* 310–320.

Goldenberg, J.L., Hart, J., Pyszczynski, T., Warnica, G.M., Landau, M., & Thomas, L. (2005). *Terror of the body: Death, neuroticism, and the flight from physical sensation*. Manuscript submitted for publication.

Goldenberg, J.L., Pyszczynski, T., Greenberg, J., Solomon, S., Kluck, B., & Cornwell, R. (2001). I am not an animal: Mortality salience, disgust, and the denial of human creatureliness. *Journal of Experimental Psychology, 130,* 427–435.

Goldenberg, J.L., Pyszczynski, T., McCoy, S.K., Greenberg, J., & Solomon, S. (1999). Death, sex, and neuroticism: Why is sex such a problem? *Journal of Personality and Social Psychology, 77,* 1173–1187.

Greenberg, J., Solomon, S., & Pyszczynski, T. (1997). Terror management theory of self-esteem and social behavior: Empirical assessments and conceptual refinements. In M.P. Zanna (Ed.), *Advances in Experimental Social Psychology* (Vol. 29, pp. 61–139). New York: Academic Press.

Haidt, J., McCauley, C.R., & Rozin, P. (1994). Individual differences in sensitivity to disgust: A scale sampling seven domains of disgust elicitors. *Personality and Individual Differences, 16,* 701–713.

Roberts, T.-A., Goldenberg, J.L., Power, C., & Pyszczynski, T. (2002). Feminine protection: The effects of menstruation on attitudes toward women. *Psychology of Women Quarterly, 26,* 131–139.

Routledge, C., Arndt, J., & Goldenberg, J.L. (2004). A time to tan: Proximal and distal effects of mortality salience on sun exposure intentions. *Personality and Social Psychology* Bulletin, *30*, 1347–1358.

Section 1: Critical Thinking Questions

1. Kajantie (2008) and Stoney (2003) reviewed factors that underlie gender differences in health at many points in the life span. Some factors, such as diet, are modifiable and others, such as family history, are not. What advice would you give to a pregnant woman about why she should try to minimize stress during pregnancy? What advice would you give to a middle-aged man to reduce his risk of cardiovascular disease? What would you tell a young woman? Would your advice differ if the woman was post-menopause? If so, how?

2. Symptoms of heart disease do not look the same for men and women, which, as explained by Stoney (2003), affect the speed in which men and women seek medical care and the likelihood of having a heart attack properly diagnosed by medical personnel. If diagnostic and referral biases were eliminated, would men and women still differ in their rates of cardiovascular disease? Explain.

3. Various factors affect how resilient or vulnerable individuals are to daily stressors and cardiovascular disease. How might gender differences in response to daily stressors (Almeida) affect risk and resiliency of men and women for cardiovascular disease (Kajantie; Stoney)?

This article has been reprinted as it originally appeared in *Current Directions in Psychological Science*. Citation information for this article as originally published appears above.

Section 2: Psychological Health and Well-Being

One of the most robust gender differences over the life span and across cultures is that females are much more likely than men to experience depression. Nolen-Hocksema explains this gender difference in terms of gender differences in power, status, and the experience of certain traumas and strains. She also addresses the gender gap in depressive symptoms by discussing differences in men's and women's biological responses, self-concepts, and coping styles when presented with the same stressors. After reviewing findings from her research and that of others, Nolen-Hocksema presents a model that integrates biological, social, and psychological factors to explain gender differences in stress experiences and stress reactivity as they relate to depression.

Relational aggression refers to harm inflicted through the manipulation of relationships and/or the threat of damage to relationships. Whereas boys are usually the targets of physical aggression, girls are thought to be the more likely victims of relational aggression. Crick, Casas, and Nelson take a developmental approach to the review of pertinent studies, focusing in part on the conflicting evidence about gender differences in the likelihood of being victimized. They also discuss the implications of relational victimization for social psychological harm.

As lesbian and gay adults more commonly are also parents and rear children from birth, questions have arisen about the consequences for children's well-being of being reared by same-sex parents. Particular concerns have surfaced in areas that involve gender such as identity development, peer relations, and sexual orientation. Patterson culls scientific evidence from studies conducted with various types of samples and research designs to conclude that the gender and sexual orientation of the parents are not nearly as important as the quality of daily interactions and family relationships. The implications of these findings are discussed as they pertain to assumptions about socialization in general and to legal and social policies that concern lesbian and gay parents.

Global feelings of self-worth, or self-esteem, fluctuate over the life span due to maturational changes in the individual and changes in the social environment. Robins, Trzesniewksi and colleagues have conducted meta-analytic reviews of studies of self-esteem across the life span and summarize those findings. A focus of the article is on the comparative waxing and waning of self-esteem for males and females. Although the overall pattern is similar for the sexes, there are some interesting gender gaps that emerge at particular points in the life span. The authors discuss possible explanations and identify directions for further research and theory on self-esteem.

A marker of the transition into later adulthood is retirement from full-time employment. Retirement ushers in a cascade of changes in roles, relationships, and routines, and carries implications for income and health. Within a life-course ecological perspective, Kim and Moen review data on whether and how retirement affects marital quality and subjective well-being, which refers to men's and women's evaluations of the quality of their lives. Gender is shown to be a key source of variability in the process of retirement and its consequences for couple and individual well-being.

Gender Differences in Depression

Susan Nolen-Hoeksema[1]

Department of Psychology, University of Michigan, Ann Arbor, Michigan

Abstract

From early adolescence through adulthood, women are twice as likely as men to experience depression. Many different explanations for this gender difference in depression have been offered, but none seems to fully explain it. Recent research has focused on gender differences in stress responses, and in exposure to certain stressors. I review this research and describe how gender differences in stress experiences and stress reactivity may interact to create women's greater vulnerability to depression.

Keywords

gender; depression; stress

Across many nations, cultures, and ethnicities, women are about twice as likely as men to develop depression (Nolen-Hoeksema, 1990; Weissman et al., 1996). This is true whether depression is indexed as a diagnosed mental disorder or as subclinical symptoms. Diagnosable depressive disorders are extraordinarily common in women, who have a lifetime prevalence for major depressive disorder of 21.3%, compared with 12.7% in men (Kessler, McGonagle, Swartz, Blazer, & Nelson, 1993).

Most explanations for the gender difference in depression have focused on individual variables, and studies have attempted to show that one variable is better than another in explaining the difference. In three decades of research, however, no one variable has single-handedly accounted for the gender difference in depression. In recent years, investigators have moved toward more integrated models, taking a transactional, developmental approach. Transactional models are appropriate because it is clear that depression impairs social and occupational functioning, and thus can have a major impact on an individual's environment. Developmental models are appropriate because age groups differ markedly in the gender difference in depression. Girls are no more likely than boys to evidence depression in childhood, but by about age 13, girls' rates of depression begin to increase sharply, whereas boys' rates of depression remain low, and may even decrease. By late adolescence, girls are twice as likely as boys to be depressed, and this gender ratio remains more or less the same throughout adulthood. The absolute rates of depression in women and men vary substantially across the life span, however.

In this review, I focus on two themes in recent research. First, because women have less power and status than men in most societies, they experience certain traumas, particularly sexual abuse, more often than men. They also experience more chronic strains, such as poverty, harassment, lack of respect, and constrained choices. Second, even when women and men experience the same stressors, women may be more likely than men to develop depression because of gender differences in biological responses to stressors, self-concepts, or coping styles.

Frequent stressful experiences and reactivity to stress are likely to have reciprocal effects on each other. Stressful experiences can sensitize both biological and psychological systems to future stress, making it more likely that individuals will react with depression. In turn, reactivity to stress is associated with impaired problem solving, and, as a result, with the accumulation or generation of new stressors, which may contribute to more depression.

STRESSFUL LIFE EVENTS

Women's lack of social power makes them more vulnerable than men to specific major traumas, particularly sexual abuse. Traumas may contribute directly to depression, by making women feel they are helpless to control their lives, and may also contribute indirectly, by increasing women's reactivity to stress. Women's social roles also carry a number of chronic strains that might contribute directly or indirectly to depression. Major changes in the frequency of traumatic events and in social roles coincide with the emergence of gender differences in depression in adolescence, and may help to explain this emergence.

Victimization

Women are the victims of sexual assault—defined as being pressured or forced into unwanted sexual contact—at least twice as often as men, and people with a history of sexual assault have increased rates of depression (see Weiss, Longhurst, & Mazure, 1999). Sexual assault during childhood has been more consistently linked with the gender difference in depression than sexual assault that first occurs during adulthood. Estimates of the prevalence of childhood sexual assault range widely. Cutler and I reviewed the most methodologically sound studies including both male and female participants and found rates of childhood sexual assault between 7 and 19% for females and between 3 and 7% for males (Cutler & Nolen-Hoeksema, 1991). We estimated that, in turn, as much as 35% of the gender difference in adult depression could be accounted for by the higher incidence of assault of girls relative to boys. A few studies have examined whether depression might be an antecedent rather than a consequence of sexual assault. Depression does appear to increase risk for sexual assault in women and men, but sexual assault significantly increases risk for first or new onsets of depression.

Childhood sexual assault may increase risk for depression throughout the life span because abuse experiences negatively alter biological and psychological responses to stress (Weiss et al., 1999). Children and adolescents who have been abused, particularly those who have been repeatedly abused over an extended period of time, tend to have poorly regulated biological response to stress. Abuse experiences can also negatively alter children's and adolescents' perspectives on themselves and others, contributing to their vulnerability to depression (Zahn-Waxler, 2000).

Chronic Strains

Women face a number of chronic burdens in everyday life as a result of their social status and roles relative to men, and these strains could contribute to their higher rates of depression (see Nolen-Hoeksema, 1990). Women make less money than men, and are much more likely than men to live in poverty. Women are more likely than men to be sexually harassed on the job. Women often have full-time paid jobs and also do nearly all the child care and domestic work of the home. In addition, women are increasingly "sandwiched" between caring for young children and caring for sick and elderly family members. This role overload is said to contribute to a sense of "burn out" and general distress, including depressive symptoms, in women.

In the context of heterosexual relationships, some women face inequities in the distribution of power over important decisions that must be made, such as the decision to move to a new city, or the decision to buy an expensive item such as a car (Nolen-Hoeksema, Larson, & Grayson, 1999). Even when they voice their opinions, women may feel these opinions are not taken seriously, or that their viewpoints on important issues are not respected and affirmed by their partners. My colleagues and I measured chronic strain by grouping inequities in workload and heterosexual relationships into a single variable, and found that this variable predicted increases in depression over time, and partially accounted for the gender difference in depression (Nolen-Hoeksema et al., 1999). Depression also contributed to increased chronic strain over time, probably because it was associated with reductions in perceptions of control and effective problem solving.

Gender Intensification in Adolescence

Social pressure to conform to gender roles is thought to increase dramatically as children move through puberty. For girls, this may mean a reduction in their opportunities and choices, either real or perceived. According to adolescents' own reports, parents restrict girls' more than boys' behaviors and have lower expectations for girls' than for boys' competencies and achievements. Girls also feel that if they pursue male-stereotyped activities and preferences, such as interests in math and science or in competitive sports, they are rejected by their peers. For many girls, especially white girls, popularity and social acceptance become narrowly oriented around appearance.

This narrowing of acceptable behavior for girls in early adolescence may contribute to the increase in depression in girls at this time, although this popular theory has been the focus of remarkably little empirical research (Nolen-Hoeksema & Girgus, 1994). There is substantial evidence that excessive concern about appearance is negatively associated with well-being in girls, but these findings may apply primarily to white girls. In addition, very little research has examined whether appearance concerns and gender roles are risk factors for depression or only correlates.

REACTIVITY TO STRESS

Even when women and men are confronted with similar stressors, women may be more vulnerable than men to developing depression and related anxiety disorders such as posttraumatic stress disorder (Breslau, Davis, Andreski, Peterson, &

Schultz, 1997). Women's greater reactivity compared with men's has been attributed to gender differences in biological responses, self-concepts, and coping styles.

Biological Responses to Stress

For many years, the biological explanations for women's greater vulnerability to depression focused on the direct effects of the ovarian hormones (especially estrogen and progesterone) on women's moods. This literature is too large and complicated to review here (but see Nolen-Hoeksema, 1990, 1995). Simply put, despite widespread popular belief that women are more prone to depression than men because of direct negative effects of estrogen or progesterone on mood, there is little consistent scientific evidence to support this belief. Although some women do become depressed during periods of hormonal change, including puberty, the premenstrual period of the menstrual cycle, menopause, and the postpartum period, it is unclear that these depressions are due to the direct effects of hormonal changes on mood, or that depressions during these periods of women's lives account for the gender differences in rates of depression.

More recent biological research has focused not on direct effects of ovarian hormones on moods, but on the moderating effects of hormones, particularly adrenal hormones, on responses to stress. The hypothalamic-pituitary-adrenal (HPA) axis plays a major role in regulating stress responses, in part by regulating levels of a number of hormones, including cortisol, which is released by the adrenal glands in response to chemicals secreted by the brain's hypothalamus and then the pituitary. In turn, cortisol levels can affect other biochemicals known to influence moods. People with major depressive disorder often show elevated cortisol responses to stress, indicating dysregulation of the HPA response.

An intriguing hypothesis is that women are more likely than men to have a dysregulated HPA response to stress, which makes them more likely to develop depression in response to stress (Weiss et al., 1999). Women may be more likely to have a dysregulated HPA response because they are more likely to have suffered traumatic events, which are known to contribute to HPA dysregulation. In addition, ovarian hormones modulate regulation of the HPA axis (Young & Korszun, 1999). Some women may have depressions during periods of rapid change in levels of ovarian hormones (the postpartum period, premenstrual period, menopause, and puberty) because hormonal changes trigger dysregulation of the stress response, making these women more vulnerable to depression, particularly when they are confronted with stress. The causal relationship between HPA axis regulation and the gender difference in depression has not been established but is likely to be a major focus of future research.

Self-Concept

Although the idea that girls have more negative self-concepts than boys is a mainstay of the pop-psychology literature, empirical studies testing this hypothesis have produced mixed results (Nolen-Hoeksema & Girgus, 1994). Several studies have found no gender differences in self-esteem, self-concept, or dysfunctional attitudes. Those studies that do find gender differences, however, tend to show that girls have poorer self-concepts than boys. Again, negative self-concepts could contribute directly to depression, and could interact with stressors to contribute to depression. Negative self-concept has been shown to predict increases in depression in some studies of children (Nolen-Hoeksema & Girgus, 1994).

One consistent difference in males' and females' self-concepts concerns interpersonal orientation, the tendency to be concerned with the status of one's relationships and the opinions others hold of oneself. Even in childhood, girls appear more interpersonally oriented than boys, and this gender difference increases in adolescence (Zahn-Waxler, 2000). When interpersonal orientation leads girls and women to subordinate their own needs and desires completely to those of others, they become excessively dependent on the good graces of others (Cyranowski, Frank, Young, & Shear, 2000). They may then be at high risk for depression when conflicts arise in relationships, or relationships end. Several recent studies have shown that girls and women are more likely than boys and men to develop depression in response to interpersonal stressors. Because depression can also interfere with interpersonal functioning, an important topic for future research is whether the gender difference in depression is a consequence or cause of gender differences in interpersonal strain.

Coping Styles

By adolescence, girls appear to be more likely than boys to respond to stress and distress with rumination—focusing inward on feelings of distress and personal concerns rather than taking action to relieve their distress. This gender difference in rumination then is maintained throughout adulthood. Several longitudinal and experimental studies have shown that people who ruminate in response to stress are at increased risk to develop depressive symptoms and depressive disorders over time (Nolen-Hoeksema et al., 1999). In turn, the gender difference in rumination at least partially accounts for the gender difference in depression. Rumination may not only contribute directly to depression, but may also contribute indirectly by impairing problem solving, and thus preventing women from taking action to overcome the stressors they face.

AN INTEGRATIVE MODEL

Women suffer certain stressors more often than men and may be more vulnerable to develop depression in response to stress because of a number of factors. Both stress experiences and stress reactivity contribute directly to women's greater rates of depression compared with men. Stress experiences and stress reactivity also feed on each other, however. The more stress women suffer, the more hyperresponsive they may be to stress, both biologically and psychologically. This hyperresponsiveness may undermine women's ability to control their environments and overcome their stress, leading to even more stress in the future. In addition, depression contributes directly to more stressful experiences, by interfering with occupational and social functioning, and to vulnerability to stress, by inciting rumination, robbing the individual of any sense of mastery she did have, and possibly sensitizing the biological systems involved in the stress response.

Important advances will be made in explaining the gender difference in depression as we understand better the reciprocal effects of biological, social, and psychological systems on each other. Key developmental transitions, particularly the early adolescent years, are natural laboratories for observing the establishment of these processes, because so much changes during these transitions, and these transitions are times of increased risk.

Additional questions for future research include how culture and ethnicity affect the gender difference in depression. The gender difference is found across most cultures and ethnicities, but its size varies considerably, as do the absolute percentages of depressed women and men. The processes contributing to the gender difference in depression may also vary across cultures and ethnicities.

Understanding the gender difference in depression is important for at least two reasons. First, women's high rates of depression exact tremendous costs in quality of life and productivity, for women themselves and their families. Second, understanding the gender difference in depression will help us to understand the causes of depression in general. In this way, gender provides a valuable lens through which to examine basic human processes in psychopathology.

Recommended Reading

Cyranowski, J.M., Frank, E., Young, E., & Shear, K. (2000). (See References)
Nolen-Hoeksema, S. (1990). (See References)
Nolen-Hoeksema, S., & Girgus, J.S. (1994). (See References)
Nolen-Hoeksema, S., Larson, J., & Grayson, C. (1999). (See References)
Young, E., & Korszun, A. (1999). (See References)

Note

1. Address correspondence to Susan Nolen-Hoeksema, Department of Psychology, University of Michigan, 525 E. University Ave., Ann Arbor, MI 48109; e-mail: nolen@umich.edu.

References

Breslau, N., Davis, G.C., Andreski, P., Peterson, E.L., & Schultz, L. (1997). Sex differences in post-traumatic stress disorder. *Archives of General Psychiatry, 54,* 1044–1048.
Cutler, S., & Nolen-Hoeksema, S. (1991). Accounting for sex differences in depression through female victimization: Childhood sexual abuse. *Sex Roles, 24,* 425–438.
Cyranowski, J.M., Frank, E., Young, E., & Shear, K. (2000). Adolescent onset of the gender difference in lifetime rates of major depression. *Archives of General Psychiatry, 57,* 21–27.
Kessler, R.C., McGonagle, K.A., Swartz, M., Blazer, D.G., & Nelson, C.B. (1993). Sex and depression in the National Comorbidity Survey I: Lifetime prevalence, chronicity, and recurrence. *Journal of Affective Disorders, 29,* 85–96.
Nolen-Hoeksema, S. (1990). *Sex differences in depression.* Stanford, CA: Stanford University Press.
Nolen-Hoeksema, S. (1995). Gender differences in coping with depression across the life span. *Depression, 3,* 81–90.
Nolen-Hoeksema, S., & Girgus, J.S. (1994). The emergence of gender differences in depression in adolescence. *Psychological Bulletin, 115,* 424–443.
Nolen-Hoeksema, S., Larson, J., & Grayson, C. (1999). Explaining the gender difference in depression. *Journal of Personality and Social Psychology, 77,* 1061–1072.

Weiss, E.L., Longhurst, J.G., & Mazure, C.M. (1999). Childhood sexual abuse as a risk factor for depression in women: Psychosocial and neurobiological correlates. *American Journal of Psychiatry, 156,* 816–828.

Weissman, M.M., Bland, R.C., Canino, G.J., Faravelli, C., Greenwald, S., Hwu, H.-G., Joyce, P.R., Karam, E.G., Lee, C.-K., Lellouch, J., Lepine, J.-P., Newman, S.C., Rubio-Stipc, M., Wells, E., Wickramaratne, P.J., Wittchen, H.-U., & Yeh, E.-K. (1996). Cross-national epidemiology of major depression and bipolar disorder. *Journal of the American Medical Association, 276,* 293–299.

Young, E., & Korszun, A. (1999). Women, stress, and depression: Sex differences in hypothalamic-pituitary-adrenal axis regulation. In E. Leibenluft (Ed.), *Gender differences in mood and anxiety disorders: From bench to bedside* (pp. 31–52). Washington, DC: American Psychiatric Press.

Zahn-Waxler, C. (2000). The development of empathy, guilt, and internalization of distress: Implications for gender differences in internalizing and externalizing problems. In R. Davidson (Ed.), *Wisconsin Symposium on Emotion: Vol. 1. Anxiety, depression, and emotion* (pp. 222–265). Oxford, England: Oxford University Press.

This article has been reprinted as it originally appeared in *Current Directions in Psychological Science*. Citation information for this article as originally published appears above.

Toward a More Comprehensive Understanding of Peer Maltreatment: Studies of Relational Victimization

Nicki R. Crick,[1] Juan F. Casas, and David A. Nelson

Institute of Child Development, University of Minnesota, Twin Cities Campus, Minneapolis, Minnesota (N.R.C.); Department of Psychology, University of Nebraska, Omaha, Nebraska (J.F.C.); and Department of Marriage, Family, and Human Development, Brigham Young University, Provo, Utah (D.A.N.)

Abstract

Although many past studies of peer maltreatment have focused on physical victimization, the importance of an empirical focus on relational victimization has only recently been recognized. In relational victimization, the perpetrator attempts to harm the target through the manipulation of relationships, threat of damage to them, or both. We review what is currently known about relational victimization with three issues in mind: (a) developmental changes in the manifestation of relational victimization, (b) gender differences in the likelihood of being victimized, and (c) evidence that relational victimization is harmful.

Keywords

victimization; gender; relational aggression

Although victimization by peers has long been considered a significant area of empirical inquiry in other countries (e.g., Olweus, 1978), in the United States it has only recently emerged as a "hot" research topic. In this country, increased interest has likely been fueled by several horrific episodes of peer violence that have attracted significant national media attention (e.g., the school shootings in Littleton, Colorado). These events have highlighted the importance of increasing understanding of peer victimization so that people can intervene before troubled interactions escalate to fatal proportions. Interestingly, even in the cases that ended in serious physical injuries and death to the victims, perpetrators (or persons close to them) often cited relational slights (e.g., being excluded from salient social groups, which is one kind of relational victimization) as significant motivating factors in their physically aggressive acts (e.g., Johnson & Brooke, 1999).

Although many past studies of peer maltreatment have focused on physical victimization (e.g., Olweus, 1978; Perry, Kusel, & Perry, 1988), the importance of an empirical focus on relational victimization has only recently been recognized (for a review, see Crick et al., 2001). Anecdotal evidence for the salience of this construct abounds, but this research area is still in its infancy.

46

WHAT IS RELATIONAL VICTIMIZATION?

In contrast to physical victimization, which involves being the frequent target of peers' physically aggressive acts, relational victimization involves being the frequent target of peers' relationally aggressive strategies. Relationally aggressive behaviors are those in which the perpetrator attempts to harm the victim through the manipulation of relationships, threat of damage to them, or both (Crick et al., 2001). Thus, for example, a relational victim may have friends who threaten to withdraw their affection unless he or she does what they want, may be excluded from important social gatherings or activities when a peer is angry with him or her, or may be the target of nasty rumors within the peer group that are designed to motivate peers to reject him or her.

Relationally aggressive acts deprive children of opportunities to satisfy their social needs for closeness, acceptance, and friendship in peer relationships, social psychological experiences that have been shown to be critical for children's development and well-being (for a review, see Baumeister & Leary, 1995). A certain degree of exposure to these behaviors is likely to be normative for most children (and adults), and is unlikely to be detrimental for most individuals. It is the children who are targeted at extreme levels that we are concerned about and whom we consider to be relationally victimized. In our studies, we have defined "extreme" as referring to greater exposure than what is average in a relevant, same-age peer group (e.g., an elementary-school classroom).

Studies of relational victimization are important not only because of the hypothesized salience of relational victimization for all children, but also because of their potential for increasing knowledge of the social development of girls (Crick & Grotpeter, 1996). This is because studies of physical victimization have shown the targets to be primarily boys, but relational victimization is more likely than physical victimization to involve girls as victims. We review what is currently known about relational victimization with three issues in mind: (a) developmental changes in the manifestation of relational victimization, (b) gender differences in the likelihood of being victimized, and (c) evidence that relational victimization is harmful. This discussion is organized with respect to three developmental periods: preschool, middle childhood, and adolescence.

DEVELOPMENTAL CHANGES IN THE MANIFESTATION OF RELATIONAL VICTIMIZATION

The manifestation of relational victimization changes with development, reflecting the social, cognitive, and emotional changes that occur with increasing maturity (Crick et al., 2001). Thus, for example, relational victimization among preschool children tends to involve direct, face-to-face behaviors, such as threatening to exclude someone from a birthday party (e.g., "You can't come to my birthday party unless you let me play in your group") or signaling ignoring by holding one's hands over one's ears (i.e., the preschool equivalent of the "silent treatment"). During middle childhood, relationally victimized children encounter more sophisticated manifestations of peer maltreatment, including both indirect and direct relationally aggressive acts. For example, a peer may spread rumors about them (an indirect act) or may refuse to choose them as team members during gym class as retaliation for a past grievance (a direct act).

These types of victimizing behaviors continue into adolescence (with increasing complexity and subtlety). In addition, the increased salience of opposite-sex friendships and romantic relationships during this developmental period provides new contexts for the expression of relational victimization. For example, a relationally victimized adolescent may find that a peer "gets even" with her for a past grievance by stealing her boyfriend. Or she may discover that her best friend has "shared" negative information about her with her boyfriend in an attempt to damage her romantic relationship. Further, her boyfriend himself may give her the silent treatment when he wants to control or manipulate her (e.g., "I won't talk to you until you do what I want"). Although cross-sectional studies show these developmental trends (Crick et al., 2001), it should be noted that no longitudinal studies of developmental changes in the manifestations of relational victimization have yet been conducted.

GENDER DIFFERENCES IN RELATIONAL VICTIMIZATION

The study of relational victimization was initiated to generate a more gender-balanced view of peer maltreatment, so it is not surprising that several studies have been conducted to evaluate whether there are indeed gender differences in relational victimization. Among preschool-age children, existing findings are mixed with regard to this issue, at least in the case of studies that have assessed victimization by using reports of teachers or peers. Specifically, results of one study showed that girls were more relationally victimized than boys (Crick, Casas, & Ku, 1999), whereas two other studies yielded no gender differences (Bonica, Yershova, & Arnold, 1999; Hart et al., 1999). In contrast, studies that have employed observational methods have shown that girls are significantly more relationally victimized than boys (e.g., Ostrov, Woods, Jansen, Casas, & Crick, 2002).

Research findings for middle childhood and adolescence are also conflicting. Studies in which children and adolescents have been asked to describe the aggressive interchanges that take place in their peer interactions indicate that relational aggression most commonly takes place in female-female interactions (e.g., Crick, Bigbee, & Howes, 1996; French, Jansen, & Pi-dada, in press). However, studies that have assessed victimization by asking children and adolescents or their teachers to answer more standardized questionnaires have yielded mixed findings, with some studies indicating that girls are more relationally victimized than boys and others showing no gender differences (Crick et al., 2001).

Given the paucity of research in this area, it is difficult to draw firm conclusions regarding gender differences in the frequency of relational victimization. However, the salience of relational victimization for increasing understanding of maltreated girls cannot be judged solely on the basis of gender differences in exposure. At least two additional issues must be considered. First, it is important to note that assessing relational victimization results in the identification of significantly more peer-victimized girls than does focusing on physical victimization only, as was done in the past (Crick & Bigbee, 1998). Second, given evidence that females are more likely than males to become distressed by negative interpersonal events (Leadbeater, Blatt, & Quinlan, 1995), the consequences of relational victimization may be more serious for girls than for boys. Thus, regardless of whether or not future research indicates the existence of gender differences in the frequency of relational victimization, the study of relational victimization is likely to have significant utility for enhancing knowledge of the social development of females.

RELATIONAL VICTIMIZATION AND SOCIAL PSYCHOLOGICAL HARM

Two approaches have been taken to establish a link between relational victimization and social psychological harm. In the first, children and adolescents have been asked to describe the types of aggressive harmful behaviors that they have observed in their peer groups (e.g., Crick et al., 1996; French et al., in press). These studies have shown that relationally aggressive acts are among the most commonly cited mean behaviors, a finding that provides evidence of the hurtful nature of relational victimization.

The second approach to assessing the potentially damaging consequences of relational victimization has focused on evaluation of the association between this type of peer maltreatment and indices of social psychological adjustment. These studies have demonstrated that, during the preschool, middle-childhood, and adolescent years, relational victimization within the general peer group is associated with significant concurrent adjustment problems, such as poor peer relationships, internalizing problems (e.g., depressive symptoms), and externalizing difficulties (e.g., delinquent behavior; for a review, see Crick et al., 2001). Recent research has also demonstrated that relational victimization predicts future difficulties such as peer rejection (Crick et al., 2001).

CONCLUSIONS AND FUTURE DIRECTIONS

Given the potentially harmful nature of relational victimization, it will be important to identify factors that predict individual differences in children's risk for exposure to this type of maltreatment and in their propensity for developing other problems related to these experiences (e.g., depressive symptoms). For example, it may be that children who have been exposed to particular kinds of aversive family environments (e.g., parental rejection or neglect, relational victimization by siblings) are more sensitive than other children to relational victimization by peers or are more likely to be viewed within the peer group as easy targets (e.g., peers may sense that these children are more vulnerable than others to social exclusion). For these children, even relatively low levels of relational victimization may be distressing and likely to result in other adjustment difficulties, as well as additional victimization in the future. In contrast, some children may be relatively resilient when confronted with relational victimization, perhaps because of supportive family environments, and may not react negatively to these experiences. This, in turn, may make them less likely to encounter relational victimization in the future (e.g., because they do not react in ways that are rewarding to the perpetrators). These and other factors warrant attention so that researchers can build theoretical models of the processes involved in relational victimization.

A number of future research directions are suggested by existing research and theory. One of the most urgent needs is for longitudinal studies. It is clear from existing studies that relational victimization is associated with concurrent difficulties in adjustment, as well as with difficulties in the short-term future; however, long-term prospective investigations are necessary to establish that relational victimization results in lasting harm. This type of research is also needed to discover whether, as we suggested in the introduction, relational victimization sometimes plays a role in physical violence directed toward peers. Studies of the factors that contribute to relational victimization (e.g., family factors, contextual factors, individual characteristics) are also sorely needed so that empirically based intervention programs can be developed for children who experience this type of peer abuse.

Studies utilizing observational approaches for assessing relational victimization are also needed, along with studies that directly compare the utility and validity of various measures of relational victimization. In addition, it would be useful for future research to evaluate chronicity and severity of relational victimization and their relative contributions to social psychological difficulties. Another important avenue for future work involves generating and applying theory to guide exploration of the impact of relational victimization on children's development. For example, this aversive peer treatment may influence children's interpretations of future peer interactions in negative ways (e.g., they may begin to interpret peers' behavior as intentionally hostile, even when it is not). Social information-processing models may be useful for understanding this phenomenon.

Finally, another issue that warrants attention in future research concerns the role of the relationship context in which victimization occurs. Most previous investigations of relational victimization have evaluated maltreatment in a large, peer-group context (e.g., a classroom). However, given recent evidence that relational peer abuse can also occur in smaller groups or dyads, such as between best friends or in a romantic relationship (for a review, see Crick et al., 2001), future research that considers and systematically compares these various contexts is needed. This may be particularly important for females because relational victimization within the dyadic context has been shown to be particularly problematic for girls (Crick & Nelson, in press).

Recommended Reading

Crick, N.R., & Bigbee, M.A. (1998). (See References)

Crick, N.R., Casas, J.F., & Ku, H. (1999). (See References)

Crick, N.R., & Grotpeter, J.K. (1996). (See References)

Crick, N.R., Nelson, D.A., Morales, J.R., Cullerton-Sen, C., Casas, J.F., & Hickman, S. (2001). (See References)

Juvonen, J., & Graham, S. (Eds.). (2001). *School-based peer harassment: The plight of the vulnerable and victimized.* New York: Guilford Press.

Acknowledgments—Preparation of this essay was supported by a FIRST Award from the National Institute of Mental Health (MH53524) and a Faculty Scholars Award from the William T. Grant Foundation to the first author and by a Child Psychology Training Grant Fellowship from the National Institute of Mental Health (T32MH15755) to the third author.

Note

1. Address correspondence to Nicki R. Crick, Institute of Child Development, University of Minnesota, 51 East River Rd., Minneapolis, MN 55455; e-mail: crick001@ umn.edu.

References

Baumeister, R.F., & Leary, M.R. (1995). The need to belong: Desire for interpersonal attachments as a fundamental human motivation. *Psychological Bulletin, 117,* 497–529.

Bonica, C., Yershova, K., & Arnold, D. (1999, April). *Relational aggression, relational victimization, and language development in preschool.* Poster presented at the biennial meeting of the Society for Research in Child Development, Albuquerque, NM.

Crick, N.R., & Bigbee, M.A. (1998). Relational and overt forms of peer victimization: A multi-informant approach. *Journal of Consulting and Clinical Psychology, 66,* 337–347.

Crick, N.R., Bigbee, M.A., & Howes, C. (1996). Gender differences in children's normative beliefs about aggression: How do I hurt thee? Let me count the ways. *Child Development, 67,* 1003–1014.

Crick, N.R., Casas, J.F., & Ku, H. (1999). Physical and relational peer victimization in preschool. *Developmental Psychology, 35,* 376–385.

Crick, N.R., & Grotpeter, J.K. (1996). Children's treatment by peers: Victims of relational and overt aggression. *Development and Psychopathology, 8,* 367–380.

Crick, N.R., & Nelson, D.A. (in press). Relational and physical victimization within friendships: Nobody told me there'd be friends like this. *Journal of Abnormal Child Psychology.*

Crick, N.R., Nelson, D.A., Morales, J.R., Cullerton-Sen, C., Casas, J.F., & Hickman, S. (2001). Relational victimization in childhood and adolescence: I hurt you through the grapevine. In J. Juvonen & S. Graham (Eds.), *School-based peer harassment: The plight of the vulnerable and victimized* (pp. 196–214). New York: Guilford Press.

French, D.C., Jansen, E.A., & Pidada, S. (in press). U. S. and Indonesian children's and adolescents' reports of relational aggression by disliked peers. *Child Development.*

Hart, C.H., Nelson, D.A., Robinson, C.C., Olsen, S.F., McNeilly-Choque, M.K., Porter, C.L., & McKee, T. (1999). Russian parenting styles and family processes: Linkages with subtypes of victimization and aggression. In K.A. Kerns (Ed.), *Explaining associations between family and peer relationships* (pp. 47–84). New York: Greenwood/Praeger.

Johnson, D., & Brooke, J. (1999, April 22). Terror in Littleton: The suspects; portrait of outcasts seeking to stand out. *The New York Times,* p. A1.

Leadbeater, B.J., Blatt, S.J., & Quinlan, D.M. (1995). Gender-linked vulnerabilities to depressive symptoms, stress, and problem behaviors in adolescents. *Journal of Research in Adolescence, 5,* 1–29.

Olweus, D. (1978). *Aggression in the schools: Bullies and whipping boys.* Washington, DC: Hemisphere.

Ostrov, J., Woods, K., Jansen, E., Casas, J.F., & Crick, N.R. (2002). *An observational study of aggression, victimization, and social-psychological adjustment: "This white crayon doesn't work."* Manuscript submitted for publication.

Perry, D.G., Kusel, S.J., & Perry, L.C. (1988). Victims of peer aggression. *Developmental Psychology, 24,* 807–814.

Children of Lesbian and Gay Parents

Charlotte J. Patterson[1]
University of Virginia

Abstract

Does parental sexual orientation affect child development, and if so, how? Studies using convenience samples, studies using samples drawn from known populations, and studies based on samples that are representative of larger populations all converge on similar conclusions. More than two decades of research has failed to reveal important differences in the adjustment or development of children or adolescents reared by same-sex couples compared to those reared by other-sex couples. Results of the research suggest that qualities of family relationships are more tightly linked with child outcomes than is parental sexual orientation.

Keywords

sexual orientation; parenting; lesbian; gay; child; socialization

Does parental sexual orientation affect child development, and if so, how? This question has often been raised in the context of legal and policy proceedings relevant to children, such as those involving adoption, child custody, or visitation. Divergent views have been offered by professionals from the fields of psychology, sociology, medicine, and law (Patterson, Fulcher, & Wainright, 2002). While this question has most often been raised in legal and policy contexts, it is also relevant to theoretical issues. For example, does healthy human development require that a child grow up with parents of each gender? And if not, what would that mean for our theoretical understanding of parent–child relations (Patterson & Hastings, in press)? In this article, I describe some research designed to address these questions.

EARLY RESEARCH

Research on children with lesbian and gay parents began with studies focused on cases in which children had been born in the context of a heterosexual marriage. After parental separation and divorce, many children in these families lived with divorced lesbian mothers. A number of researchers compared development among children of divorced lesbian mothers with that among children of divorced heterosexual mothers and found few significant differences (Patterson, 1997; Stacey & Biblarz, 2001).

These studies were valuable in addressing concerns of judges who were required to decide divorce and child custody cases, but they left many questions unanswered. In particular, because the children who participated in this research had been born into homes with married mothers and fathers, it was not obvious how to understand the reasons for their healthy development. The possibility that children's early exposure to apparently heterosexual male and female role models had contributed to healthy development could not be ruled out.

When lesbian or gay parents rear infants and children from birth, do their offspring grow up in typical ways and show healthy development? To address this question, it was important to study children who had never lived with heterosexual parents. In the 1990s, a number of investigators began research of this kind.

An early example was the Bay Area Families Study, in which I studied a group of 4- to 9-year-old children who had been born to or adopted early in life by lesbian mothers (Patterson, 1996, 1997). Data were collected during home visits. Results from in-home interviews and also from questionnaires showed that children had regular contact with a wide range of adults of both genders, both within and outside of their families. The children's self-concepts and preferences for same-gender playmates and activities were much like those of other children their ages. Moreover, standardized measures of social competence and of behavior problems, such as those from the Child Behavior Checklist (CBCL), showed that they scored within the range of normal variation for a representative sample of same-aged American children. It was clear from this study and others like it that it was quite possible for lesbian mothers to rear healthy children.

STUDIES BASED ON SAMPLES DRAWN FROM KNOWN POPULATIONS

Interpretation of the results from the Bay Area Families Study was, however, affected by its sampling procedures. The study had been based on a convenience sample that had been assembled by word of mouth. It was therefore impossible to rule out the possibility that families who participated in the research were especially well adjusted. Would a more representative sample yield different results?

To find out, Ray Chan, Barbara Raboy, and I conducted research in collaboration with the Sperm Bank of California (Chan, Raboy, & Patterson, 1998; Fulcher, Sutfin, Chan, Scheib, & Patterson, 2005). Over the more than 15 years of its existence, the Sperm Bank of California's clientele had included many lesbian as well as heterosexual women. For research purposes, this clientele was a finite population from which our sample could be drawn. The Sperm Bank of California also allowed a sample in which, both for lesbian and for heterosexual groups, one parent was biologically related to the child and one was not.

We invited all clients who had conceived children using the resources of the Sperm Bank of California and who had children 5 years old or older to participate in our research. The resulting sample was composed of 80 families, 55 headed by lesbian and 25 headed by heterosexual parents. Materials were mailed to participating families, with instructions to complete them privately and return them in self-addressed stamped envelopes we provided.

Results replicated and expanded upon those from earlier research. Children of lesbian and heterosexual parents showed similar, relatively high levels of social competence, as well as similar, relatively low levels of behavior problems on the parent form of the CBCL. We also asked the children's teachers to provide evaluations of children's adjustment on the Teacher Report Form of the CBCL, and their reports agreed with those of parents. Parental sexual orientation was not related to children's adaptation. Quite apart from parental sexual orientation, however, and consistent with findings from years of research on children of heterosexual parents, when parent–child relationships were marked by warmth and affection, children were more likely to be developing well. Thus, in this sample drawn from a known population, measures of children's adjustment were unrelated to parental sexual orientation (Chan et al., 1998; Fulcher et al., 2005).

Even as they provided information about children born to lesbian mothers, however, these new results also raised additional questions. Women who conceive children at sperm banks are generally both well educated and financially comfortable. It was possible that these relatively privileged women were able to protect children from many forms of discrimination. What if a more diverse group of families were to be studied? In addition, the children in this sample averaged 7 years of age, and some concerns focus on older children and adolescents. What if an older group of youngsters were to be studied? Would problems masked by youth and privilege in earlier studies emerge in an older, more diverse sample?

STUDIES BASED ON REPRESENTATIVE SAMPLES

An opportunity to address these questions was presented by the availability of data from the National Longitudinal Study of Adolescent Health (Add Health). The Add Health study involved a large, ethnically diverse, and essentially representative sample of American adolescents and their parents. Data for our research were drawn from surveys and interviews completed by more than 12,000 adolescents and their parents at home and from surveys completed by adolescents at school.

Parents were not queried directly about their sexual orientation but were asked if they were involved in a "marriage, or marriage-like relationship." If parents acknowledged such a relationship, they were also asked the gender of their partner. Thus, we identified a group of 44 12- to 18-year-olds who lived with parents involved in marriage or marriage-like relationships with same-sex partners. We compared them with a matched group of adolescents living with other-sex couples. Data from the archives of the Add Health study allowed us to address many questions about adolescent development.

Consistent with earlier findings, results of this work revealed few differences in adjustment between adolescents living with same-sex parents and those living with opposite-sex parents (Wainright, Russell, & Patterson, 2004; Wainright & Patterson, 2006). There were no significant differences between teenagers living with same-sex parents and those living with other-sex parents on self-reported assessments of psychological well-being, such as self-esteem and anxiety; measures of school outcomes, such as grade point averages and trouble in school; or measures of family relationships, such as parental warmth and care from adults and peers. Adolescents in the two groups were equally likely to say that they had been involved in a romantic relationship in the last 18 months, and they were equally likely to report having engaged in sexual intercourse. The only statistically reliable difference between the two groups—that those with same-sex parents felt a greater sense of connection to people at school—favored the youngsters living with same-sex couples. There were no significant differences in self-reported substance use, delinquency, or peer victimization between those reared by same- or other-sex couples (Wainright & Patterson, 2006).

Although the gender of parents' partners was not an important predictor of adolescent well-being, other aspects of family relationships were significantly associated with teenagers' adjustment. Consistent with other findings about adolescent development, the qualities of family relationships rather than the gender of parents' partners were consistently related to adolescent outcomes. Parents who reported having close relationships with their offspring had adolescents who reported more favorable adjustment. Not only is it possible for children and adolescents who are parented by same-sex couples to develop in healthy directions, but—even when studied in an extremely diverse, representative sample of American adolescents—they generally do.

These findings have been supported by results from many other studies, both in the United States and abroad. Susan Golombok and her colleagues have reported similar results with a near-representative sample of children in the United Kingdom (Golombok et al., 2003). Others, both in Europe and in the United States, have described similar findings (e.g., Brewaeys, Ponjaert, Van Hall, & Golombok, 1997).

The fact that children of lesbian mothers generally develop in healthy ways should not be taken to suggest that they encounter no challenges. Many investigators have remarked upon the fact that children of lesbian and gay parents may encounter anti-gay sentiments in their daily lives. For example, in a study of 10-year-old children born to lesbian mothers, Gartrell, Deck, Rodas, Peyser, and Banks (2005) reported that a substantial minority had encountered anti-gay sentiments among their peers. Those who had had such encounters were likely to report having felt angry, upset, or sad about these experiences. Children of lesbian and gay parents may be exposed to prejudice against their parents in some settings, and this may be painful for them, but evidence for the idea that such encounters affect children's overall adjustment is lacking.

CONCLUSIONS

Does parental sexual orientation have an important impact on child or adolescent development? Results of recent research provide no evidence that it does. In fact, the findings suggest that parental sexual orientation is less important than the qualities of family relationships. More important to youth than the gender of their parent's partner is the quality of daily interaction and the strength of relationships with the parents they have.

One possible approach to findings like the ones described above might be to shrug them off by reiterating the familiar adage that "one cannot prove the null hypothesis." To respond in this way, however, is to miss the central point of these studies. Whether or not any measurable impact of parental sexual orientation on children's development is ever demonstrated, the main conclusions from research to date remain clear: Whatever correlations between child outcomes and parental sexual orientation may exist, they are less important than those between child outcomes and the qualities of family relationships.

Although research to date has made important contributions, many issues relevant to children of lesbian and gay parents remain in need of study. Relatively few studies have examined the development of children adopted by lesbian or gay parents or of children born to gay fathers; further research in both areas would be welcome (Patterson, 2004). Some notable longitudinal studies have been reported, and they have found children of same-sex couples to be in good mental health. Greater understanding of family relationships and transitions over time would, however, be helpful, and longitudinal studies would be valuable. Future research could also benefit from the use of a variety of methodologies.

Meanwhile, the clarity of findings in this area has been acknowledged by a number of major professional organizations. For instance, the governing body of the American Psychological Association (APA) voted unanimously in favor of a statement that said, "Research has shown that the adjustment, development, and psychological well-being of children is unrelated to parental sexual orientation and that children of lesbian and gay parents are as likely as those of heterosexual parents to flourish" (APA, 2004). The American Bar Association, the American Medical Association, the American Academy of Pediatrics, the American Psychiatric Association, and other mainstream professional groups have issued similar statements.

The findings from research on children of lesbian and gay parents have been used to inform legal and public policy debates across the country (Patterson et al., 2002). The research literature on this subject has been cited in amicus briefs filed by the APA in cases dealing with adoption, child custody, and also in cases related to the legality of marriages between same-sex partners. Psychologists serving as expert witnesses have presented findings on these issues in many different courts (Patterson et al., 2002). Through these and other avenues, results of research on lesbian and gay parents and their children are finding their way into public discourse.

The findings are also beginning to address theoretical questions about critical issues in parenting. The importance of gender in parenting is one such issue. When children fare well in two-parent lesbian-mother or gay-father families, this suggests that the gender of one's parents cannot be a critical factor in child development. Results of research on children of lesbian and gay parents cast doubt upon the traditional assumption that gender is important in parenting. Our data suggest that it is the quality of parenting rather than the gender of parents that is significant for youngsters' development.

Research on children of lesbian and gay parents is thus located at the intersection of a number of classic and contemporary concerns. Studies of lesbian- and gay-parented families allow researchers to address theoretical questions that had previously remained difficult or impossible to answer. They also address oft-debated legal questions of fact about development of children with lesbian and gay parents. Thus, research on children of lesbian and gay parents contributes to public debate and legal decision making, as well as to theoretical understanding of human development.

Recommended Reading

Golombok, S., Perry, B., Burston, A., Murray, C., Mooney-Somers, J., Stevens, M., & Golding, J. (2003). (See References)
Patterson, C.J., Fulcher, M., & Wainright, J. (2002). (See References)

Stacey, J., & Biblarz, T.J. (2001). (See References)
Wainright, J.L., & Patterson, C.J. (2006). (See References)
Wainright, J.L., Russell, S.T., & Patterson, C.J. (2004). (See References)

Note

1. Address correspondence to Charlotte J. Patterson, Department of Psychology, P.O. Box 400400, University of Virginia, Charlottesville, VA 22904; e-mail: cjp@virginia.edu.

References

American Psychological Association (2004). Resolution on sexual orientation, parents, and children. Retrieved September 25, 2006, from http://www.apa.org/pi/lgbc/policy/parentschildren.pdf

Brewaeys, A., Ponjaert, I., Van Hall, E.V., & Golombok, S. (1997). Donor insemination: Child development and family functioning in lesbian mother families. *Human Reproduction, 12,* 1349–1359.

Chan, R.W., Raboy, B., & Patterson, C.J. (1998). Psychosocial adjustment among children conceived via donor insemination by lesbian and heterosexual mothers. *Child Development, 69,* 443–457.

Fulcher, M., Sutfin, E.L., Chan, R.W., Scheib, J.E., & Patterson, C.J. (2005). Lesbian mothers and their children: Findings from the Contemporary Families Study. In A. Omoto & H. Kurtzman (Eds.), *Recent research on sexual orientation, mental health, and substance abuse* (pp. 281–299). Washington, DC: American Psychological Association.

Gartrell, N., Deck., A., Rodas, C., Peyser, H., & Banks, A. (2005). The National Lesbian Family Study: 4. Interviews with the 10-year-old children. *American Journal of Orthopsychiatry, 75,* 518–524.

Golombok, S., Perry, B., Burston, A., Murray, C., Mooney-Somers, J., Stevens, M., & Golding, J. (2003). Children with lesbian parents: A community study. *Developmental Psychology, 39,* 20–33.

Patterson, C.J. (1996). Lesbian mothers and their children: Findings from the Bay Area Families Study. In J. Laird & R.J. Green (Eds.), *Lesbians and gays in couples and families: A handbook for therapists* (pp. 420–437). San Francisco: Jossey-Bass.

Patterson, C.J. (1997). Children of lesbian and gay parents. In T. Ollendick & R. Prinz (Eds.), *Advances in clinical child psychology* (Vol. 19, pp. 235–282). New York: Plenum Press.

Patterson, C.J. (2004). Gay fathers. In M.E. Lamb (Ed.), *The role of the father in child development* (4th ed., pp. 397–416). New York: Wiley.

Patterson, C.J., Fulcher, M., & Wainright, J. (2002). Children of lesbian and gay parents: Research, law, and policy. In B.L. Bottoms, M.B. Kovera, & B.D. McAuliff (Eds.), *Children, social science and the law* (pp. 176–199). New York: Cambridge University Press.

Patterson, C.J., & Hastings, P. (in press). Socialization in context of family diversity. In J. Grusec & P. Hastings (Eds.), *Handbook of socialization.* New York: Guilford Press.

Stacey, J., & Biblarz, T.J. (2001). (How) Does sexual orientation of parents matter? *American Sociological Review, 65,* 159–183.

Wainright, J.L., & Patterson, C.J. (2006). Delinquency, victimization, and substance use among adolescents with female same-sex parents. *Journal of Family Psychology, 20,* 526–530.

Wainright, J.L., Russell, S.T., & Patterson, C.J. (2004). Psychosocial adjustment and school outcomes of adolescents with same-sex parents. *Child Development, 75,* 1886–1898.

This article has been reprinted as it originally appeared in *Current Directions in Psychological Science*. Citation information for this article as originally published appears above.

Self-Esteem Development Across the Life Span

Richard W. Robins[1]
Department of Psychology, University of California, Davis
Kali H. Trzesniewski
Institute of Psychiatry, King's College, London, United Kingdom

Abstract

After decades of debate, a consensus is emerging about the way self-esteem develops across the lifespan. On average, self-esteem is relatively high in childhood, drops during adolescence (particularly for girls), rises gradually throughout adulthood, and then declines sharply in old age. Despite these general age differences, individuals tend to maintain their ordering relative to one another: Individuals who have relatively high self-esteem at one point in time tend to have relatively high self-esteem years later. This type of stability (i.e., rank-order stability) is somewhat lower during childhood and old age than during adulthood, but the over all level of stability is comparable to that found for other personality characteristics. Directions for further research include (a) replication of the basic trajectory using more sophisticated longitudinal designs, (b) identification of the mediating mechanisms underlying self-esteem change, (c) the development of an integrative theoretical model of the life-course trajectory of self-esteem.

Keywords

self-esteem; development; change; stability

As he was nearing the end of his life, Michelangelo began working on what many people believe to be his most important work, the Florentine Pietà. After working intensely for almost a decade, he entered his studio one day and took a sledge-hammer to the sculpture. He broke away the hands and legs and nearly shattered the work before his assistants dragged him away. Why did Michelangelo attempt to destroy one of his greatest creations, a statue that has been described as among the finest works of the Renaissance? Disillusioned and isolated in the last decades of his life, Michelangelo had a heightened sense of perfectionism that was exacerbated by his failure to live up to the expectations of his father, who viewed being a sculptor as akin to being a manual laborer. Michelangelo, it seems, had self-esteem issues. Was Michelangelo's low self-esteem normative for someone his age? Was he likely to have been plagued by self-doubts throughout his life? An emerging body of evidence is beginning to offer answers to these kinds of questions.

In this article, we review the current state of scientific evidence regarding the development of self-esteem across the lifespan.[2] After decades of debate, a consensus is emerging about the way self-esteem changes from childhood to old age. We focus here on two forms of change: (a) normative changes in self-esteem, which reflect whether individuals, on average, increase or decrease over time (assessed by mean differences in self-esteem across age groups); and (b) the stability of individual differences in self-esteem, which reflect the degree to which the relative ordering of individuals is maintained over time (assessed by correlations between self-esteem scores across two time points, i.e., test–retest correlations).[3]

THE NORMATIVE TRAJECTORY OF SELF-ESTEEM ACROSS THE LIFE SPAN

As we go through life, our self-esteem inevitably waxes and wanes. These fluctuations in self-esteem reflect changes in our social environment as well as maturational changes such as puberty and cognitive declines in old age. When these changes are experienced by most individuals at about the same age and influence individuals in a similar manner, they will produce normative shifts in self-esteem across developmental periods.

The findings from three recent studies—a meta-analysis of 86 published articles (Trzesniewski, Donnellan, & Robins, 2001; see also Twenge & Campbell, 2001); a large, cross-sectional study of individuals aged 9 to 90 (Robins, Trzesniewski, Tracy, Gosling, & Potter, 2002); and a cohort-sequential longitudinal study of individuals aged 25 to 96 (Trzesniewski & Robins, 2004)—paint a portrait of the normative trajectory of self-esteem across the life span (see Fig. 1). Below, we summarize the major changes that occur from childhood to old age.

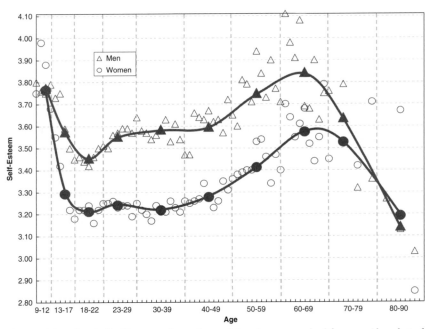

Fig. 1. Mean level of self-esteem for males and females across the life span. Also plotted are year-by-year means, separately for males (open triangles) and females (open circles). From "Global Self-Esteem Across the Life span," by R. W. Robins, K.H. Trzesniewski, J.L. Tracy, S.D. Gosling, and J. Potter, 2002, *Psychology and Aging, 17,* p. 428. Copyright 2002 by the American Psychological Association. Reprinted with permisson.

Childhood

Young children have relatively high self-esteem, which gradually declines over the course of childhood. Researchers have speculated that children have high self-esteem because their self-views are unrealistically positive. As children develop cognitively, they begin to base their self-evaluations on external feedback and social comparisons, and thus form a more balanced and accurate appraisal of their academic competence, social skills, attractiveness, and other personal characteristics. For example, as children move from preschool to elementary school they receive more negative feedback from teachers, parents, and peers, and their self-evaluations correspondingly become more negative.

Adolescence

Self-esteem continues to decline during adolescence. Researchers have attributed the adolescent decline to body image and other problems associated with puberty, the emerging capacity to think abstractly about one's self and one's future and therefore to acknowledge missed opportunities and failed expectations, and the transition from grade school to the more academically challenging and socially complex context of junior high school.

Adulthood

Self-esteem increases gradually throughout adulthood, peaking sometime around the late 60s. Over the course of adulthood, individuals increasingly occupy positions of power and status, which might promote feelings of self-worth. Many lifespan theorists have suggested that midlife is characterized by peaks in achievement, mastery, and control over self and environment (e.g., Erikson, 1985). Consistent with these theoretical speculations, the personality changes that occur during adulthood tend to reflect increasing levels of maturity and adjustment, as indicated by higher levels of conscientiousness and emotional stability (Trzesniewski, Robins, Roberts, & Caspi, 2004).

Old Age

Self-esteem declines in old age. The few studies of self-esteem in old age suggest that self-esteem begins to drop around age 70 (about the age when Michelangelo began working on the Florentine Pietà). This decline may be due to the dramatic confluence of changes that occur in old age, including changes in roles (e.g., retirement), relationships (e.g., the loss of a spouse), and physical functioning (e.g., health problems), as well as a drop in socioeconomic status. The old-age decline may also reflect a shift toward a more modest, humble, and balanced view of the self in old age (Erikson, 1985). That is, older individuals may maintain a deep-seated sense of their own worth, but their self-esteem scores drop because they are increasingly willing to acknowledge their faults and limitations and have a diminished need to present themselves in a positive light to others. Consistent with this interpretation, narcissism tends to decline with age (Foster, Campbell, & Twenge, 2003).

Gender Differences

Overall, males and females follow essentially the same trajectory: For both genders, self-esteem is relatively high in childhood, drops during adolescence, rises gradually throughout adulthood, and then declines in old age. Nonetheless, there are some interesting gender divergences. Although boys and girls report similar levels of self-esteem during childhood, a gender gap emerges by adolescence, such that adolescent boys have higher self-esteem than adolescent girls (Kling, Hyde, Showers, & Buswell, 1999; Robins et al., 2002). This gender gap persists throughout adulthood, and then narrows and perhaps even disappears in old age (Kling et al., 1999; Robins et al., 2002). Researchers have offered numerous explanations for the gender difference, ranging from maturational changes associated with puberty to social-contextual factors associated with the differential treatment of boys and girls in the classroom or gender differences in body image ideals. However, no generally accepted integrative theoretical model exists.

RANK-ORDER STABILITY OF SELF-ESTEEM

Over the past several decades, researchers have debated the degree to which self-esteem should be thought of as a trait-like construct that remains relatively stable over time or as a state-like process that continually fluctuates in response to environmental and situational stimuli. If self-esteem is more state-like over the long term than other personality characteristics, then it may not be a useful predictor of important real-world outcomes.

The findings of a recent meta-analysis support the claim that self-esteem is a stable, trait-like construct (Trzesniewski, Donnellan, & Robins, 2003). The stability of self-esteem across all age groups, as determined by test-retest correlations, is comparable to that of the major dimensions of personality, including Extraversion, Agreeableness, Conscientiousness, Neuroticism, and Openness to Experience (Roberts & DelVecchio, 2000). Thus, individuals who have relatively high self-esteem at one point in time tend to have high self-esteem years later; likewise those with low self-esteem earlier in life tend to have low self-esteem later.

However, self-esteem is more stable in some periods of life than in others. Stability is relatively low during early childhood, increases throughout adolescence and early adulthood, and then declines during midlife and old age. This curvilinear trend holds for men and women, for U.S. and non-U.S. participants, and for different self-esteem scales.

The lower levels of stability found during childhood and old age may reflect the dramatic life changes, shifting social circumstances, and relatively rapid maturational changes that characterize both the beginning and end of life. For example, during old age, important life events such as retirement and becoming a grandparent may transform one's sense of self, producing higher levels of self-esteem in some individuals and lower levels in others. These life events can lead to lower levels of self-esteem stability if they are experienced at different ages (e.g., some people retire earlier than others) or differentially affect individuals (e.g., only some retirees decline in self-esteem). Moreover, Erikson (1985) noted that as individuals grow older they begin to review their lifelong accomplishments and experiences, leading in some cases to more critical self-appraisals (ego despair) and in other cases to increased self-acceptance (ego integrity). Thus, a developmental shift toward greater self-reflection in old age may produce increases in self-esteem for some individuals but decreases for others.

IMPLICATIONS

Until recently, the self-esteem literature had been caught in a quagmire of conflicting findings and there was little agreement about the way self-esteem develops. The research reviewed in this article will hopefully move the field toward consensus, and help address questions such as: When in the life span is self-esteem relatively high or low? Is self-esteem more like a state (relatively transitory) or more like a trait (relatively unchanging)?

Understanding the trajectory of self-esteem may provide insights into the underlying processes that shape self-esteem development. For example, the fact that self-esteem drops during both adolescence and old age suggests that there might be something common to both periods (e.g., the confluence of multiple social and physical changes) that negatively affects self-esteem.

Knowledge about self-esteem development also has implications for the timing of interventions. For example, the normative trajectory of self-esteem across the life span suggests that interventions should be timed for pre- or early adolescence because by late adolescence much of the drop in self-esteem has already occurred. Moreover, developmental periods during which rank-order stability is relatively low may be ideal targets of intervention programs because self-esteem may be particularly malleable during these times of relative upheaval in the self-concept.

CONCLUSIONS AND FUTURE DIRECTIONS

Research accumulating over the past several years paints an increasingly clear picture of the trajectory of self-esteem across the life span. Self-esteem shows remarkable continuity given the vast array of experiences that impinge upon a lived life. At the same time, self-esteem also shows systematic changes that are meaningfully connected to age-related life experiences and contexts. These normative changes illustrate the role of the self as an organizing psychological construct that influences how individuals orient their behavior to meet new demands in their environment and new developmental challenges.

Several difficult but tractable issues remain. First, some of the findings reported here require further replication and exploration. In particular, relatively few studies have documented the decline in self-esteem during old age. Establishing the robustness of this effect is important given inconsistent findings in the literature about whether emotional well-being and other aspects of adjustment drop during old age (Mroczek, 2001). In addition, a more fine-grained analysis of age trends might reveal important fluctuations (e.g., changes from early to late adulthood) that were obscured in the present studies.

Second, although the methodological quality of self-esteem research has increased dramatically over the past decade, there is still room for improvement. Greater attention should be paid to measurement issues, including analyses of whether self-esteem scales show different forms of measurement invariance (e.g., does the meaning of self-esteem items vary across age groups?). The use of more representative samples would increase the generalizability of the findings and allow for a deeper exploration into the potential moderating effects of gender, race, ethnicity, and social class. Sophisticated statistical models should be used to better understand dynamic, reciprocal causal influences (e.g., is self-esteem a cause or consequence of important life experiences; e.g., Ferrer & McArdle, 2003). Cohort-sequential longitudinal studies, in which individuals from different age groups are followed over time, are needed to tease apart aging and cohort effects (e.g., will all older individuals develop lower self-esteem or just the particular cohort of individuals who experienced the Great Depression and other life events unique to that cohort?). Finally, genetically informed designs are needed to explore the mutual influence of nature and nurture on self-esteem development; researchers have yet to appreciate the profound implications of the finding that global self-esteem, like most traits, has a genetic basis (e.g., McGuire et al., 1999).

Third, research is needed on the mediating mechanisms underlying self-esteem change. Chronological age has no causal force per se. We need to understand what else changes with age that might produce changes in self-esteem at different developmental periods. One approach is to document the social-contextual factors associated with chronological age, such as the key social roles and events that define and shape one's position in the life course. However, it is important to recognize that such factors can only influence self-esteem through intrapsychic mechanisms, such as perceptions of control and agency and feelings of pride and shame, which shape the way people react to and internalize the events that occur in their lives. In our view, the best way to understand self-esteem development is to understand the self-evaluative mechanisms that drive the self system—that is, the cognitive and affective processes presumed to play a role in how self-evaluations are formed, maintained, and changed. Although experimental studies have linked a number of self-evaluative processes to short-term changes in self-evaluation, we know little about the influence of such processes on self-esteem change over long periods of time. Life span research on the self should draw on this experimental work to develop hypotheses about long-term change in self-esteem and explore how self-evaluative processes documented in the lab play out in real-world contexts.

Finally, the literature on self-esteem development lacks an overarching theoretical framework. Most past theoretical work has focused on particular developmental periods (e.g., the transition to adolescence) and particular life domains (e.g., work). Consequently, although the literature has generated a laundry list of possible reasons why self-esteem might drop during adolescence (and why this might be particularly true for girls), there is no integrative model of how the various proposed processes work together to shape self-esteem development. We also do not know whether these same processes can be invoked to account for the drop in self-esteem during old age. Given the complexity of self-esteem development, such a model would necessarily incorporate biological, social, and psychological factors; account for reciprocal and dynamic causal influences; and include mechanisms of continuity as well as change (e.g., various forms of person–environment interaction). Our hope is that, by examining patterns of findings across developmental contexts (childhood to old age) and across life domains (work, relationships, health), the field will move toward an overarching theory of the life-course trajectory of self-esteem.

Recommended Reading

Harter, S. (1999). *The construction of the self: A developmental perspective.* New York: Guilford.

Robins, R.W., Trzesniewski, K.H., Tracy, J.L., Gosling, S.D., & Potter, J. (2002). (See References)

Trzesniewski, K.H., Donnellan, M.B., & Robins, R.W. (2003). (See References)

Acknowledgments—This research was supported by Grant AG022057 from the National Institute of Aging.

Notes

1. Address correspondence to Richard W. Robins, Department of Psychology, University of California, Davis, CA 95616-8686; e-mail: rwrobins@ucdavis.edu.

2. The focus of this article is on explicit (i.e., conscious) global evaluations of self-worth, not implicit (i.e., unconscious) or domain-specific (e.g., math ability) self-evaluations.

3. These two forms of change are conceptually and statistically distinct. Individuals in a sample could increase substantially in self-esteem but the rank ordering of individuals would be maintained if everyone increased by the same amount. Similarly, the rank ordering of individuals could change substantially over time without producing any aggregate increases or decreases (e.g., if the number of people who decreased offset the number of people who increased).

References

Erikson, E.H. (1985). *The life cycle completed: A review.* New York: W.W. Norton.

Ferrer, E., & McArdle, J.J. (2003). Alternative structural models for multivariate longitudinal data analysis. *Structural Equation Modeling, 10,* 493–524.

Foster, J.D., Campbell, W.K., & Twenge, J.M. (2003). Individual differences in narcissism: Inflated self-views across the lifespan and around the world. *Journal of Research in Personality, 37,* 469–486.

Kling, K.C., Hyde, J.S., Showers, C.J., & Buswell, B.N. (1999). Gender differences in self-esteem: A meta-analysis. *Psychological Bulletin, 125,* 470–500.

McGuire, S., Manke, B., Saudino, K., Reiss, D., Hetherington, E.M., & Plomin, R. (1999). Perceived competence and self-worth during adolescence: A longitudinal behavioral genetic study. *Child Development, 70,* 1283–1296.

Mroczek, D.K. (2001). Age and emotion in adulthood. *Current Directions in Psychological Science, 10,* 87–90.

Roberts, B.W., & DelVecchio, W.F. (2000). The rank-order consistency of personality from childhood to old age: A quantitative review of longitudinal studies. *Psychological Bulletin, 126,* 3–25.

Robins, R.W., Trzesniewski, K.H., Tracy, J.L., Gosling, S.D., & Potter, J. (2002). Global self-esteem across the lifespan. *Psychology and Aging, 17,* 423–434.

Trzesniewski, K.H., Donnellan, M.B., & Robins, R.W. (2001, April). *Self-esteem across the life span: A meta-analysis.* Poster session presented at the biennial meeting of the Society for Research on Child Development, Minneapolis, MN.

Trzesniewski, K.H., Donnellan, M.B., & Robins, R.W. (2003). Stability of self-esteem across the life span. *Journal of Personality and Social Psychology, 84,* 205–220.

Trzesniewski, K.H., & Robins, R.W. (2004). *A cohort-sequential study of self-esteem from age 25 to 96*. Poster presented at the Society for Personality and Social Psychology. Austin, Texas.

Trzesniewski, K.H., Robins, R.W., Roberts, B.W., & Caspi, A. (2004). Personality and self-esteem development across the life span. In P.T. Costa, Jr. & I.C. Siegler (Eds), *Recent advances in psychology and aging* (pp. 163–185). Amsterdam, the Netherlands: Elsevier.

Twenge, J.M., & Campbell, W.K. (2001). Age and birth cohort differences in self-esteem: A cross-temporal meta-analysis. *Personality and Social Psychology Review, 5,* 321–344.

This article has been reprinted as it originally appeared in *Current Directions in Psychological Science*. Citation information for this article as originally published appears above.

Is Retirement Good or Bad for Subjective Well-Being?

Jungmeen E. Kim[1] and Phyllis Moen

Mt. Hope Family Center and Clinical and Social Sciences in Psychology, University of Rochester, Rochester, New York (J.E.K.), and Department of Human Development and Cornell Careers Institute, Cornell University, Ithaca, New York (P.M.)

Abstract

Retirement has been viewed either as a transition that is accompanied by psychological distress or as a time of continued, or even enhanced, subjective well-being. Existing evidence is mixed, with some studies reporting retirement as positively related to well-being and others reporting a negative relationship or none at all. Our research indicates that developmental and social contexts shape an individual's retirement decisions and experiences, so that retirement should be studied in its ecological and life-course context. Research on marital quality and subjective well-being in retirement has demonstrated both similarities and differences between men and women, as well as the need to consider couples conjointly (rather than viewing individuals in isolation). Future research focusing on the retirement process as it unfolds over time and in ecological context can serve to illuminate the circumstances under which retirement promotes or detracts from the quality of life.

Keywords

retirement; life quality; subjective well-being; life course; ecological approach

Retiring from full-time employment has been regarded as a milestone marking passage into later adulthood. Exiting from one's primary "career" job can be a key life change, transforming one's social and physical worlds. Roles, relationships, and daily routines change, with concomitant shifts in income and health. These transformations may well affect how individuals perceive themselves, their abilities, and the quality of their lives. In this article, we draw on existing research evidence to address the question of whether and how retirement influences subjective well-being (i.e., people's evaluations of the quality of their lives) and marital quality for men and women.

SUBJECTIVE WELL-BEING IN RETIREMENT

Several theoretical perspectives suggest potential links between retirement and subjective well-being. First, role theory points to employment as a fundamental role, central to the individual's identity. Role theory, however, lends itself to two opposite formulations. From the role-enhancement perspective, men and women who retire from their career jobs are vulnerable to feeling that they have lost an important role, and such feelings can lead to psychological distress. Alternatively, from the role-strain perspective, retirement from the demands of a career job may reduce the role strain (i.e., felt difficulty of managing overload and conflict) related to that job, thereby enhancing subjective well-being. Second, continuity theory proposes that people tend to maintain earlier lifestyle patterns, self-esteem, and values, even as they leave their primary career jobs. Therefore, retirement need not lead to maladjustment and distress.

The evidence concerning the relationship between retirement and subjective well-being has been inconsistent. Some studies have shown statistically significant associations between retirement and decreased life satisfaction and greater psychological distress. Others have found no deleterious effects, and some have even found positive effects (see Kim & Moen, in press, for a recent review). One explanation for these diverse findings is that most earlier research compared snapshots of retirees and nonretirees, ignoring the heterogeneity in both populations and the possibility of shifts in well-being around the time of the transition from employment to retirement (Kim & Moen, 1999).

Research evidence points to three factors that contribute to retirees' subjective well-being: (a) economic resources, (b) social relationships, and (c) personal resources. First, people with inadequate incomes and financial problems are especially likely to experience dissatisfaction and maladjustment in retirement. Perceptions of having an adequate income are also related to adjustment to retirement (Kim & Moen, 1999). Second, studies have shown that marriage and family relationships play an important role in predicting well-being following retirement. For instance, a study of retirees and workers ages 58 to 64 found that being married is associated with positive attitudes toward retirement, possibly because being married buffers the uncertainty of retirement (Mutran, Reitzes, & Fernandez, 1997). We (Kim & Moen, 1999) further showed that marital quality, rather than simply marital status, is positively related to retirement adjustment. Third, personal resources include not only sociodemographic status but also health and personality variables. Having a higher education and higher-prestige job prior to retirement has been linked to greater satisfaction with retirement and higher morale after retirement (George, Fillenbaum, & Palmore, 1984). A substantial body of research has shown that health is positively correlated to adjustment to retirement (e.g., Shaw, Patterson, Semple, & Grant, 1998). Personality characteristics also play a crucial role: Self-efficacy (i.e., an individual's belief that he or she can deal with specific activities or problems appropriately, and with reasonable prospect of success) and self-esteem are major factors facilitating successful adjustment to retirement (Mutran et al., 1997).

MARITAL QUALITY IN RETIREMENT

Although studies show retirement to be related to marital quality, findings regarding the direction of influence are inconclusive. Some studies suggest that retirement promotes marital satisfaction by reducing competition from other roles, thereby increasing opportunities for marital companionship and intimacy. But retirement often means changes in income, health, residence, friends, and the division of household labor, and such changes are all potential sources of marital stress.

Most previous research focused on individuals (typically husbands), but marital quality may be different if both spouses are retired than if only one is retired, and any effects of an individual's retirement may be contingent on his or her spouse's employment status. In a longitudinal study of married workers and retirees (ages 50–74), we found that being retired is positively related to marital quality for both husbands and wives, whereas moving into retirement actually reduces marital quality, at least in the short term. Having a nonemployed wife was positively related to husbands' marital satisfaction, whether the husbands were retired or not. The lowest marital satisfaction was reported by wives who were still in the work-force but whose husbands were not (Moen, Kim, & Hofmeister, 2001). These findings point to the importance of investigating the distinction between being or becoming retired and examining both spouses' employment circumstances.

A LIFE-COURSE, ECOLOGICAL APPROACH

We propose that the link between retirement and well-being can be best understood through the lens of a life-course, ecological perspective. The life-course approach (Elder, 1995) highlights the dynamic processes of development and change over the life span. The ecology of human development (Bronfenbrenner, 1995) suggests that transitions should be viewed in the social contexts of other roles, relationships, and developmental processes. Viewing retirement as a life-course, ecological transition suggests a focus on process and timing in historical as well as situational contexts, the interdependency of linked lives, and the importance of human agency, as we explain more specifically later in this section.

Scholars are coming to regard retirement not as an "either or" proposition but as a process played out over time, often involving a number of transitions between paid and unpaid work. An important principle of the life-course approach is that to understand any transition (such as retirement), one must place it in the larger context of both current exigencies (e.g., a health crisis) and other life pathways (e.g., whether one's children are grown, one's spouse is about to retire, or one has decided to go back to school; Elder, 1995). Research shows that family, educational, employment, and other experiences all help to shape the transition into retirement. Studies show differential psychological impacts of "early" versus "late" versus "on time" retirement (e.g., Williamson, Rinehart, & Blank, 1992), pointing to the importance of understanding the circumstances shaping the timing of retirement.

Another key tenet of a life-course, ecological perspective is that lives are interdependent. Developmental processes always take place in the context of ongoing social relations. Individuals frequently base their decision to retire on changes in others' health or retirement plans, and the retirement experience is played out in a network of shifting social relations.

Finally, this perspective emphasizes human agency, the idea that individuals take an active role in designing and redesigning their life biographies in the context of available options and existing constraints (such as the availability of pensions and eligibility for retirement). Today, retirement is being transformed, with many people exiting their primary career jobs only to seek other employment and possibly even second and third careers. Growing numbers of people retire from their primary career jobs in their 50s and early 60s. Earlier retirement, in combination with increases in longevity, means that retirement is becoming more of a midlife transition, rather than a transition to old age; people who retire often acquire new roles (e.g., volunteer), continue in other roles (e.g., worker, friend, or spouse), and develop new self-identities.

THE CONTEXTS OF GENDER AND MARRIAGE

Retirement has typically been studied as an individual, principally male, passage. But almost half the workforce is female, and the majority of workers are now married to other workers, and these facts are having enormous impacts on how retirement is conceptualized.

First, gender is a key source of heterogeneity in the nature and impact of retirement. The whole process of retirement may be qualitatively different for women than for men, in part because of the differences in their experience in the labor force (Han & Moen, 1999). Women are more likely than men to experience discontinuity, moving in and out of the labor force as their family responsibilities shift. Correspondingly, women tend to have more negative attitudes toward retirement, plan for it less, adjust to it more poorly, and are more likely to experience depression following retirement (Kim & Moen, 1999, in press). Moreover, women's adjustment to retirement is more adversely affected by poor health and inadequate incomes than men's (Quick & Moen, 1998; Seccombe & Lee, 1986).

Second, joint retirement among dual-earner couples is increasingly common, so a key influence on an individual's retirement decisions is the employment status of his or her spouse. A study of married, full-time workers (ages 58–64) found that having a working spouse encourages both men and women to remain employed (Reitzes, Mutran, & Fernandez, 1998). In a sample of married, retired couples (ages 50–72), even one spouse's retirement was a decision made by the couple, with wives typically influenced by their husbands' retirement timing (but not the reverse; Smith & Moen, 1998).

Recent research findings point to the importance of knowing couples' joint employment status for understanding their adjustment to retirement. In a study of couples ages 50 to 72, Szinovacz (1996) found that couples with employed wives and retired husbands reported lower marital quality than dual-earner couples. Our own findings, from a study of men and women ages 50 to 74, indicate there are significant gender differences in the relationship between couples' retirement and subsequent subjective well-being and marital quality (Kim & Moen, 1999; Moen et al., 2001). Interviews conducted 2 years apart showed that men who were newly or continuously retired tended to have increased morale, especially if their wives remained employed. By contrast, women who were newly retired tended to have increased depressive symptoms, especially if their husbands remained employed. In addition, for women, lower marital satisfaction was associated with decreased morale after retirement, even after we controlled for age, income, and health. Our results document that couples' conjoint retirement patterns matter for the subjective well-being of both men and women after retirement, with retiring men experiencing higher morale but also greater marital conflict if their wives do not retire at the same time they do. Retiring wives experience both more depressive symptoms and greater marital conflict if their husbands remain employed. Note, however, that we found both men and women who had been retired for more than 2 years reported better life quality (subjective well-being and marital quality) than those who had not yet retired from their primary career jobs, or who had recently made the transition to retirement.

CONCLUSION

The literature on retirement and life quality suggests both methodological and theoretical challenges. First, most studies on retirement have been cross-sectional. Developmental, ecological, and life-course perspectives point to the need to study continuity and change across the transition into retirement, as well as how this passage shapes long-term development. Cross-sectional studies on retirement exacerbate the difficulties in interpreting differences across age groups. Are they cohort effects (e.g., unique to pre-baby boomers) or age effects (a function not of retirement, but of growing older)? Dynamic, longitudinal analyses can capture the actual process of moving from a primary career job to (eventually) ending all participation in the labor force and can illuminate the developmental consequences of this transition.

Second, the evidence on retirement and well-being documents mostly men's retirement experiences in cohorts for which retiring at age 65 is the norm. Even in studies involving women, many researchers rely on a male model of retirement, investigating women whose careers are most similar to men's. Much is left to learn about women's unique experiences in their pathways to and through retirement (see Han & Moen, 1999). There is a similar dearth of evidence on the retirement experiences of members of diverse ethnic and cultural groups.

Finally, investigators studying retirement have yet to develop and test models of the psychological precursors of this transition (i.e., factors that influence the decision to retire). Psychologists know little about how the psychological resources individuals bring to this life stage affect their retirement experiences. The retirement process itself, as well as adjustment to it, is a product of biological (e.g., aging and health), societal (e.g., economic and social conditions), interpersonal (e.g., relations with spouse and co-workers), and psychological (e.g., self-concept and self-efficacy) factors. Future studies of adjustment to retirement would do well to adopt a holistic approach that incorporates all these aspects of this transition.

To conclude, we reiterate that retirement is a process rather than an event, and spans a period of time. As a critical life transition in late midlife, it involves developmental, social-relational, and psychological antecedents and consequences. Our research suggests that psychological adaptation processes involved in retirement are affected by factors relating to social contexts apart from sociodemographic and health variables. Gender is a key factor in shaping the ways in which individuals experience the passage into retirement. This transition can be best understood when it is socially and temporally situated in individuals' life biographies and their ecological contexts. By investigating retirement in its ecological, life-course contexts, future research can capture the complexity of the processes by which retirement may influence the subjective well-being of men and women in late midlife.

Recommended Reading

Calasanti, T.M. (1996). Gender and life satisfaction in retirement: An assessment of the male model. *Journal of Gerontology: Social Sciences, 51B,* S18–S29.

Kim, J.E., & Moen, P. (in press). (See References)

Moen, P. (1996). A life course perspective on retirement, gender, and well-being. *Journal of Occupational Health Psychology, 1,* 131–144.

Shaw, W.S., Patterson, T. L., Semple, S., & Grant, I. (1998). (See References)

Acknowledgments—Preparation of this article was supported in part by Grants 96-6-9 and 99-6-23 from the Alfred P. Sloan Foundation (Phyllis Moen, principal investigator) and by Grant IT50 AG11711 from the National Institute on Aging (Karl Pillemer and Phyllis Moen, co-principal investigators).

Note

1. Address correspondence to Jungmeen E. Kim, Mt. Hope Family Center, 187 Edinburgh St., Rochester, NY 14608; e-mail: jungmeen@psych.rochester.edu.

References

Bronfenbrenner, U. (1995). The bioecological model from a life course perspective: Reflections of a participant observer. In P. Moen, G.H. Elder, Jr., & K. Lüscher, (Eds.), *Examining lives in context: Perspectives on the ecology of human development* (pp. 599–618). Washington, DC: American Psychological Association.

Elder, G.H., Jr. (1995). The life course paradigm: Social change and individual development. In P. Moen, G.H. Elder, Jr., & K. Lüscher (Eds.), *Examining lives in context: Perspectives on the ecology of human development* (pp. 101–140). Washington, DC: American Psychological Association.

George, L.K., Fillenbaum, G.G., & Palmore, E.B. (1984). Sex differences in the antecedents and consequences of retirement. *Journal of Gerontology, 39,* 364–371.

Han, S.K., & Moen, P. (1999). Clocking out: Temporal patterning of retirement. *American Journal of Sociology, 105,* 191–236.

Kim, J.E., & Moen, P. (1999). *Work/retirement transitions and psychological well-being in late midlife* (Bronfenbrenner Life Course Center Working Paper No. 99-10). Ithaca, NY: Cornell University.

Kim, J.E., & Moen, P. (in press). Moving into retirement: Preparation and transitions in late midlife. In M.E. Lachman (Ed.), *Handbook of midlife development*. New York: John Wiley.

Moen, P., Kim, J.E., & Hofmeister, H. (2001). Couples' work/retirement transitions, gender, and marital quality. *Social Psychology Quarterly, 64,* 55–71.

Mutran, E.J., Reitzes, D.C., & Fernandez, M.E. (1997). Factors that influence attitudes toward retirement. *Research on Aging, 19,* 251–273.

Quick, H.E., & Moen, P. (1998). Gender, employment, and retirement quality: A life course approach to the differential experiences of men and women. *Journal of Occupational Health Psychology, 3,* 44–64.

Reitzes, D.C., Mutran, E.J., & Fernandez, M.E. (1998). The decision to retire: A career perspective. *Social Science Quarterly, 79,* 607–619.

Seccombe, K., & Lee, G.R. (1986). Gender differences in retirement satisfaction and its antecedents. *Research on Aging, 8,* 426–440.

Shaw, W.S., Patterson, T.L., Semple, S., & Grant, I. (1998). Health and well-being in retirement: A summary of theories and their implications. In M. Hersen & V.B. Van Hasselt (Eds.), *Handbook of clinical geropsychology* (pp. 383–409). New York: Plenum.

Smith, D.B., & Moen, P. (1998). Spouse's influence on the retirement decision: His, her, and their perceptions. *Journal of Marriage and the Family, 60,* 734–744.

Szinovacz, M. (1996). Couples' employment/retirement patterns and perceptions of marital quality. *Research on Aging, 18,* 243–268.

Williamson, R.C., Rinehart, A.D., & Blank, T.O. (1992). *Early retirement: Promises and pitfalls.* New York: Insight Books/Plenum.

Section 2: Critical Thinking Questions

1. How could girls' greater susceptibility to relational victimization (Crick and colleagues) be causally related to gender differences in depression (Nolen-Hocksema)?

2. Patterson presents research to show that parent gender and sexual orientation do not have major consequences for children's behavior. Discuss the implications of this research for evaluating the importance of parental influence on children's gender roles and behaviors.

3. In what ways could the transitional event of retirement (Kim & Moen) affect changes in self-esteem from middle to late adulthood (Robins & Trzesniewski)? What protective factors might help adults' self-esteem at this life stage?

This article has been reprinted as it originally appeared in *Current Directions in Psychological Science.* Citation information for this article as originally published appears above.

Section 3: Cognitive Functioning

The articles in this section address gender in relation to cognitive functioning, starting with infancy and moving up the life span into older age. Young infants show a preference for looking at faces over other forms of visual stimuli. However, not all faces are equally processed. Ramsey-Rennels and Langlois have uncovered an asymmetry in infants' cognitive processing of faces based on gender . . . of the face. Infants more readily form summary representations, or prototypes, of female faces than male faces. They also prefer to look at female faces and look at them longer than male faces. Both nature and nurture explanations are considered to explain these asymmetries. Differences in the processing of male and female faces have implications for later face-recognition abilities, learning about gender categories, and social-information processing.

Even young children are skilled at detecting gender cues in the world around them. Martin and Ruble weave together gender schema theory and cognitive developmental theory to explain developmental changes in children's understanding of gender in relation to their cognitive abilities. Children use the information they gather to categorize themselves as male or female and to develop and apply stereotypes about the genders. Children also follow similar paths in the waxing and waning of rigidity in their thinking about stereotypes. As they conclude their review of evidence to support cognitive theories of gender development, Martin and Ruble argue that gendered cognitions influence children's behavior.

Episodic memory is the branch of long-term memory that captures conscious recollection of the content, time, and place of unique personal experiences. Recall and recognition studies have tended to find gender differences favoring women in verbal episodic-memory tasks and differences favoring men when the tasks rely on visual-spatial processing. Herlitz and Rehman review research on gender difference in tasks that involve both verbal and visual-spatial processing. They also present data from a series of face recognition experiments that vary the gender-typedness of the face. The nature of the material affects whether one finds the apparent female advantage in episodic memory tasks.

For men and women, there are age-related changes in cognitive processes that occur with the normal aging process. Although not all changes are negative, declines in verbal and working memory, processing speed, and reasoning are frequently noted consequences of normal brain aging that accelerate after age 50. Results from research have been equivocal as to whether or not estrogen therapy protects women against aspects of cognitive decline. Following a review of this literature, Sherwin forwards the critical-period hypothesis to explain contradictory findings about the estrogen-cognition connection.

Halpern's article begins with a discussion of the controversy that surrounds the study of gender *differences*. She first tackles the meaning and interpretation of differences and then introduces an information process-oriented rubric for understanding gender differences on cognitive tasks. This taxonomy is applied to tasks that have shown a female advantage and a male advantage, and to cross-cultural data on reading, math, and science achievement. The approach proves useful for addressing the paradox between girls' and boys' school grades and scores on standardized tests. The article ends with depiction of a psychobiosocial model to capture contributions of nature and nurture to gender differences in cognitive abilities.

Infants' Differential Processing of Female and Male Faces

Jennifer L. Ramsey-Rennels[1]
University of Nevada, Las Vegas

Judith H. Langlois
The University of Texas at Austin

Abstract

Infants show an interesting asymmetry in face processing: They are more fluent in processing female faces than they are at processing male faces. We hypothesize that such processing asymmetry results from greater experience with female faces than with male faces early in development. Asymmetrical face processing may have long-lasting implications for development of face recognition, development of knowledge structures regarding females and males, and social-information processing. We encourage researchers to use both female and male faces in their face-perception research and to conduct separate analyses for female and male faces.

Keywords

face processing; gender categorization; face recognition; knowledge structures; information processing

Categorization is a fundamental information-processing capability that allows reliable recognition and response to novel examples of familiar category members. For example, if Ariana walks into an unfamiliar room containing a telephone, she knows she can use the phone to talk to someone even though she has never before seen this particular telephone. Categorization of objects enables people to allocate cognitive resources efficiently—Ariana will expend more energy in figuring out what to say on the phone than in determining how it works.

Because of the adaptive nature of categorization, it is not surprising that categorization abilities emerge early in infancy (e.g., Quinn, 2002). Such abilities facilitate infants' early and rapid learning about the many different objects in the world. But what about categorization of people? Like categorizing objects, categorizing people has important benefits. For example, categorizing age allows one to interact with infants and children in a developmentally appropriate manner. Categorizing gender allows one to determine if a person would be an appropriate mate. There are, however, problems related to categorization of people—these categories could become linked to positive and negative attributions that might not be accurate characterizations of a particular member of that group. Thus, one byproduct of this otherwise adaptive process of categorization is the formation of stereotypes (e.g., Bargh & Chartrand, 1999).

Our work has focused on infants and the early origins of stereotypes, particularly on how infants recognize, evaluate, and categorize the facial appearance of adults. Our research in this area has led us to conclude that there is a potentially important asymmetry in how infants process male and female faces. Most of our research successes involved infants' responses to female faces (e.g., Rubenstein, Kalakanis, & Langlois, 1999). Yet, our research failures were equally illuminating because they almost always involved infants' responses to male faces (see Ramsey, Langlois, & Marti, 2005, for an overview).

ASYMMETRIES IN INFANT PROCESSING OF FACES

Two different types of studies illustrate the asymmetry we observed. First, as part of our research program to understand the cognitive mechanisms underlying infants' preferences for attractive faces, we examined infants' ability to abstract an averaged (summary) representation, or prototype, of sets of female or male faces. Abstracting a facial prototype from category examples is important because a prototype (a) can facilitate processing of new exemplar faces from that category; and (b) may guide interest toward faces, as infants visually prefer faces most similar to their prototype (Rubenstein et al., 1999). Although we found that infants formed prototypes of female faces (Rubenstein et al., 1999), we could not find evidence that they formed prototypes of male faces. This asymmetry suggests that infants' initial prototype or representation of faces may be more female-like than male-like (Ramsey et al., 2005).

A second type of study, in which infants view male and female faces when they are paired together, shows another asymmetry: Infants look longer at female faces than they do at male faces (Quinn, Yahr, Kuhn, Slater, & Pascalis, 2002). We posit that infants visually prefer female faces to male faces because female faces are more similar than male faces are to the infant's facial prototype. Interestingly, however, when infants view female faces only or male faces only, they spend more time looking at male faces than they do at female faces, particularly when the task is complex (Ramsey et al., 2005). Because female faces are not available to "compete" for infants' attention in studies presenting male faces, longer looking times may reflect infants' lack of expertise and lack of efficiency in processing male faces. Longer looking at male faces in the absence of female faces is particularly evident when the task requires recognition or categorical abstraction, perhaps because infants do not yet have a fully developed male face prototype to facilitate processing (Ramsey et al., 2005).

These asymmetries in our work and that of Quinn et al. (2002) prompted us to explore the infant face-perception literature further for asymmetries in other areas of face processing. We discovered that most studies use only female faces to evaluate infants' reactions to faces. The lack of male-face studies caused us to question whether conclusions about infants' face recognition, interest in faces, understanding of emotion, and development of social expectancies from the existing infant face-perception literature really generalized to all faces, male and female, as is typically assumed.

When we examined the few studies that included male stimulus faces, we found further evidence of differences in infants' processing of female and male faces. First, 3- to 4-month-olds have more difficulty discriminating among male faces and subsequently recognizing them than they do female faces (Quinn et al., 2002). Second, older infants are more skilled at categorizing female faces than they are at categorizing male faces: Whereas 10-month-olds easily recognize that a sex-ambiguous female face does not belong with a group of sex-typical female faces, they have more difficulty excluding a sex-ambiguous male face from a group of sex-typical male faces (data interpretation of Younger & Fearing, 1999, by Ramsey et al., 2005). In addition, there is a lag between when infants recognize that female voices are associated with female faces and when male voices are associated with male faces; infants reliably match female faces and voices at 9 months (Poulin-Dubois, Serbin, Kenyon, & Derbyshire, 1994) but do not reliably match male faces and voices until 18 months. Even at 18 months, infants are more accurate at matching female faces and voices than they are at matching male faces and voices (Poulin-Dubois, Serbin, & Derbyshire, 1998).

Thus, the infant perception literature shows that (a) infants have more difficulty processing male faces than female faces, (b) infants prefer female to male faces, and (c) differential processing of male and female faces is related to the fluency with which infants form categories of male versus female faces. Why?

THE ROLE OF EXPERIENCE WITH FACES

Early visual experience with faces appears to be very important for specialized processing of upright relative to inverted faces and within-species face recognition (e.g., Nelson, 2001; Pascalis, de Haan, & Nelson, 2002). In most instances, infants have significantly more exposure to adult female faces than they have to adult male faces. For example, the primary caregiver is female for the majority of infants, and infants spend approximately 50% of their personal interactions with her during the first year. Also, parents of 2-, 5-, 8-, and 11-month-olds report twice as many interactions between their infant and female strangers than between their infant and male strangers during a typical week (Ramsey & Simmons, 2005). There are also qualitative differences in how adults interact with infants (e.g., females play more visual games than males), which may cause females to elicit more attention from infants during social interactions than males do (Ramsey et al., 2005). Therefore, we posit that infants' typical experience with female faces early in development facilitates expert processing (discrimination, recognition, and categorization) of female faces. Greater experience with female faces than with male faces should result in more fluent processing of female faces.

An alternate hypothesis is that experience with faces is not formative; rather, evolution has predisposed infants to attend to female faces because mothers were generally the primary caregivers. Research, however, shows that experience is important for face processing: Babies who have fathers as their primary caregivers show more interest in male faces than in female faces (Quinn et al., 2002). Moreover, 3-month-olds more easily recognize faces from the race with which they are most familiar than they recognize faces from a different race (Sangrigoli & de Schonen, 2004). Thus, it seems unlikely that experience is irrelevant. Rather, predominant experience with faces from a particular sex, race, species, orientation, etc. should result in more fluent processing of the commonly experienced faces.

Once infants become more expert at processing female faces than male faces, the asymmetry may cascade because ease of processing is linked to affective preferences (Winkielman & Cacioppo, 2001). Increased positive affect toward female faces increases the likelihood that infants will look at female faces, further skewing experience and expertise with female faces. Infants' lack of experience with male faces may be compounded by an additional complexity: Male faces are more variable and less perceptually similar than female faces (Ramsey et al., 2005). Measurements of male faces show greater deviation from the mean than measurements of female faces do. This greater deviation means male faces are less prototypical (i.e., less representative of their sex category on average) than female faces are. Thus, infants not only have less experience with male faces than with female faces, but their experience with male faces is less productive because categories with more variable members can be difficult for infants to learn (e.g., Quinn, 2002). Such impediments may cause developmental delays in the attainment of coherent prototype formation for male faces (Ramsey et al., 2005).

Much as how early language input causes specialized processing of the native language, abundant experience with certain faces (e.g., female) during infancy results in expert processing of those faces (Nelson, 2001). Indeed, 9-month-olds perform almost like adults in being better able to recognize human faces than monkey faces, whereas 6-month-olds perform equally well in their recognition of human and monkey faces (Pascalis et al., 2002). The similarities between 9-month-olds and adults in their poorer recognition of monkey faces, as compared to 6-month-olds, is likely due to their greater experience with and specialization in processing human faces over monkey faces. Unlike infants' experience with the native language relative to other languages and with human faces relative to monkey faces, the disparity between infants' experience with female faces and their experience with male faces is not as large, making this a unique type of problem regarding discrepancies in experience. We suggest, therefore, that differences in early experience with faces can have qualitative, long-lasting impact on how male and female faces are processed, but that these processing disparities may be subtle.

IMPLICATIONS OF EARLY DIFFERENTIAL PROCESSING

What might be the enduring implications of differential processing of female and male faces? The fluency or ease with which infants more expertly discriminate, recognize, and categorize female faces relative to male faces has the potential to contribute to later face-recognition abilities, knowledge acquisition of the sex categories, and social-information processing.

Early fluency in processing female faces during infancy should contribute to a later advantage in adults' recognition of female faces. Indeed, adult females are better at recognizing female faces than they are at recognizing male faces, and they perform better than males do at recognizing female faces (e.g., Lewin & Herlitz, 2002). Why should the advantage seen in both female and male infants' recognition of female faces be sustained only in female adults? An important developmental task for young children is to learn about their gender. Because preschoolers typically learn about their own gender before they learn about the other gender (Martin & Halverson, 1981), girls may maintain or enhance their processing of female faces whereas boys may "lose" some of their expertise in processing female faces as male faces begin to compete for their attention. Obviously this proposed developmental pathway requires investigation and there are other mediating variables, but in a legal system that places great reliance on eyewitness testimony, a clear understanding of why females may possess an advantage in recognizing female faces relative to male faces is needed (e.g., Lewin & Herlitz, 2002).

Fluent processing of female faces should allow infants to more easily structure the female face category than the male face category, which should enable infants and young children to more readily learn about females than males because it is less effortful to make associations to the female face category (e.g., Quinn, 2002). Lack of experience with male faces will make it difficult to attain conceptual knowledge about the male face category, suggesting that knowledge structures associated with females should emerge earlier and be more elaborate than those associated with males, at least early in development. Furthermore, the variability of the male face category should make it difficult to associate and organize the conceptual knowledge that is attained. These proposed differences in knowledge structures for females and males would suggest that linking, organizing, and retrieving information should occur with greater ease when processing social information about female targets, relative to male targets.

FUTURE DIRECTIONS

Infants' differential experience with female and male faces influences their discrimination, recognition, and categorization of faces, although more work is needed to understand the full extent and origins of those differences. We suggest that particular attention be paid to experience with faces and to when interactions with males increase during development. Examining when (or if) the visual preference for female faces over male faces subsides or reverses should provide insight into face-processing changes due to experience and will likely require testing older children and perhaps even adults. Because categorization is inherently linked to knowledge acquisition, it is also important to investigate how the category structure for female and male faces develops, evolves, and reorganizes over time, with attention to both perceptual and conceptual components of the categories.

Unlike other research assessing the role of experience when there is overwhelming exposure to the commonly experienced category (e.g., native language) and minimal experience with alternate categories (e.g., foreign languages), the difference between infants' experience with female and male faces is more subtle. Understanding how subtleties in early exposure subsequently impact later face processing could be informative for researchers interested in sensitive periods in development. One question concerns whether limited early exposure to male faces extends the window for expert processing of male faces to develop or if fluency of processing male faces never develops to the same level that it does for female faces. Testing older children and adults, who should have more experience with male faces, is necessary for addressing this issue, but methods assessing reaction time or psychophysiological responses may be necessary to capture subtle differences in fluency of processing female and male faces.

Regardless of the age group being studied, we urge face-perception researchers to use both female and male faces in their studies, to make a priori hypotheses about potential differences in processing, and to conduct separate analyses for female and male faces in order to carefully examine the nature of any disparities in processing female and male faces (quantitative or qualitative divergence). Because aspects of adult face processing have roots in infancy, we suggest that researchers check the developmental literature for clues when they cannot identify why face-processing discrepancies occur among adult participants.

Recommended Reading

Pascalis, O., de Haan, M., & Nelson, C.A. (2002). (See References)
Quinn, P.C., Yahr, J., Kuhn, A., Slater, A.M., & Pascalis, O. (2002). (See References)
Ramsey, J.L., Langlois, J.H., & Marti, C.N. (2005). (See References)
Winkielman, P., & Cacioppo, J.T. (2001). (See References)

Acknowledgments—Preparation of this manuscript was supported by two Grants from the National Institute of Child Health and Human Development, one to Jennifer Ramsey-Rennels (HD48467) and one to Judith Langlois (HD21332).

Note

1. Address correspondence to Jennifer L. Ramsey-Rennels, Department of Psychology, University of Nevada, Las Vegas, 4505 Maryland Parkway Box 455030, Las Vegas, NV 89154-5030; e-mail: ramseyj2@unlv.nevada.edu.

References

Bargh, J.A., & Chartrand, T.L. (1999). The unbearable automaticity of being. *American Psychologist, 54*, 462–479.
Lewin, C., & Herlitz, A. (2002). Sex differences in face recognition—women's faces make the difference. *Brain & Cognition, 50*, 121–128.
Martin, C.L., & Halverson, F., Jr. (1981). A schematic processing model of sex-typing and stereotyping in children. *Child Development, 52*, 1119–1134.
Nelson, C.A. (2001). The development and neural bases of face recognition. *Infant & Child Development, 10*, 3–18.
Pascalis, O., de Haan, M., & Nelson, C.A. (2002). Is face processing species-specific during the first year of life? *Science, 296*, 1321–1323.
Poulin-Dubois, D., Serbin, L.A., & Derbyshire, A. (1998). Toddlers' intermodal and verbal knowledge about gender. *Merrill-Palmer Quarterly, 44*, 338–354.
Poulin-Dubois, D., Serbin, L.A., Kenyon, B., & Derbyshire, A. (1994). Infants' intermodal knowledge about gender. *Developmental Psychology, 30*, 436–442.
Quinn, P.C. (2002). Beyond prototypes: Asymmetries in infant categorization and what they teach us about the mechanisms guiding knowledge acquisition. In R. Kail & H. Reese (Eds.), *Advances in child development and behavior: Vol. 29* (pp. 161–193). San Diego: Academic Press.
Quinn, P.C., Yahr, J., Kuhn, A., Slater, A.M., & Pascalis, O. (2002). Representation of the gender of human faces by infants: A preference for female. *Perception, 31*, 1109–1121.
Ramsey, J.L., Langlois, J.H., & Marti, C.N. (2005). Infant categorization of faces: Ladies first. *Developmental Review, 25*, 212–246.
Ramsey, J.L., & Simmons, R.E. (2005). [Two, 5, 8, and 11 month olds' interactions with familiar and unfamiliar individuals during a typical week]. Unpublished raw data.
Rubenstein, A.J., Kalakanis, L., & Langlois, J.H. (1999). Infant preferences for attractive faces: A cognitive explanation. *Developmental Psychology, 35*, 848–855.

Sangrigoli, S., & de Schonen, S. (2004). Recognition of own-race and other-race faces by three-month-old infants. *Journal of Child Psychology and Psychiatry, 45,* 1219–1227.

Winkielman, P., & Cacioppo, J.T. (2001). Mind at ease puts smile on the face: Psychophysiological evidence that processing facilitation elicits positive affect. *Journal of Personality and Social Psychology, 81,* 989–1000.

Younger, B.A., & Fearing, D.D. (1999). Parsing items into separate categories: Developmental change in infant categorization. *Child Development, 70,* 291–303.

This article has been reprinted as it originally appeared in *Current Directions in Psychological Science*. Citation information for this article as originally published appears above.

Children's Search for Gender Cues: Cognitive Perspectives on Gender Development

Carol Lynn Martin[1]
Arizona State University

Diane Ruble
New York University

Abstract

Young children search for cues about gender—who should or should not do a particular activity, who can play with whom, and why girls and boys are different. From a vast array of gendered cues in their social worlds, children quickly form an impressive constellation of gender cognitions, including gender self-conceptions (gender identity) and gender stereotypes. Cognitive perspectives on gender development (i.e., cognitive developmental theory and gender-schema theory) assume that children actively search for ways to make sense of the social world that surrounds them. Gender identity develops as children realize that they belong to one gender group, and the consequences include increased motivation to be similar to other members of their group, preferences for members of their own group, selective attention to and memory for information relevant to their own sex, and increased interest in activities relevant to their own sex. Cognitive perspectives have been influential in increasing understanding of how children develop and apply gender stereotypes, and in their focus on children's active role in gender socialization.

Keywords

gender development; gender stereotypes; cognitive theories

Erin, a 4-year-old, explained to her aunt about a drawing she had done: "The ones with eyelashes are girls; boys don't have eyelashes."

In an Italian restaurant, a four-year-old noticed his father and another man order pizza and his mother order lasagna. On his way home in the car, he announced that he had figured it out: "Men eat pizza and women don't." (Bjorklund, 2000, p. 361)

Children are gender detectives who search for cues about gender—who should or should not engage in a particular activity, who can play with whom, and why girls and boys are different. Cognitive perspectives on gender development assume that children are actively searching for ways to find meaning in and make sense of the social world that surrounds them, and they do so by using the gender cues provided by society to help them interpret what they see and hear. Children are wonderfully skilled in using these cues to form expectations about other people and to develop personal standards for behavior, and they learn to do this very quickly and often with little direct training. By the age of 5, children develop an impressive constellation of stereotypes about gender (often amusing and incorrect) that they apply to themselves and others. They use these stereotypes to form impressions of others, to help guide their own behavior, to direct their attention, and to organize their memories.

The first cognitive theory of gender development was Kohlberg's (1966) cognitive developmental approach, which was based on the ideas of Piaget. Kohlberg's theory emphasized the active role of the child in gender development, and proposed that children's understanding of gender concepts influences their behavior, and that this influence becomes more pronounced once children reach a relatively sophisticated understanding of gender—knowing that a person's sex is stable and unchanging. In the 1970s, a new group of cognitive approaches to gender emerged—gender-schema theories. Gender-schema theory is based on the idea that children form organized knowledge structures, or *schemas,* which are gender-related conceptions of themselves and others, and that these schemas influence children's thinking and behavior. Although similar to Kohlberg's theory in the assumption that children play an active role in gender development, gender-schema theory assumes a more basic understanding of gender is all that is required to motivate children's behavior and thinking. Gender-schema theory was further elaborated with contributions from developmental and social psychologists (Liben & Bigler, 2002; for reviews, see Martin, Ruble, & Szkrybalo, 2002). Over time, these two cognitive perspectives—that is, cognitive developmental and gender-schema theories—have been influential in promoting the idea that children actively construct gender on the basis of both the nature of the social environment and how they think about the sexes. Other perspectives also have incorporated cognitive mechanisms to account for gender development (e.g., Bussey & Bandura, 1999).

MAJOR THEMES OF COGNITIVE THEORIES OF GENDER DEVELOPMENT

We believe that cognitive theories of gender development are characterized by three central features.

The Emergence of Gender Identity and Its Consequences

A central tenet of cognitive approaches is that there are immediate consequences of children's recognition that there are two gender groups and that they belong to one of them. These consequences are both evaluative and motivational-informational.

Evaluative Consequences   Considerable research with diverse kinds of social groups suggests that an individual evaluates a group positively as soon as he or she identifies, even in a very minimal way, with that group (see Ruble et al., in press). For instance, children as young as 3 years of age have been shown to like their own sex more than the other. Similarly, young children attribute more positive characteristics to their own sex than to the other (see Ruble & Martin, 1998). One of the most powerful developmental phenomena is children's striking tendency to segregate by sex when they can choose play partners (Maccoby, 1998). Young children seldom play exclusively with members of the other sex. Evaluative consequences of group identification are particularly likely when group membership is salient (e.g., when groups differ in appearance) and when it is made functionally significant by authority figures; both of these conditions are true for gender (Bigler, Jones, & Lobliner, 1997).

Motivational and Informational Consequences   The emergence of gender identity and growing understanding of the stability of social group membership affects children's motivation to learn about gender, to gather information about their gender group, and to act like other group members (Ruble & Martin, 1998). For example, experimental studies using novel toys find that at an age when children have achieved gender identity, they pay more attention to and remember more information relevant to toys they believe are appropriate for their own gender group than for toys they believe to be for the other sex (Bradbard, Martin, Endsley, & Halverson, 1986).

Once they recognize their gender group, children make broad assumptions about similarities within the gender groups and about differences between girls and boys. In numerous studies, children have been found to use the sex of a person to form impressions and make judgments about him or her (e.g., judgments about whether they would like the person, what the person may like to do, and what the person is like). For instance, using gender stereotypes, a girl may not approach a new neighbor who is a boy because she suspects that he will not share her interests. By acting on their assumptions about what other members of their gender like to do, children further differentiate the sexes.

Active, Self-Initiated View of Gender Development

When cognitive theorists refer to the motivational consequences of self-identification as a boy or girl, they mean something quite specific. Gender identification produces a new motivation that is initiated by and emanates from the child. This motivation involves the child's deliberate efforts to learn about a social category that he or she is actively constructing as part of a process of finding meaning in the social world.

Perhaps the clearest evidence for this kind of active construction is found when the process goes awry and children draw faulty conclusions about gender distinctions and show distorted perception of and memory for gender-role-inconsistent information. There are numerous examples of such errors in the literature. In one study, after being shown equal numbers of pictures of people engaged in gender-stereotypic activities (e.g., a girl sewing) and gender-inconsistent activities (e.g., a boy cooking), children were three times more likely to misremember the inconsistent than the stereotypic pictures. For example, instead of remembering that they had been shown a picture of a *girl* sawing wood, children reported having seen a picture of a *boy* sawing wood (Martin & Halverson, 1983). Children also seem to want to generate or exaggerate male-female differences, even if none exist. In our own studies, it has been difficult to generate neutral stimuli because children appear to seize on any element that may implicate a gender norm so that they may categorize it as male or female. Experimental research also suggests that young children are quick to jump to conclusions about sex differences, even on the basis of only a single instance. For example, when 3-year-olds were told that a particular boy likes a sofa and a particular girl likes a table, they generalized this information to draw the conclusion that another girl would also like the table (Bauer & Coyne, 1997).

Developmental Patterns

A major feature of cognitive theories of gender is an emphasis on developmental changes in understanding of gender, which may be accounted for by children's changing cognitive abilities (e.g., abilities to classify on multiple dimensions) and their evolving understanding of concepts. Because of such changes, the relative strength (rigidity) of children's gender-related beliefs and behaviors is predicted to wax and wane across development. The early learning of gender categories and associated attributes (stereotypes) appears to set off a sequence of events that results in, first, very rigid beliefs (that only boys or only girls can do or be something), which are followed by more flexible, realistic beliefs (that either sex can do almost anything). Specifically, considerable evidence suggests that gender stereotyping shows a developmental pattern that can be characterized by three ordered phases (Trautner et al., 2003):

- First, children begin learning about gender-related characteristics. This phase takes place mainly during the toddler and preschool years.
- Second, the newly acquired gender knowledge is consolidated in a rigid either-or fashion, reaching its peak of rigidity between 5 and 7 years.
- Third, after this peak of rigidity, a phase of relative flexibility follows.

This phase pattern (see Fig. 1) received striking support by an analysis of data collected on a sample of children over a period of 6 years (Trautner et al., 2003). The children reached peak rigidity in their gender stereotypes at age 5 to 6, then showed a dramatic increase in flexibility 2 years later (i.e., at age 7 or 8). Moreover,

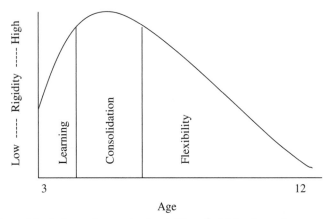

Fig. 1. A model of phase changes in the rigidity of children's gender stereotypes as a function of age.

although the children varied considerably in their maximal levels of rigidity at age 5 to 6, there was little difference in levels of flexibility by age 8. These findings provide strong support for a cognitive perspective by showing that all children take basically the same path of waxing and waning of stereotype rigidity across development, despite variations in when the path begins and what level it reaches. Although this developmental sequence of gender stereotyping is no doubt associated with more general cognitive processes and abilities, such as understanding of gender constancy and categorization and classifications skills, the exact mechanisms underlying changes in gender stereotyping are not yet fully understood.

Gender-related preferences and behaviors show more mixed developmental patterns than stereotyping (Liben & Bigler, 2002; Ruble & Martin, 1998), with some showing clear rigidity in preschool (Maccoby, 1998) and others showing little developmental change in rigidity (Serbin, Powlishta, & Gulko, 1993). These differences are probably due to varying influences of socialization, biological, and cognitive developmental factors.

On the basis of an extensive review of the literature, we have recently suggested the following developmental hypothesis: The consequences of gender identity may differ at different levels of understanding. Specifically, lower levels of understanding (recognizing one's sex) may serve to orient children to the importance of gender, thereby increasing their in-group biases and their motivation to attend to information about gender, whereas higher levels of understanding (recognizing the invariance of the category) may heighten children's behavioral responsiveness to gender-related social norms (Martin et al., 2002). A parallel hypothesis has received support in research on ethnic-related identity and consequences, but the hypothesis remains to be tested for gender (Ruble et al., in press).

THE EARLY ORIGINS OF GENDER

Researchers have been fascinated for years with questions about the early origins of gendered behavior and thinking. The two most pressing issues are, at what age do children begin to think of themselves and other people in terms of gender, and how do these gender cognitions influence their behavior and thinking?

Development of Gender-Based Perceptual Discriminations

In the quest to understand the earliest origins of gender development, researchers have been conducting studies with infants and toddlers. The latest research on this topic has yielded surprising findings: Six-month-old infants can distinguish the voices of women and men, and most 9-month-olds are able to discriminate between photographs of men and women. Even more surprising is that between the ages of 11 and 14 months, infants learn to recognize the associations between women's and men's photographs and their voices (e.g., that men's faces "go with" low voices), showing that they can form associations across sensory modalities. These studies suggest that by the time children can talk, they have in place perceptual categories that distinguish "male" from "female" (for a review, see Martin et al., 2002).

Linking Thought and Behavior

If cognitions play a role in guiding behavior, one would expect that the onset of gender-related cognitions precedes behavior that reflects sex differences. Developmental trends tend to support this pattern, but not always. For instance, girls show preferences for dolls and boys for transportation toys at a very early age, before gender cognitions develop. Yet most sex differences do not become apparent until after age 2, when children have at least rudimentary gender cognitions.

Do young children's gender cognitions actually influence behavior? Specifically, do children who recognize their gender identity or know gender stereotypes behave in more gender-differentiated ways than children who do not recognize gender identity or know gender stereotypes? Establishing clear causal linkages between knowing about gender and acting on the basis of that knowledge has been challenging (Martin et al., 2002). In natural settings, it is difficult to assess the role of cognition because patterns of behavior are also influenced by children's prior experiences. Nevertheless, a few longitudinal analyses have shown that once children know gender stereotypes, their personal preferences become more gender typed (Miller, Trautner, & Ruble, in press).

These links have also been studied in the laboratory by giving novel toys or activities gender-related labels, either directly (e.g., "I think that boys like this toy better than girls") or subtly (e.g., "this is a test to see how good you would be at mechanics or operating machinery"). Such studies have shown that children pay more attention to toys and activities that they believe are for their own sex than to toys and activities they think are for the other sex. Similarly, children have better memory for, perform better with, and have greater expectations of success with toys and activities they think are for their own sex. Essentially, these studies illustrate that when a toy or activity is stereotyped, with either overt or covert cues, children respond according to whether the toy or activity is appropriate for their own sex.

FUTURE DIRECTIONS

In conclusion, several lines of evidence support cognitive theories of gender development. First, children's growing knowledge about and identification with gender categories has evaluative and motivational consequences. For instance, knowledge of gender stereotypes is linked to behavior, especially in carefully designed experimental and correlational studies. Second, children show developmental changes in stereotyping that parallel other cognitive developmental changes. Third, knowledge about gender categories may be found in primitive forms in infancy, well before the emergence of many gender-typed behaviors.

However, many fundamental questions remain to be tackled by future research. For example, it is not yet known at what age children begin to identify with gender in some form. Is it possible that toddlers have developed gender preferences based on primitive gender identities by the time they are able to talk? Researchers also do not know what processes underlie the waxing and waning of rigidity and flexibility in gender beliefs and behaviors. Do socialization processes interact with cognitive-developmental factors to determine when children attend to gender information and adopt rigid beliefs about it?

Recently, interest in integrating multiple perspectives on gender has been heightened by research on children and adults who either have a mismatch between their biological sex and their gender identity or are born with ambiguous genitalia. Collaborative efforts with biologically oriented theorists could address such important issues as whether there is a critical or sensitive period for gender identity and how social, biological, and cognitive factors affect its development. How, for example, do the gender-identification processes unfold for children born with ambiguous genitalia? What cues might children use to lead them to conclude that their gender is different from their biological sex? Are there interpersonal and mental health consequences of whether or not they forge a clear identity as one sex or the other? Such questions have been asked for decades, and have critical implications for health and mental health, but convincing answers have remained elusive.

Recommended Reading

Liben, S.L., & Bigler, R.S. (2002). (See References)
Martin, C.L., Ruble, D.N., & Szkrybalo, J. (2002). (See References)
Ruble, D.N., & Martin, C.L. (1998). (See References)
Ruble, D.N., & Martin, C.L. (2002). Conceptualizing, measuring, and evaluating the developmental course of gender differentiation: Compliments, queries, and quandaries. *Monographs of the Society for Research in Child Development, 67*(2, Serial No. 269), 148–166.

Acknowledgments—Preparation of this article was supported by Grants from the MacArthur Foundation, the Russell Sage Foundation, and the National Institute of Mental Health (R01 37215).

Note

1. Address correspondence to Carol Martin, Department of Family and Human Development, Arizona State University, Tempe, AZ 85287-2502; e-mail: cmartin@asu.edu.

References

Bauer, P.J., & Coyne, M.J. (1997). When the name says it all: Preschoolers' recognition and use of the gendered nature of common proper names. *Social Development, 6,* 271–291.
Bigler, R.S., Jones, L.C., & Lobliner, D.B. (1997). Social categorization and the formation of intergroup attitudes in children. *Child Development, 68,* 530–543.
Bjorklund, D.F. (2000). *Children's thinking: Developmental function and individual differences.* Belmont, CA: Wadsworth.
Bradbard, M.R., Martin, C.L., Endsley, R.C., & Halverson, C.F. (1986). Influence of sex stereotypes on children's exploration and memory: A competence versus performance distinction. *Developmental Psychology, 22,* 481–486.
Bussey, K., & Bandura, A. (1999). Social-cognitive theory of gender development and differentiation. *Psychological Review, 106,* 676–713.
Kohlberg, L.A. (1966). A cognitive-developmental analysis of children's sex role concepts and attitudes. In E. Maccoby (Ed.), *The development of sex differences* (pp. 82–173). Stanford, CA: Stanford University Press.
Liben, S.L., & Bigler, R.S. (2002). The developmental course of gender differentiation: Conceptualizing, measuring and evaluating constructs and pathways. *Monographs of the Society for Research in Child Development, 67*(2, Serial No. 269), 1–147.

Maccoby, E.E. (1998). *The two sexes: Growing up apart, coming together*. Cambridge, MA: Belknap Press.

Martin, C.L., & Halverson, C.F. (1983). The effects of sex-stereotyping schemas on young children's memory. *Child Development, 54,* 563–574.

Martin, C.L., Ruble, D.N., & Szkrybalo, J. (2002). Cognitive theories of early gender development. *Psychological Bulletin, 128,* 903–933.

Miller, C.F., Trautner, H.M., & Ruble, D.N. (in press). The role of gender knowledge in children's gender-typed preferences. In C. Tamis-LeMonda & L. Balter (Eds.), *Child psychology: A handbook of contemporary issues*. Philadelphia: Psychology Press.

Ruble, D.N., Alvarez, J., Bachman, M., Cameron, J., Fuligni, A., Garcia-Coll, C., & Rhee, E. (in press). The development and implications of children's social self or the "we." In M. Bennett & F. Sani (Eds.), *The development of the social self*. East Sussex, England: Psychological Press.

Ruble, D.N., & Martin, C.L. (1998). Gender development. In W. Damon (Ed.), *Handbook of child psychology: Vol. 3* (pp. 933–1016). New York: Wiley.

Serbin, L.A., Powlishta, K.K., & Gulko, J. (1993). The development of sex typing in middle childhood. *Monographs of the Society for Research in Child Development, 58*(2, Serial No. 232).

Trautner, H.M., Ruble, D.N., Cyphers, L., Kirsten, B., Behrendt, R., & Hartmann, P. (2003). *Rigidity and flexibility of gender stereotypes in childhood: Developmental or differential?* Manuscript submitted for publication.

This article has been reprinted as it originally appeared in *Current Directions in Psychological Science*. Citation information for this article as originally published appears above.

Sex Differences in Episodic Memory

Agneta Herlitz[1] and Jenny Rehnman
*Aging Research Center, Karolinska Institutet,
Stockholm, Sweden, and Stockholm University,
Stockholm, Sweden*

Abstract

Research shows sex differences in episodic memory. These differences vary in magnitude as a function of the type of material to be remembered. Throughout the life span, verbal episodic-memory tasks yield differences favoring women. In contrast, episodic-memory tasks requiring visuospatial processing result in differences favoring men. There are also sex differences favoring women on episodic-memory tasks requiring both verbal and visuospatial processing and on face-recognition tasks. Thus, there may be a small, general episodic-memory advantage for women— an advantage that can increase by the advantage women have over men in verbal production and can be reversed by the male advantage in visuospatial tasks. In addition, environmental factors affect the magnitude of the sex differences in episodic memory.

Keywords

sex differences; episodic memory; visuospatial; verbal

Being able to remember events from one's past is essential for functioning in society. By now, it is well known that a number of factors, among them age and education, affect one's ability to remember. Whether one's sex also influences the ability to remember everyday events is less well researched. One reason may be that, in the first comprehensive review of this subject, Maccoby and Jacklin (1974) did not find sex differences in memory. However, the theoretical model of memory used by those researchers was different from that of current theories, which may explain why they did not find sex differences.

EPISODIC MEMORY

Although several theories of memory exist today, most investigators would agree that memory can be subdivided into two broad categories: working memory (or short-term memory) and long-term memory. Long-term memory can in turn be divided into subsystems, one being episodic memory. Episodic memory refers to the conscious recollection of unique personal experiences in terms of their content (what), location (where), and temporal occurrence (when; Tulving, 2001). Episodic memory is typically assessed by first presenting some information (e.g., episodes, words, objects, or faces), and by then asking the person to recall or recognize the earlier-presented information.

What Impact Does Task Material Have on Sex Differences in Episodic Memory?

Although Maccoby and Jacklin (1974) did not find sex differences in memory, many more recent studies have found sex differences favoring women in episodic-memory tasks. For example, in a large population-based study of 1,000 adults between 35 and 80, we found sex differences on episodic-memory tasks in which the participants were told to try to remember lists of words, objects, or activities that had been presented earlier (Herlitz, Nilsson, & Bäckman, 1997). The difference between men and women on a word-recall task was $d = .25$ (see Fig. 1). d is computed by calculating the difference between the means of women and men, divided by the pooled standard deviation. Here, a positive value indicates that women perform at a higher level than men, and a negative value indicates that men outperform women. The closer the value is to zero, the smaller the difference. A d of .20 indicates that 59% of all women perform at a higher level than the average man. The comparable numbers for $d = .40$ and $d = .60$ are 66% and 73%, respectively. Notably, most tests used to assess episodic memory in clinical situations, such as the California Verbal Learning Test and subtests of the Wechsler Memory Scale, use similar materials as we did—that is, word lists, lists of objects, or pictures of objects. Women are typically found to perform at a higher level than men on these tests (e.g., Kramer, Delis, Kaplan, O'Donnell, & Prifitera, 1997).

Maccoby and Jacklin (1974) noted that girls excel on verbal tasks and that boys perform at a higher level than girls on visuospatial tasks. Sex differences in verbal and visuospatial tasks have since then been confirmed in numerous studies (e.g., Hyde & Linn, 1988; Voyer, Voyer, & Bryden, 1995). Because women excel on verbal-production tasks—for example, tasks requiring participants to rapidly retrieve words starting with the letter f ($d = .33$; Hyde & Linn, 1988)—it may not be surprising that women also excel when they are asked to recall events that happened during the past year, day, or minute. Women may simply be

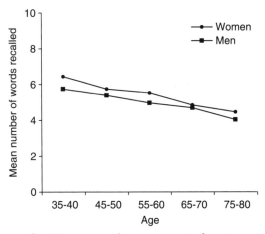

Fig. 1. Performance of 1,000 women and men on an episodic-memory task requiring participants to recall an earlier-presented list of words (Herlitz, Nilsson, & Bäckman, 1997).

at an advantage on such episodic-memory tasks due to their superior verbal-production abilities. Analogously, as men typically perform at a higher level than women on visuospatial tasks—such as understanding what an irregular figure looks like when it is rotated in space ($d = .56$; Voyer et al., 1995)—men can be expected to perform at a higher level than women on episodic-memory tasks requiring visuospatial processing. Although relatively few studies have examined sex differences in visuospatial episodic-memory tasks, it is clear that the pattern of sex differences is different than for verbal episodic-memory tasks (Lewin, Wolgers, & Herlitz, 2001). The magnitude of the male advantage seems to vary as a function of the extent to which the task relies on visuospatial processing versus the extent to which verbal processing can be utilized. As can be seen in Figure 2, which shows typical effect sizes (d) in various episodic-memory tasks, a task requiring participants to remember the route walked in a maze with little or no external information results in large sex differences favoring men (e.g., Astur, Ortiz, & Sutherland, 1998), whereas smaller sex differences are found in other route-finding tasks when external verbal information can support memory performance (e.g., Crook, Youngjohn, & Larrabee, 1993). Translated into real-life situations, a greater male advantage can be expected when walking back from the

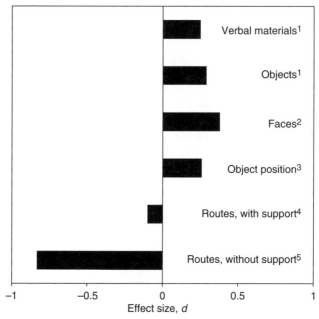

Fig. 2. Representative examples illustrating the pattern and magnitude of sex differences in episodic memory across different types of materials. The material to be remembered is, from the top, words,[1] objects,[1] faces,[2] object positions,[3] routes with environmental information,[4] and routes without environmental information.[5] A positive effect size, d, indicates that women perform at a higher level than men, and a negative d indicates that men perform at a higher level than women. Note: [1]Herlitz, Nilsson, & Bäckman (1997); [2]Lewin, Wolgers, & Herlitz (2001); [3]Voyer, Postma, Brake, & Imperato-McGinley (2007); [4]Crook, Youngjohn, & Larrabee (1993); [5]Astur, Ortiz, & Sutherland (1998).

glade in a pine forest than when walking back from the museum to the hotel in Rome, as more varied and easily verbalized information is available in Rome, compared to the forest.

Of interest is also whether there are sex differences on episodic-memory tasks requiring both verbal and visuospatial processing. Notably, women outperform men on tasks requiring remembering an object's position, such as when playing the game Memory or when trying to remember where they last saw their keys (Voyer, Postma, Brake, & Imperato-McGinley, 2007; see Fig. 2). Thus, even though such tasks clearly require visuospatial processing, women may be able to use their verbal advantage to remember objects' positions. Are there sex differences on episodic-memory tasks requiring minimal verbal or visuospatial processing, such as when remembering unfamiliar odors? This is of interest, as the presence of sex differences on such tasks may suggest that there is an underlying sex difference in basic episodic-memory capacity that is present irrespective of the type of material to be remembered. Although not many studies have addressed this issue and more studies are needed, there are findings suggesting that women have a slight advantage over men on such tasks (Öberg, Larsson, & Bäckman, 2002).

Face Recognition

Many studies have shown that women outperform men on face-recognition tasks (e.g., Lewin et al., 2001; Lewin & Herlitz, 2002). Although face recognition cannot readily be assumed to rely on verbal processing, it was hypothesized that women can utilize their greater verbal abilities to encode faces by verbalizing them—for example, "a dark, blue-eyed handsome man." This hypothesis was investigated by showing faces without hair, ears, or pieces of clothing in rapid succession, preventing the participants from verbalizing the faces (Lewin & Herlitz, 2002). It was found that women recognized more faces than men did, irrespective of whether verbal encoding was suppressed or not—thus providing no support for the hypothesis that women use their greater verbal abilities to encode faces. However, the results also revealed that the female recognition advantage was magnified for female faces. This tendency for females to remember faces of their own sex more accurately than faces of the opposite sex (i.e., "the own-sex effect") is found across age, so that both young girls and adult women remember more female faces, irrespective of the age of the faces (e.g., faces of young girls or adult women) and across ethnicity (i.e., ethnically familiar or unfamiliar faces). In contrast, men tend to remember male and female faces equally well (e.g., Rehnman & Herlitz, 2006, 2007). Why might this be the case?

To address this intriguing issue, we created a set of androgynous faces (see Fig. 3) and showed the same set to three groups of men and women (Rehnman, Lindholm, & Herlitz, 2007). The three groups saw the same group of androgynous faces but received somewhat different instructions—that they would be presented with a series of either (a) "female faces," (b) "male faces," or (c) "faces," and that their task was to remember the faces for a later recognition task. Interestingly, women who were told that they should remember female faces remembered more faces than women who were told to remember male faces or

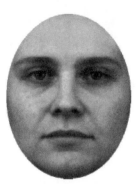

Fig. 3. An example of the androgynous faces used in the Rehnman, Lindholm, & Herlitz (2007) study of face recognition.

just faces. By contrast, men performed at similar levels across instructional conditions. In addition, women remembered more androgynous faces than men did when they were told to remember just (gender-unspecified) faces.

We interpret these findings to mean that women allocate more attention to female than to male faces. Studies on infants have shown that infant girls devote more attention to faces than infant boys do (Conellan, Baron-Cohen, Wheelwright, Batki, & Ahluwalia, 2000). Speculatively, the attention infant girls devote to faces may form the basis of women's superior face-recognition ability. Moreover, developmentally, categorization of female faces precedes that of male faces for both sexes, possibly as a result of greater early exposure to female than to male faces (Ramsey-Rennels & Langlois, 2006). With increasing age, girls may develop their interest in other females, which also might be strengthened through their interactions with other women. By contrast, developing boys may orient themselves toward other males, losing their early advantage for categorization of female faces and resulting in an absence of bias.

DEVELOPMENTAL TRENDS AND ENVIRONMENTAL FACTORS

In research on sex differences, one focus has been on whether the magnitude of the differences varies across the life span. Explanation of the differences to some extent rests on whether or not it does. For example, a change in the magnitude or direction of sex differences around puberty would suggest that the biological (e.g., hormonal) changes taking place around that time are important in explaining the differences. With regard to sex differences in verbal episodic-memory tasks, it is clear that there are sex differences in the recall of word lists favoring girls at a young age (i.e., age 5; $d \approx .39$) and that those differences are of similar magnitude in young adults (i.e., age 15; $d \approx .43$; e.g., Kramer et al., 1997), middle-aged adults, and old adults ($d \approx .25$; e.g., Herlitz et al., 1997). The same appears to be true for sex differences in face recognition (age 9, $d \approx .47$, adults $d \approx .53$; Rehnman & Herlitz, 2006, 2007), although much less research has been conducted in this area. Thus, data seem to suggest that the major biological changes associated with development and aging do not influence the pattern and magnitude of sex differences in these episodic-memory tasks.

Another important question is whether sex differences in episodic memory exist throughout the world. Large variations in the pattern and magnitude of sex differences would suggest that cultural factors influence the differences to a considerable degree. To our knowledge, sex differences in episodic memory have been examined in 23 out of 192 United Nations member states, and although the bulk of studies come from Europe and North America, there are a sufficiently large number of studies of verbal episodic memory conducted in Australia to conclude that sex differences are present also in this part of the world. Whether the same pattern of data exists on the African continent and in South America remains unknown, whereas studies emanating from Southeast Asia (e.g., Kim & Kang, 1999) seem to indicate a similar pattern of sex differences in verbal episodic memory as in Australia, Europe, and North America.

Factors such as education and public exposure may influence the magnitude, rather than the pattern, of sex differences. This is illustrated in a study in which we compared the magnitude and pattern of cognitive sex differences in literate and illiterate older adults from Bangladesh and Sweden (Herlitz & Kabir, 2006). The participants were tested on a brief cognitive test. In general, men performed at a higher level than women on a spatial-visualization task (drawing or forming, with sticks, a geometrical form), whereas women performed at a higher level than men on the episodic-memory task (a short word list). Among illiterate Bangladeshis, there were large differences favoring men—even on tasks for which no differences were expected, such as providing accurate information about the neighborhood they lived in. In fact, the only task in which men did not outperform women was the episodic-memory task. Illiterate Bangladeshi women, in contrast to Bangladeshi men, have little or no access to the world outside the immediate home and family. Therefore, we interpreted the results as indicating that the pattern of cognitive sex differences is similar irrespective of nationality and literacy but that the magnitude of the differences is related to both education and sociocultural factors. Importantly, the low performance of the illiterate women demonstrated the inhibiting effect restrictions in public exposure might have on cognitive performance.

CONCLUSIONS AND FUTURE DIRECTIONS

Gender influences performance on episodic-memory tasks: Women consistently outperform men on tasks that require remembering items that are verbal in nature or can be verbally labeled. However, women also excel on tasks requiring little or no verbal processing, such as recognition of unfamiliar odors or faces. In contrast, there is a male advantage on episodic-memory tasks requiring visuospatial processing. These findings suggest that women's episodic-memory advantage can increase or be reversed, depending on the nature of the material to be remembered. For example, if the material is verbal or evokes women's attention (e.g., female faces), women outperform men, whereas men outperform women on visuospatial episodic-memory tasks (e.g., remembering a route).

Are these statistically rather small sex differences in episodic memory sufficiently large to be detected in everyday life? Are the anecdotal reports claiming that men do not remember people they have met, the location of misplaced objects, or who said what at the last party as well as women do real-life illustrations of these differences? Or are such memory failures just as commonly found for women? Besides exploring sex differences in everyday memory failures, future studies should investigate whether such differences are merely a function of sex differences in other areas (e.g., verbal, visuospatial) or whether there is, in addition to material-specific effects, a general episodic-memory advantage for women. If the latter is true, empirical attention should be directed at delineating the origins of this female superiority. Could the difference be understood in terms of the different pressures evolution has put on males and females and does it have biologically plausible neural correlates? Clearly, further research is needed before we fully can understand the causes and mechanisms behind sex differences in episodic memory.

Recommended Reading

Halpern, D.F. (2000). *Sex differences in cognitive abilities* (3rd ed.). Mahwah, NJ: Erlbaum. A comprehensive and clearly written review for readers who wish to expand on their knowledge of sex differences in cognitive abilities.

Herlitz, A. (1997). (See References). One of the first papers to raise attention about sex differences in episodic memory.

Tulving, E. (2001). (See References). A thorough and theoretical analysis of episodic memory.

Note

1. Address correspondence to Agneta Herlitz, Aging Research Center, Karolinska Institutet, Gävlegatan 16, S-113 30 Stockholm, Sweden; e-mail: agneta.herlitz@ki.se.

References

Astur, R.S., Ortiz, M.L., & Sutherland, R.J. (1998). A characterization of performance by men and women in a virtual Morris water task: A large and reliable sex difference. *Behavioural Brain Research, 93,* 185–190.

Connellan, J., Baron-Cohen, S., Wheelwright, S., Batki, A., & Ahluwalia, J. (2000). Sex differences in human neonatal social perception. *Infant Behavior & Development, 23,* 113–118.

Crook, T.H., Youngjohn, J.R., & Larrabee, G.J. (1993). The influence of age, gender, and cues on computer-simulated topographic memory. *Developmental Neuropsychology, 9,* 41–53.

Herlitz, A., & Kabir, Z.N. (2006). Sex differences in cognition among illiterate Bangladeshis: A comparison with literate Bangladeshis and Swedes. *Scandinavian Journal of Psychology, 47,* 441–447.

Herlitz, A., Nilsson, L.-G., & Bäckman, L. (1997). Gender differences in episodic memory. *Memory & Cognition, 25,* 801–811.

Hyde, J.S., & Linn, M.C. (1988). Gender differences in verbal ability: A meta-analysis. *Psychological Bulletin, 104,* 53–69.

Kim, J.K., & Kang, Y. (1999). Normative study of the Korean-California Verbal Learning Test (K-CVLT). *The Clinical Neuropsychologist, 13,* 365–369.

Kramer, J.H., Delis, D.C., Kaplan, E., O'Donnell, L., & Prifitera, A. (1997). Developmental sex differences in verbal learning. *Neuropsychology, 11,* 577–584.

Lewin, C., & Herlitz, A. (2002). Sex differences in face recognition: Women's faces make the difference. *Brain and Cognition, 50,* 121–128.

Lewin, C., Wolgers, G., & Herlitz, A. (2001). Sex differences favoring women in verbal but not in visuospatial episodic memory. *Neuropsychology, 15,* 165–173.

Maccoby, E.E., & Jacklin, C.N. (1974). *The psychology of sex differences*. Stanford: Stanford University Press.

Öberg, C., Larsson, M., & Bäckman, L. (2002). Differential sex effects in olfactory functioning: The role of verbal processing. *Journal of the International Neuropsychological Society, 8*, 691–698.

Ramsey-Rennels, J.L., & Langlois, J.H. (2006). Infants' differential processing of female and male faces. *Current Directions in Psychological Science, 15*, 59–62.

Rehnman, J., & Herlitz, A. (2006). Higher face recognition in girls: Magnified by own-sex and own-ethnicity bias. *Memory, 14*, 289–296.

Rehnman, J., & Herlitz, A. (2007). Women recognize more faces than men do. *Acta Psychologica, 124*, 344–355.

Rehnman, J., Lindholm, T., & Herlitz, A. (2007). *Why women remember women: Gender labeling of androgynous faces produces a female own-sex bias.* Manuscript submitted for publication.

Tulving, E. (2001). Episodic memory and common sense: How far apart? *Philosophical Transactions of the Royal Society of London, Series B—Biological Sciences, 356*, 1505–1515.

Voyer, D., Postma, A., Brake, B., & Imperato-McGinley, J. (2007). Gender differences in object location memory: A meta-analysis. *Psychonomic Bulletin & Review, 14*, 23–38.

Voyer, D., Voyer, S., & Bryden, M.P. (1995). Magnitude of sex differences in spatial abilities: A meta-analysis and consideration of critical variables. *Psychological Bulletin, 117*, 250–270.

This article has been reprinted as it originally appeared in *Current Directions in Psychological Science*. Citation information for this article as originally published appears above.

Does Estrogen Protect Against Cognitive Aging in Women?

Barbara B. Sherwin[1]

McGill University, Montreal, Quebec, Canada

Abstract

Although there is evidence from randomized controlled trials that estrogen therapy protects against aspects of cognitive decline that occur with normal aging in women, findings from the Women's Health Initiative Memory Study and from some cross-sectional and longitudinal studies failed to find neuroprotective effects of estrogen in older women. There is growing empirical support for the critical-period hypothesis, formulated in the attempt to resolve these discrepancies. It holds that estrogen therapy has protective effects on verbal memory and on working memory only when it is initiated closely in time to menopause, whereas starting treatment many years following menopause does not protect and may even be harmful. Supporting evidence for this hypothesis from basic neuroscience and from animal and human studies is evaluated for its ability to explain the inconsistencies and to describe the conditions under which estrogen may protect cognitive function in aging women.

Keywords

estrogen; cognition; aging; postmenopausal women

The intense interest in the causes and prevention of degenerative diseases common in older age can be attributed to a variety of factors. First, there has been a dramatic increase in life expectancy in industrialized countries during the past century due, in part, to the decrease in maternal and childhood mortality, the availability of vaccines to control many infectious diseases, the development of antibiotics and other drugs to treat chronic illnesses, and improvements in the standard of living. These medical and social advances mean that, on average, people in industrialized countries are living well into their eighth decade of life. Unfortunately, however, this increase in life expectancy has not been paralleled by a decrease in the rate of disability before death, so that more people are living longer but with a disability toward the end of life that causes considerable suffering for them and their families and a heavy financial and social burden for society. Prominent among the degenerative diseases of older age are those that affect cognitive functioning. In this article I evaluate the degree to which estrogen, whose production declines drastically at midlife, is implicated in cognitive aging in women and address possible reasons for the inconsistencies in this literature.

NORMAL COGNITIVE AGING

There is now a considerable amount of evidence to suggest that age-related changes in cognition occur with normal aging. Declines in cognitive function occur in several cognitive domains including memory, processing speed, and reasoning

(Salthouse, 2004). Although cognitive decline begins in early adulthood, it accelerates after age 50. Moreover, the integrity of some brain areas is more vulnerable to some aging processes than that of others. Changes tend to occur most profoundly in the hippo-campus and prefrontal cortex (PFC), the same brain areas that subserve the specific cognitive functions that decline with normal aging, including verbal memory and working memory, respectively (Esiri, 2007). While pathological cognitive decline is related to the loss of synapses, neurons, neurotransmitters, and neural networks, neuronal loss may not be an inevitable feature of normal brain aging. Indeed, neurogenesis, the synthesis of new neurons, continues throughout life, including in old age.

ESTROGEN AND COGNITIVE FUNCTIONING

After age 40, the ovaries become less and less efficient as a result of the gradual depletion of ovarian follicles along with age-related changes in the hypothalamic-pituitary-ovarian axis (the feedback system that controls the production of estrogen). The perimenopausal period, when the ovarian production of estrogen is decreasing, encompasses several years leading up to the spontaneous or natural menopause, the cessation of menstrual cycles, which occurs at an average age of 51.8 years in industrialized countries. A surgical menopause occurs whenever the ovaries are surgically removed from premenopausal women and is associated with an abrupt decrease in estrogen levels. Both types of menopause can give rise to symptoms such as hot flashes, cold sweats, disturbances in memory, and mood changes. Although estrogen therapy (ET) is effective in relieving some of these symptoms, naturally menopausal women are required to take progesterone along with estrogen in order to protect the uterus against estrogen's stimulatory effects, whereas women who have had their uteri surgically removed can receive estrogen alone.

Many investigators have sought to determine whether post-menopausal ET might protect against the decline in aspects of cognition that occur with normal aging. To provide a rationale for these clinical trials, it is important to first establish that estrogen actually influences aspects of brain anatomy and physiology that are important for cognitive functions. In fact, estrogen receptors are found in the hippocampus and in the PFC, and estrogen can affect neurons in these areas directly by interacting with receptors in the nucleus of a neuron or, indirectly, by interacting with nonnuclear receptors (Lee & McEwen, 2001). Through these mechanisms, estrogen is able to enhance neurotransmission by increasing the number of possible connections between neurons in the hippocampus, by indirectly increasing the production of the neurotransmitter acetylcholine that is critically important for memory, and by its numerous mechanisms that enhance the growth and survival of neurons (Lee & McEwen, 2001). Neuroimaging studies show that ET is associated with different patterns of activation in some regions of the brain that subserve memory and other cognitive functions and that estrogen seems to attenuate the decline in hippocampal volume that occurs with aging (Resnick, Pham, Kraut, Zonderman & Davatzikos, 2003).

Animal studies also provide evidence that estrogen influences learning and memory in a task-dependent fashion, suggesting that the hormone differentially affects specific brain regions. When estrogen was administered to young and aged female rats whose ovaries had been surgically removed, performance on hippocampally dependent spatial-memory tasks was enhanced (Gibbs & Gabor, 2003). Similarly, when aged monkeys whose ovaries had been removed were exposed to alternating treatments with estradiol, the most potent estrogen, and a placebo, only estradiol improved performance on a spatial-memory task (Lacreuse, Wilson, & Herndon, 2002). No treatment effects were observed on a delayed-response task, which assesses visuo-spatial working memory and is associated with PFC function. Therefore, in both rats and nonhuman primates, estrogen specifically protects memory functions that are dependent on the hippocampus.

There is now a voluminous body of literature on the putative protective effect of ET on aspects of cognitive functioning in women. While I will not undertake a comprehensive account of the findings here, I will attempt to summarize and interpret this body of knowledge. Prospective, randomized controlled trials (RCTs) of healthy, surgically menopausal women (mean age, 44 years) were the first to show the specificity of the beneficial effects of ET on verbal memory (Phillips & Sherwin, 1992; Fig. 1) and, more recently, on working memory (Grigorova, Sherwin, & Tulandi, 2006). Whereas these findings were supported by some other RCTs of naturally menopausal women, not all cross-sectional and longitudinal studies have provided confirmation (Sherwin, 2003). Although numerous critical analyses of this literature have attempted to account for the inconsistencies between studies, disagreement remains.

The inconsistencies regarding whether estrogen protected, failed to protect, or even caused harm with regard to cognitive decline in postmenopausal women were compounded when the findings from the Women's Health Initiative Memory

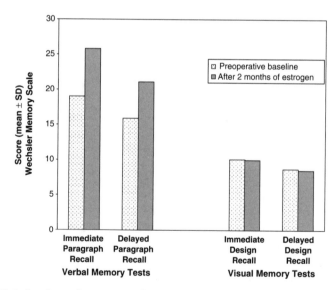

Fig. 1. Verbal and visual memory performance (as measured by the Wechsler Memory Scale) before and after 2 months of estrogen treatment in surgically menopausal women. Data from Phillips & Sherwin (1992).

Study (WHIMS), the largest RCT ever undertaken, were published in 2004 (Espeland et al., 2004). Approximately 3,000 naturally menopausal women randomly received conjugated equine estrogen (CEE) plus medroxyprogesterone acetate (MPA) or a placebo, and 4,500 surgically menopausal women received treatment with CEE alone or a placebo for 5 years. All participants were tested annually with the modified Mini Mental State Examination (3MSE), a measure of global cognitive function. Contrary to expectations, the risk for mild cognitive impairment and for probable all-cause dementia were nonsignificantly higher in the groups that received CEE alone or CEE plus MPA compared with the placebo (Espeland et al., 2004). Although the magnitude of the differences in 3MSE scores between the hormone- and placebo-treated groups was too small to be clinically meaningful, these findings failed to support the idea that estrogen protected against cognitive deterioration in women.

A second ancillary study to the Women's Health Initiative (WHI), the WHI Study of Cognitive Aging (WHISCA) was begun 3 years following randomization of women to CEE plus MPA or a placebo; it longitudinally evaluated specific cognitive functions in naturally postmenopausal women whose mean age was 73.7 years at the time of their recruitment from the WHI (Resnick et al., 2006). After an average of 1.35 years of follow-up, scores of women taking CEE plus MPA had declined significantly on a test of verbal learning and memory and had increased significantly on a test of short-term visual memory compared to the women on the placebo. The absence of pretreatment scores, the low 2-year adherence rate in the CEE plus MPA group (47.4%), and the fact that MPA was coadministered with CEE suggests that these findings should be interpreted cautiously.

THE CRITICAL-PERIOD HYPOTHESIS

Why did ET not only fail to protect against cognitive decline but possibly even cause harm to the postmenopausal women in WHIMS, whereas neuroprotective effects had been apparent in other, smaller RCTs and in some cross-sectional and longitudinal studies? An examination of some differences between the study populations and treatments administered in the WHIMS compared to those of the smaller RCTs that found beneficial effects of estrogen may help to understand these discrepancies. Perhaps the most striking observation is that the studies finding a protective effect of estrogen on cognitive aging came from the smaller RCTs in which premenopausal women in their forties had received estradiol alone or a placebo immediately following surgical removal of their uteri and ovaries (Sherwin, 2003), whereas the average age of the women in the WHIMS was 72 years at baseline.

Recently, the critical-period hypothesis was formulated in the attempt to resolve the inconsistencies in the estrogen-and-cognition literature (Resnick & Henderson, 2002). It holds that ET optimally protects against cognitive decline when treatment is begun close in time to menopause whereas starting treatment decades afterward is not beneficial and may even cause harm. Indeed, there is a growing body of evidence from basic neuroscience and from rodent, nonhuman primate, and human studies supporting the idea that ET protects against a deterioration in memory performance when treatment is started shortly following removal of the ovaries but not when estrogen is administered after a considerable delay or when it is given to very old individuals (Sherwin, 2005). Similarly, there is evidence that ET protects against memory decline in women when started soon after a natural or surgical menopause but not when treatment is delayed for many years (Sherwin, 2005).

Why might ET be neuroprotective when administered to women shortly following menopause but not when it is initiated decades later? One way to understand these findings is to consider that brain aging results in a decrease in brain volume and neuron size and a 46% reduction in dendritic spine numbers in humans over the age of 50 (Esiri, 2007). Therefore, ET given to the 72-year-old women in the WHIMS was administered against the background of two decades of accrued brain aging, whereas the neuroprotective influences of ET in the 44-year-old surgically menopausal women (Sherwin, 2003) were not confounded by brain aging. Indeed, findings that estradiol increased hippocampal spine density in young, but not in aged, rats (Gibbs & Gabor, 2003) and enhanced working memory in middle-aged animals when given immediately after ovary removal, but not when administered after a prolonged period of estrogen deprivation (Daniel, Hulst, & Berbling, 2006; Fig. 2), support the idea that brain aging

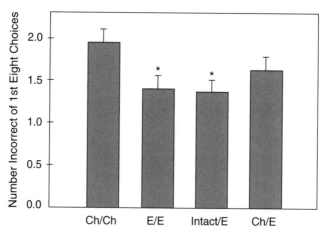

Fig. 2. Working memory performance (as mean number of incorrect choices in the first eight visits to a maze averaged over 24 training days) in four groups of rats subjected to ovary removal and cholesterol and/or estradiol treatment. Three groups were ovariectomized at 12 months of age and received cholesterol treatment 5 months before and during training in a radial arm maze (Ch/Ch), estradiol treatment 5 months before and during training (E/E), or cholesterol treatment for 5 months followed by estradiol treatment beginning 1 week before training (Ch/E). The fourth group underwent sham surgery at 12 months of age and was ovariectomized and treated with estradiol 1 week before training at 17 months of age (Intact/E). Reprinted from "Estradiol Replacement Enhances Working Memory in Middle-Aged Rats When Initiated Immediately After Ovariectomy But Not After a Long-Term Period of Ovarian Hormone Deprivation," by J.M. Daniel, J.L. Hulst, & J.L. Berbling, 2006, *Endocrinology, 147*, p. 610. Copyright 2006, The Endocrine Society. Reproduced with permission.

modulates responses to the hormone, although other, unknown factors may also be operative.

The results of recent reanalyses of the WHI data that examined risk for adverse events in other organ systems as a function of age at the time of the trial also accord with the critical-period hypothesis. Although the risks for both coronary heart disease and stroke were significantly elevated in the 60- to 79-year-old hormone-treated women, the risks for coronary heart disease and for total mortality were reduced by hormone therapy in the 50- to 59-year-old hormone-treated women, compared to those receiving a placebo (Rossouw et al., 2007). Of more direct relevance is the preliminary reanalysis of the WHIMS data, which found that women who took ET before the age of 65 (prior to their enrollment in the WHI) were 50% less likely to develop Alzheimer's disease and all-cause dementia (Henderson, Espeland, Hogan, Rapp, & Stefanick, 2007) compared to nonusers. Both reanalyses support the notion that ET has protective effects in younger, healthier women and may cause harm when given to older women.

Because of the considerable controversy concerning ET and breast cancer risk, it is important to consider yet another WHI data reanalysis, which found nonsignificant reductions in the risk for breast cancer for women who took CEE alone compared to placebo after 7 years of treatment, although the risk was elevated in naturally menopausal women given CEE plus MPA (Stefanick et al., 2006). Whether other synthetic progestins or natural progesterone may have a more benign effect when co-administered with estrogen is currently unknown.

SUMMARY AND CONCLUSIONS

Taken as a whole, the literature on estrogen and cognitive aging in women is marked by disagreement that needs to be resolved for both theoretical and clinical reasons. Results from basic neuroscience and from animal and human studies provide substantial empirical support for the critical-period hypothesis. This evidence suggests, but does not prove, that estrogen alone is neuroprotective when treatment is begun close in time to menopause in healthy women and is administered for a few years and that it is potentially harmful when administered to women over the age of 65. Moreover, recent reanalyses of the WHI data support the critical-period hypothesis and suggest that it may be generalizable to organ systems other than the brain.

OTHER MODULATORS OF THE ESTROGEN–COGNITION RELATIONSHIP

An analysis of the estrogen–cognition literature reveals that several variables modulate this hormone–behavior relationship and require careful consideration in designing future studies. First, because normal brain aging and the risk for the development of neuropathology increases in older women, it would be important for future RCTs to recruit same-aged women in individual investigations to eliminate the confound of aging. Second, in view of the specificity of the estrogenic effects on aspects of cognition, future studies need to administer valid and reliable measures of specific cognitive domains rather than tests that measure only global cognitive function such as the 3MSE. Third it is important to consider the effects of estrogen and progesterone (or synthetic progestins) separately on cognitive function in women; although the effects on the brain of the numerous available chemical formulations of progestins are poorly described, it is clear that progestins affect the brain in ways that, in some cases, are opposite to estrogen (Lee & McEwen, 2001). Therefore, a future priority is to establish the distinctive effects of each sex hormone on cognitive functions before dealing with the possible influence on the brain of administering them together.

Finally, in view of the potential benefits of ET in younger menopausal women, it is important to acknowledge that its efficacy most likely lies in its ability to delay cognitive decline and the clinical manifestations of Alzheimer's disease. That is, there is currently no reason to believe that this hormone would have direct effects on the actual causal factors that underlie cognitive decline and Alzheimer's disease, which are currently unknown. However, in view of the continuing increase in life expectancy in industrialized countries, the implementation of strategies that could delay cognitive decline would result in enormous personal and societal benefits with regard to maintaining the quality of life for our elderly populations.

Recommended Reading

Hogervorst, E., Yaffe, K., Richards, M., & Huppert, F. (2002). Hormone replacement therapy for cognitive functioning in postmenopausal women. *Cochrane Database of Systematic Reviews,* Issue 2, Art. No. CD003122. DOI:10.1002/14651858.

Lee, S.J., & McEwen, B.S. (2001). (See References)

Sherwin, B.B. (2003). (See References)

Sherwin, B.B. (2006). Estrogen and cognitive aging in women. *Neuroscience, 138,* 1021–1026.

Acknowledgments—The preparation of this manuscript was supported by a Grant from the Canadian Institutes of Health Research (#MOP-77773) awarded to B.B. Sherwin.

Note

1. Address correspondence to Barbara B. Sherwin, McGill University, Department of Psychology, 1205 Dr. Penfield Ave., Montreal, Quebec, Canada H3A 1B1; e-mail: barbara.sherwin@mcgill.ca.

References

Daniel, J.M., Hulst, J.L., & Berbling, J.L. (2006). Estradiol replacement enhances working memory in middle-aged rats when initiated immediately after ovariectomy but not after a long-term period of ovarian hormone deprivation. *Endocrinology, 147,* 607–614.

Esiri, M.M. (2007). Aging and the brain. *Journal of Pathology, 211,* 181–187.

Espeland, M.A., Rapp, S.R., Shumaker, S.A., Brunne, E., Manson, J.E., Sherwin, B.B., et al. (2004). The effect of conjugated equine estrogens on global cognitive function in postmenopausal women: Women's Health Initiative Memory Study. *JAMA: Journal of the American Medical Association, 291,* 2959–2968.

Gibbs, R.B., & Gabor, R. (2003). Estrogen and cognition: Applying preclinical findings to clinical perspectives. *Journal of Neuroscience Research, 74,* 637–643.

Grigorova, M., Sherwin, B.B., & Tulandi, T. (2006). Effects of treatment with leuprolide acetate depot on working memory and executive functions in young premenopausal women. *Psychoneuroendocrinology, 31,* 935–947.

Henderson, V.W., Espeland, M.A., Hogan, P.E., Rapp, S.R., & Stefanick, M.L. (2007). Prior use of hormone therapy and incident Alzheimer's disease in the Women's Health Initiative Study. *Neurology, 68*(Suppl. 1), A205.

Lacreuse, A., Wilson, M.E., & Herndon, J.G. (2002). Estradiol, but not raloxifene, improves aspects of spatial working memory in aged ovariectomized rhesus monkeys. *Neurobiology of Aging, 23,* 589–600.

Lee, S.J., & McEwen, B.S. (2001). Neurotrophic and neuroprotective actions of estrogens and their therapeutic implications. *Annual Review of Pharmacology & Pharmacological Toxicology, 41,* 569–591.

Phillips, S.M., & Sherwin, B.B. (1992). Effects of estrogen on memory function in surgically menopausal women. *Psychoneuroendocrinology, 17,* 485–495.

Resnick, S.M., & Henderson, V.W. (2002). Hormone therapy and risk of Alzheimer's disease: A critical time. *JAMA: The Journal of the American Medical Association, 288,* 2170–2172.

Resnick, S.M., Maki, P.M., Rapp, S.R., Espeland, M.A., Brunner, R., Coker, L.H., et al. (2006). Effects of combined estrogen plus progestin hormone treatment on cognition and affect. *Journal of Clinical Endocrinology and Metabolism, 91,* 1802–1810.

Resnick, S.M., Pham, D.L., Kraut, M.A., Zonderman, A.B., & Davatzikos, C. (2003). Longitudinal magnetic resonance imaging studies of older adults: A shrinking brain. *Journal of Neuroscience, 23,* 3295–3301.

Rossouw, J.E., Prentice, R.L., Manson, J.E., Wu, L., Barnabei, V.M., Ko, M., et al. (2007). Postmenopausal hormone therapy and risk of cardiovascular disease by age and years since menopause. *JAMA: The Journal of the American Medical Association, 297,* 1465–1477.

Salthouse, T.A. (2004). What and when of cognitive aging. *Current Directions in Psychological Science, 13,* 140–144.

Sherwin, B.B. (2003). Estrogen and cognition in women. *Endocrine Reviews, 24,* 133–151.

Sherwin, B.B. (2005). Estrogen and memory in women: How can we reconcile the findings? *Hormones and Behavior, 47,* 371–375.

Stefanick, M.L., Anderson, G.L., Margolis, K.L., Rodabough, R.J., Paskett, E.D., Lane, D.S., & Hubbell, F.A. (2006). Effects of conjugated equine estrogens on breast cancer and mammography screening in postmenopausal women with hysterectomy. *JAMA: The Journal of the American Medical Association, 295,* 1647–1657.

This article has been reprinted as it originally appeared in *Current Directions in Psychological Science*. Citation information for this article as originally published appears above.

A Cognitive-Process Taxonomy for Sex Differences in Cognitive Abilities

Diane F. Halpern[1]

Claremont McKenna College

Abstract

Females and males show different average patterns of academic achievement and scores on cognitive ability tests. Females obtain higher grades in school, score much higher on tests of writing and content-area tests on which the questions are similar to material that was learned in school, attain a majority of college degrees, and are closing the gap in many careers that were traditionally male. By contrast, males score higher on standardized tests of mathematics and science that are not directly tied to their school curriculum, show a large advantage on visuospatial tests (especially those that involve judgments of velocity and navigation through three-dimensional space), and are much more knowledgeable about geography and politics. A cognitive-process taxonomy can shed light on these differences.

Keywords

cognitive abilities; sex differences; academic achievement

As Bob Dylan wrote in 1964, "The times they are a-changin'." Every industrialized country in the world is on the cusp of one of the most profound social changes in history, with women entering and, in some cases, dominating professions that have been primarily male, including law, medicine, accounting, and veterinary practice. But women have been slow to enter jobs that require strenuous physical labor, as well as jobs in the technical fields and the physical sciences, and far fewer men are entering traditionally female occupations, such as clerical work, or occupations that require direct personal care, such as child care.

Predictions about future trends in employment can be made by looking at the statistics for educational pipelines. A substantial majority of college students are women; American women have received more college degrees than men every year since 1982, and the gap is widening every year. Among persons between 25 and 34 years old, 33% of women have completed college, compared with 29% of men. In addition, women get higher grades in school in every subject area. Women are still enrolled disproportionately in the humanities, social sciences, and education (Willingham & Cole, 1997).

These changes in the work lives of women and men raise the question: Why are some fields, such as engineering and physics, still dominated by men, while others, such as business, economics, veterinary medicine, and accounting, are now majority-female fields (among young adults)? At the heart of this question is the basic search to understand how women and men are similar and different. For cognitive psychologists, this is a question about intelligence and the relationship among cognitive abilities, academic achievement, being female or male, and career choice.

THE POLITICS AND PSYCHOLOGY
OF GROUP DIFFERENCES

The "battle of the sexes"[2] has assumed center stage in the classroom as popular writers have advanced different social agendas by declaring that there is a "war against boys" (Sommers, 2000) or that "schools shortchange girls" (American Association of University Women. 1992). Psychologists who are contemplating research into this emotionally charged topic will learn an applied lesson about the pervasiveness of the bias to prefer research findings that confirm hypotheses consistent with one's own worldview (commonly known as confirmation bias), as well as about the social psychology of research. There are many psychologists who believe that research into the many questions about sex differences should not be conducted because the results will be damaging to women. But it is only through careful research that psychologists can separate false stereotypes from those that have a basis in fact (i.e., are supported by statistical data). Of course, no research is ever free from bias, but research, even though it is imperfect, is the best method we have for understanding emotionally charged social issues. All research takes place in a sociohistorical framework that determines the questions asked, the research methods used, and, most important, how results are interpreted. If we required that research be free from bias, psychologists could never study important social issues.

What Is the Meaning of Differences?

A finding that two or more groups differ with respect to some variable does not mean that one of the groups is inferior, especially as is the case here, with differences found across many different types of measures, sometimes favoring males and other times favoring females. Perhaps even more important, differences are not immutable. It would be difficult to argue that our understanding of scientific issues would be better if research was censored or that the world would be better if all groups were the same. Girls and boys, and women and men, are both similar and different—it is a false dichotomy to ask if they are similar or different. The theoretically interesting questions concern the ways in which they are similar and different and the contexts and reasons for the findings.

Why Are We So Afraid of Differences?

The potential for misuse of research on differences is a legitimate concern, but there is greater potential harm for claims made in the absence of data. There is also concern that research on differences obscures and minimizes the many ways males and females are similar, so that people come to exaggerate differences and think of females and males as so dissimilar that it is as though they come from alien planets. But research has shown that most people understand the fact that the ranges of abilities (within-group variability) for males and females overlap, and, in fact, most people underestimate the size of female-male differences (Swim, 1994).

Jensen (1998) reviewed several cognitive-achievement tests that, unlike traditional tests of intelligence, were not written to yield equal scores for females and males. He concluded that there are no overall sex differences in intelligence, but he did find sex differences on several of the individual tests. It is important to note that there are many cognitive tests and academic indicators that show no difference in the academic achievement and cognitive ability of males and females, but there are also measures that show large and consistent differences favoring females, and still others that show large and consistent differences favoring males. The size and direction of the sex difference depends on what and how you measure. The emerging picture is complex, but there are consistencies across time and place that suggest that the sex differences in cognitive abilities and academic achievement are systematic and not due to random variance.

A COGNITIVE-PROCESS APPROACH

A useful taxonomy for understanding cognitive sex differences is based on similarities and differences in underlying cognitive processes and offers a more fine-grained analysis than a simple comparison that sums across all tests—an analysis that considers how information is retrieved from memory, the nature of the representation of meaning in memory, and what females and males, on average, do when they work on different types of cognitive tasks. Older rubrics for understanding differences between females and males grouped cognitive tasks as though they were topics in a typical school curriculum (e.g., verbal, quantitative, and visuospatial). By contrast, a cognitive-process taxonomy relies on the understanding that information is acquired, stored, selected, retrieved, and used, and that each of these component processes has its own probability of being successfully completed and can vary in processing speed. For example, working memory (the portion of memory that is actively involved in the immediate task being performed, e.g., in performing arithmetic or processing language while you are listening to someone or figuring out a route from a map) is separated into multiple component processing subsystems—phonological, visuospatial, and meaning subsystems— and information stored in memory has different representational codes—visuospatial and verbal. The following differences between females and males, most of which have been documented early in childhood and across all industrialized societies, can be understood using a cognitive-process approach. Cognitive processes are categorized in the taxonomy as favoring women or men on the basis of the results of the preponderance of empirical studies (Halpern, 2000).

Compared with men, women have more rapid access to phonological, semantic, and episodic information in long-term memory, and obtain higher scores on tests of verbal learning and the production and comprehension of complex prose. A writing test was added to the standardized tests for college admissions because writing is an essential academic skill needed for every discipline, and the female advantage on writing tests increased the number of females who receive scholarships. Psychologists who have argued that the female advantage in fluent retrieval (writing and speaking) is small have overlooked those abilities for which females show the largest advantages—writing, retrieval from long-term memory, and speech articulation. Girls have the advantage on quantitative tasks in early elementary school, when math involves learning math facts and arithmetic calculations, showing rapid memory retrieval similar to that needed in language production and comprehension, and in later grades they perform better than males on algebra problems when the cognitive components of the solution strategy are similar to those of language processing (Gallagher, Levin, & Cahalan, 2002). By contrast, males have the advantage on tests of verbal analogies, which may seem to be verbal but at a cognitive-process level involve mapping relationships in working memory.

Males have large advantages on tasks that require transformations in visuospatial working memory; sex differences are found by age 4—probably the youngest age at which this ability can be measured reliably. The difference between males and females on mental rotation tests is very large (close to 1 standard deviation), so large that many statisticians maintain that tests of statistical significance are not needed. Males also excel at tasks that require velocity judgments about moving objects, tracking movement through three-dimensional space, and aiming at a moving or stationary target, and they show a large advantage in their knowledge of politics and geography (Willingham & Cole, 1997). The global consistency in female-male cognitive patterns is shown in Figure 1, which compares male and female achievement in reading literacy, science, and mathematics in 33 countries.

The Advantages of a Cognitive-Process Taxonomy

A troubling problem for psychologists who want to understand cognitive sex differences is the fact that females achieve better grades in school and on tests in all subject areas when the material closely resembles what has been taught in school, but boys achieve higher grades on standardized tests if the test questions are not tied to any specific curriculum or in-class learning experience. These results can be partly explained by the fact that more women than men take advanced standardized tests like the Graduate Record Examination (GRE), so their overall mean on these tests would be expected to be lower than the mean for men (because the larger number of women test takers suggests that overall the group of women who take the tests is less select than the group of men who take them). However, this reasoning does not apply for tests taken by approximately equal numbers of females and males, for which similar results are found.

Kimball (1989) hypothesized that girls' learning is more rote than boys' learning, so girls' learning is assessed best with familiar problems, but this theory ignores the fact that writing is a highly creative act involving novel topics, and girls perform particularly well on writing tests. Other theories designed to explain why boys and girls have different (average) patterns of achievement depending on the type of test also overlook the fact that the differences are not easy to categorize. Other explanations have focused on learning preferences or styles. But girls' preference for cooperative learning activities and boys' preference for more competitive ones cannot explain the finding that girls and boys learn in a variety of classrooms and that differences are found as a function of the type of test that is used to assess learning and not as a function of the learning activities. The notion that girls perform particularly well in school because their temperament is better suited to sitting for long periods of time has achieved considerable popularity, but it is hard to see how the inability to sustain attention at a sedentary task would apply to students in advanced studies.

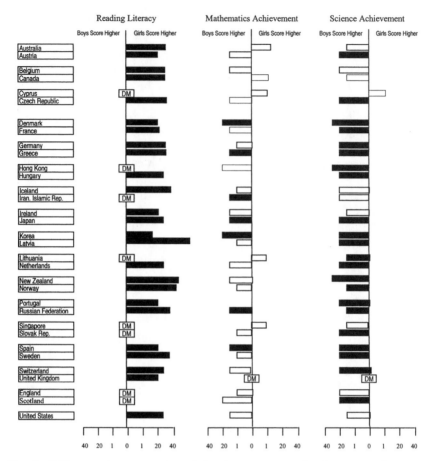

Fig. 1. Differences between male and female scores in reading literacy, mathematics achievement, and science achievement in 33 countries. The reading-literacy data are from 15-year-olds who participated in the Program for International Student Assessment (PISA; National Center for Education Statistics, 2002). The mathematics- and science-achievement data are from eighth graders who participated in The International Mathematics and Science Study (TIMSS; National Center for Education Statistics, 2000). Each bar represents the average score difference between boys and girls on combined tests. Black bars indicate statistically significant results. "DM" indicates missing data.

The cognitive-process taxonomy (Halpern, 2000) offers a solution to the puzzle of the mismatch between school grades and scores on standardized tests. In a recent study, Gallagher et al. (2002) examined cognitive patterns of sex differences in success at solving math problems on the GRE using the proposed cognitive-process taxonomy. They found the usual sex differences favoring males when there was an advantage to using a spatially based solution strategy (i.e., a strategy using a spatial representation), but not when solution strategies were more verbal or similar to the ones presented in popular math textbooks. Similarly, the usual male advantage was found with math problems that had multiple possible solution paths, but not problems that had multiple steps and therefore taxed working memory. Thus, the differences in the performance of males and females on GRE math problems lie in the recognition and selection of solution strategies and not in the load on working memory. Gallagher et al. found that average performance of different groups on standardized math tests can be minimized or maximized by altering the way problems are presented and the type of cognitive processes that are optimal for generating solutions.

The Psychobiosocial Model: Cause and Effect are Circular

Psychologists and virtually everyone else who studies cognitive sex differences want to know the proportion of variability in performance that can be explained by innate (nature) or learned (nurture) variables. This is the wrong question because it rests on the assumptions that there are "true" values that exist "out there" for clever experimenters to discover and that variables can be divided into the mutually exclusive categories of "nature," "nurture," and their interaction. Research has shown that nature and nurture alter each other in sequentially interacting ways. What people learn influences the structure of their neurons (e.g., their branching and size); brain architectures, in turn, support certain skills and abilities, which may lead people to select additional experiences. Differences in the interests of females and males both derive from differences in the areas in which they have achieved success and lead to further differential success in these areas because of differential knowledge and experience. Learning is both a biological and an environmental variable, and biology and environment are as inseparable as conjoined twins who share a common heart. A diagram of this psychobiosocial model is shown in Figure 2.

Humans face pervasive and inescapable life experiences that teach appropriate sex roles and often punish violators. The influences range from explicit messages like the one spoken by that international spokesdoll for femininity, Barbie, who told little girls that "math is tough," to the implicit effects of common stereotypes that can depress test performance among members of groups that are expected to score low on a test (Steele, 1997), to the inductive lessons learned by realizing, for example, that the overwhelming majority of secretaries are female and engineers are male. But there is also considerable evidence for sex-related biological influences. The prenatal hormones that shape a fetus's developing genitals also influence the development of the fetus's brain in a female or male direction. Research has shown that cognitive abilities vary systematically over the menstrual cycle for women and over the daily and annual testosterone cycles for men (Kimura, 1996). Female-to-male transsexuals show changes in their results on cognitive tests from typical female patterns to typical male patterns soon after beginning cross-hormone treatments to prepare them for life as a man (Van Goozen, Cohen-Kettenis, Gooren, Frijda, & Van De Poll, 1995). Estrogen has a cumulative effect over a lifetime such that women who had greater exposure to estrogen (early menarche and late menopause) have higher scores on selected batteries of (mostly verbal) cognitive tasks than women with shorter exposures to estrogen (Smith et al., 1999), and gay men frequently show cognitive patterns that are more similar to those of females than to those of heterosexual men (Gladue, Beatty, Larson, & Staton, 1990). These effects have been

111

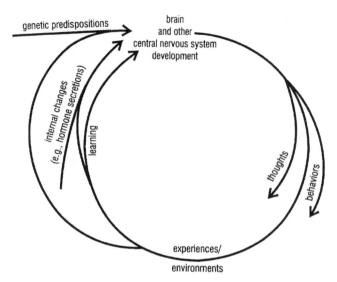

Fig. 2. A psychobiosocial model that can be used as a framework for understanding cognitive sex differences. It replaces the older idea that nature and nurture are separate influences and instead indicates that biological and psychosocial variables exert mutual influences on each other (graphically represented as a circle). From *Sex Differences in Cognitive Abilities,* 3rd ed. (p. 18), by D.F. Halpern, 2000, Mahwah, NJ: Erlbaum. Copyright 2000 by Lawrence Erlbaum Associates. Reprinted with permission.

confirmed using methodologically strong experimental designs with nonhuman mammals.

CAVEATS, CONCLUSIONS, AND CRITIQUES

There are still many unanswered questions about the cognitive abilities of females and males. Researchers do not know why girls and women excel on most long-term memory tests and why boys and men have the advantage on tasks with visuospatial components. The explanation that these differences are remnants from hunter-gatherer societies is appealing, but weak as an explanatory construct because any result can be explained post hoc, and the spatial skills used to solve math or physics problems are conceptually closer to those used for female-typical spatial tasks like weaving or fitting objects in small spaces than to those used to cross large distances. New work in testing shows that test scores can be manipulated by the way in which problems are posed and by whether there is an advantage to using verbal or visuospatial solution processes; these findings create new problems for researchers interested in test measurement (psychometricians), as well as for test developers.

What can we conclude from this complex picture? Given the seesaw nature of cognitive sex differences, there is no evidence that one sex is smarter than the other. Experimental results are based on group averages, and no one is average. Cognitive ability is a prerequisite for success in any field, but success depends on much more. Readers are urged to remember that everyone can improve in any cognitive area—that is the reason for education—and rapid changes in the proportion of men and women in some fields show that huge changes can occur across populations by changing educational opportunities and social expectations. People do not have to be the same to be equal.

Recommended Reading

Gallagher, A., Levin, J., & Cahalan, C. (2002). (See References)
Halpern, D.F. (2000). (See References)
Halpern, D.F., & Collaer, M.L. (in press). Sex differences in visuospatial abilities: More than meets the eye. In P. Shah & A. Miyake (Eds.), *Higher-level visuospatial thinking and cognition*. Cambridge, MA: Cambridge University Press.

Notes

1. Address correspondence to Diane F. Halpern, Berger Institute for Work, Family, and Children, Claremont McKenna College, 850 Columbia Ave., Claremont, CA 91711; e-mail: diane.halpern@claremontmckenna.edu.

2. Some authors prefer to use the term "gender" when referring to female-male differences that are social in origin and "sex" when referring to differences that are biological in origin. In keeping with the psychobiosocial model that I am advocating and with the belief that these two types of influences are interdependent and cannot be separated, I use only one term here. The two terms are often used inconsistently in the literature.

References

American Association of University Women. (1992). *How schools shortchange girls: The AAUW report*. New York: Marlowe.

Gallagher, A., Levin, J., & Cahalan, C. (2002). *GRE research: Cognitive patterns of gender differences on mathematics admissions tests* (ETS Report No. 02-19). Princeton, NJ: Educational Testing Service.

Gladue, B.A., Beatty, W.W., Larson, J., & Staton, R.D. (1990). Sexual orientations and spatial ability in men and women. *Psychobiology, 18*, 101–108.

Halpern, D.F. (2000). *Sex differences in cognitive abilities* (3rd ed.). Mahwah, NJ: Erlbaum.

Jensen, A.R. (1998). *The g factor: The science of mental ability*. New York: Praeger.

Kimball, M.M. (1989). A new perspective on women's math achievement. *Psychological Bulletin, 105*, 198–214.

Kimura, D. (1996). Sex, sexual orientation, and sex hormones influence human cognitive function. *Current Opinion in Neurobiology, 6*, 259–263.

National Center for Education Statistics. (2000). *Pursuing excellence: Comparisons of international eighth-grade mathematics and science achievement from a U.S. perspective, 1995 and 1999* (NCES 2001-028). Washington, DC: U.S. Government Printing Office.

National Center for Education Statistics. (2002). *Outcomes of learning: Results from the 2000 Program for International Student Assessment of 15-year-olds in reading, mathematics, and science literacy* (NCES 2002-115). Washington, DC: U.S. Government Printing Office.

Smith, C.A., McCleary, C.A., Murdock, G.A., Wilshire, T.W., Buckwalter, D.K., Bretsky, P., Marmol, L., Gorsuch, R.L., & Buckwalter, J.G. (1999). Lifelong estrogen exposure and cognitive performance in elderly women. *Brain & Cognition, 39*, 203–218.

Sommers, C. (2000). *The war against boys: How misguided feminism is harming our young men*. New York: Simon & Schuster.

Steele, C.M. (1997). A threat in the air: How stereotypes shape intellectual identity and performance. *American Psychologist, 52*, 613–629.

Swim, J.K. (1994). Perceived versus meta-analytic effect sizes: An assessment of the accuracy of gender stereotypes. *Journal of Personality and Social Psychology, 66*, 21–36.

Van Goozen, S.H.M., Cohen-Kettenis, P.T., Gooren, L.J.G., Frijda, N.H., & Van De Poll, N.E. (1995). Gender differences in behaviour: Activating effects of cross-sex hormones. *Psychoneuroendocrinology, 20,* 171–177.

Willingham, W.W., & Cole, N.S. (1997). *Gender and fair assessment.* Hillsdale, NJ: Erlbaum.

Section 3: Critical Thinking Questions

1. Is there overlap in the domains in which the genders show different cognitive abilities (Ramsey-Rennels & Langlois; Herlitz & Rehnman) and the areas in which they show cognitive deficits (Sherwin)?

2. Apply the psychobiosocial model for gender differences in cognitive abilities (Halpern) to children's development of gender-related stereotypes (Martin & Ruble).

3. Thinking ahead ten years or so, do you expect gendered stereotypes to become less rigid (Martin & Ruble)? Do you expect the achievement gap between the genders to lessen (Halpern)? Why or why not?

This article has been reprinted as it originally appeared in *Current Directions in Psychological Science.* Citation information for this article as originally published appears above.

Section 4: Evolution and Human Sexuality

Over the past century, prevailing wisdom has shifted several times concerning the extent of similarity and difference in men's and women's sexuality. Peplau attends to four aspects of sexuality that have differed for men and women regardless of whether they are heterosexual or homosexual. She marshals scientific evidence in support of greater sexual desire among men, more emphasis on committed relationships by women, aggression more strongly linked to sexuality for men, and more malleability in women's sexual attitudes and behaviors. However, Peplau also identifies limits in this body of research and urges a reconceptualization of assumptions about gender and sexuality.

Men and women make inferences about what is going on in the minds of the other sex. In this article, Buss presents two theories to support different evolutionary pressures on men and women in the domains of mating and sexuality. He argues that gender differences in mating strategies lead to specific forms of sexual conflict and predictable errors in social inference. Error management theory can be used to identify cognitive biases that vary by gender, and that are, Buss claims, adaptive errors. Strategic management theory is invoked to understand the emotion component to the sexual conflict that arises between men and women. Presented, too, is the potential evolutionary adaptiveness of negative emotions such as jealousy.

In what can be seen as the counterpoint piece to the Buss article, Miller, Putcha-Bhagavatula, & Pedersen debunk the claim that men and women have evolved gender-distinct sexual strategies for short-term and long-term mating. They review research on primate and human mating, parental investment, and jealousy, and do not find much support for male and female asymmetries. They also invoke sociocultural explanations rather than gender per se to account for mate preferences. By presenting additional data and new analyses of college students' mating preferences, Miller and colleagues offer a challenge to Buss' sexual strategies theory.

Romantic love and sexual desire . . . do they go hand in hand? Diamond distinguishes the two, making a case for different underpinnings for affectional bonding compared to the desire for sexual activities. Evolutionary arguments are given, and both animal and human research are reviewed. The interplay of love and desire are discussed for gay and straight men and women. Diamond explains some apparent incongruities between established patterns of desire and affection and the formation of sexual and non-sexual bonds, invoking social, cultural factors, and evolutionary factors.

Research on mating pressures typically focuses on competition to be the sexual partner. New thinking about sexual selection extends to competition among males post-copulation. Shackelford and Goetz argue that sperm competition for fertilization has led to evolved adaptations to aid sperm in outcompeting rivals' sperm. Competition among sperm arises when females have sperm from two or more males into their reproductive tract at the same time. Working from an evolutionary perspective, the authors discuss the interplay among female infidelity, rape, sperm competition, male anatomy, and paternal investment.

Human Sexuality: How Do Men and Women Differ?

Letitia Anne Peplau[1]

*Psychology Department, University of California,
Los Angeles, Los Angeles, California*

Abstract

A large body of scientific research documents four important gender differences in sexuality. First, on a wide variety of measures, men show greater sexual desire than do women. Second, compared with men, women place greater emphasis on committed relationships as a context for sexuality. Third, aggression is more strongly linked to sexuality for men than for women. Fourth, women's sexuality tends to be more malleable and capable of change over time. These male-female differences are pervasive, affecting thoughts and feelings as well as behavior, and they characterize not only heterosexuals but lesbians and gay men as well. Implications of these patterns are considered.

Keywords

human sexuality; sexual desire; sexual orientation; sexual plasticity

A century ago, sex experts confidently asserted that men and women have strikingly different sexual natures. The rise of scientific psychology brought skepticism about this popular but unproven view, and the pendulum swung toward an emphasis on similarities between men's and women's sexuality. For example, Masters and Johnson (1966) captured attention by proposing a human sexual response cycle applicable to both sexes. Feminist scholars cautioned against exaggerating male-female differences and argued for women's sexual equality with men. Recently, psychologists have taken stock of the available scientific evidence. Reviews of empirical research on diverse aspects of human sexuality have identified four important male-female differences. These gender differences are pervasive, affecting thoughts and feelings as well as behavior, and they characterize not only heterosexuals but lesbians and gay men as well.

SEXUAL DESIRE

Sexual desire is the subjective experience of being interested in sexual objects or activities or wishing to engage in sexual activities (Regan & Berscheid, 1999). Many lines of research demonstrate that men show more interest in sex than women (see review by Baumeister, Catanese, & Vohs, 2001). Compared with women, men think about sex more often. They report more frequent sex fantasies and more frequent feelings of sexual desire. Across the life span, men rate the strength of their own sex drive higher than do their female age-mates. Men are more interested in visual sexual stimuli and more likely to spend money on such sexual products and activities as X-rated videos and visits to prostitutes.

Men and women also differ in their preferred frequency of sex. When heterosexual dating and marriage partners disagree about sexual frequency, it is usually the man who wants to have sex more often than the woman does. In heterosexual couples, actual sexual frequency may reflect a compromise between the desires of the male and female partners. In gay and lesbian relationships, sexual frequency is decided by partners of the same gender, and lesbians report having sex less often than gay men or heterosexuals. Further, women appear to be more willing than men to forgo sex or adhere to religious vows of celibacy.

Masturbation provides a good index of sexual desire because it is not constrained by the availability of a partner. Men are more likely than women to masturbate, start masturbating at an earlier age, and do so more often. In a review of 177 studies, Oliver and Hyde (1993) found large male-female differences in the incidence of masturbation. In technical terms, the meta-analytic effect size[2] (d) for masturbation was 0.96, which is smaller than the physical sex difference in height (2.00) but larger than most psychological sex differences, such as the performance difference on standardized math tests (0.20). These and many other empirical findings provide evidence for men's greater sexual interest.

SEXUALITY AND RELATIONSHIPS

A second consistent difference is that women tend to emphasize committed relationships as a context for sexuality more than men do. When Regan and Berscheid (1999) asked young adults to define sexual desire, men were more likely than women to emphasize physical pleasure and sexual intercourse. In contrast, women were more likely to "romanticize" the experience of sexual desire, as seen in one young woman's definition of sexual desire as "longing to be emotionally intimate and to express love for another person" (p. 75). Compared with women, men have more permissive attitudes toward casual premarital sex and toward extramarital sex. The size of these gender differences is relatively large, particularly for casual premarital sex ($d = 0.81$; Oliver & Hyde, 1993). Similarly, women's sexual fantasies are more likely than men's to involve a familiar partner and to include affection and commitment. In contrast, men's fantasies are more likely to involve strangers, anonymous partners, or multiple partners and to focus on specific sex acts or sexual organs.

A gender difference in emphasizing relational aspects of sexuality is also found among lesbians and gay men (see review by Peplau, Fingerhut, & Beals, in press). Like heterosexual women, lesbians tend to have less permissive attitudes toward casual sex and sex outside a primary relationship than do gay or heterosexual men. Also like heterosexual women, lesbians have sex fantasies that are more likely to be personal and romantic than the fantasies of gay or heterosexual men. Lesbians are more likely than gay men to become sexually involved with partners who were first their friends, then lovers. Gay men in committed relationships are more likely than lesbians or heterosexuals to have sex with partners outside their primary relationship.

In summary, women's sexuality tends to be strongly linked to a close relationship. For women, an important goal of sex is intimacy; the best context for pleasurable sex is a committed relationship. This is less true for men.

SEXUALITY AND AGGRESSION

A third gendered pattern concerns the association between sexuality and aggression. This link has been demonstrated in many domains, including individuals' sexual self-concepts, the initiation of sex in heterosexual relationships, and coercive sex.

Andersen, Cyranowski, and Espindle (1999) investigated the dimensions that individuals use to characterize their own sexuality. Both sexes evaluated themselves along a dimension of being romantic, with some individuals seeing themselves as very passionate and others seeing themselves as not very passionate. However, men's sexual self-concepts were also characterized by a dimension of aggression, which concerned the extent to which they saw themselves as being aggressive, powerful, experienced, domineering, and individualistic. There was no equivalent aggression dimension for women's sexual self-concepts.

In heterosexual relationships, men are commonly more assertive than women and take the lead in sexual interactions (see review by Impett & Peplau, 2003). During the early stages of a dating relationship, men typically initiate touching and sexual intimacy. In ongoing relationships, men report initiating sex about twice as often as their female partners or age-mates. To be sure, many women do initiate sex, but they do so less frequently than their male partners. The same pattern is found in people's sexual fantasies. Men are more likely than women to imagine themselves doing something sexual to a partner or taking the active role in a sexual encounter.

Rape stands at the extreme end of the link between sex and aggression. Although women use many strategies to persuade men to have sex, physical force and violence are seldom part of their repertoire. Physically coercive sex is primarily a male activity (see review by Felson, 2002). There is growing recognition that stranger and acquaintance rape are not the whole story; some men use physical force in intimate heterosexual relationships. Many women who are battered by a boyfriend or husband also report sexual assaults as part of the abuse.

In summary, aggression is more closely linked to sexuality for men than for women. Currently, we know little about aggression and sexuality among lesbians and gay men; research on this topic would provide a valuable contribution to our understanding of gender and human sexuality.

SEXUAL PLASTICITY

Scholars from many disciplines have noted that, in comparison with men's sexuality, women's sexuality tends to have greater plasticity. That is, women's sexual beliefs and behaviors can be more easily shaped and altered by cultural, social, and situational factors. Baumeister (2000) systematically reviewed the scientific evidence on this point. In this section, I mention a few of the many supportive empirical findings.

One sign of plasticity concerns changes in aspects of a person's sexuality over time. Such changes are more common among women than among men. For example, the frequency of women's sexual activity is more variable than men's. If a woman is in an intimate relationship, she might have frequent sex with her partner. But following a breakup, she might have no sex at all, including masturbation, for several months. Men show less temporal variability: Following a romantic breakup, men may substitute masturbation for interpersonal sex and so maintain a more constant frequency of sex. There is also growing evidence that women are more likely than men to change their sexual orientation over time. In an illustrative longitudinal study (Diamond, 2003), more than 25% of 18- to 25-year-old women who initially identified as lesbian or bisexual changed their sexual identity during the next 5 years. Changes such as these are less common for men.

A further indication of malleability is that a person's sexual attitudes and behaviors are responsive to social and situational influences. Such factors as education, religion, and acculturation are more strongly linked to women's sexuality than to men's. For example, moving to a new culture may have more impact on women's sexuality than on men's. The experience of higher education provides another illustration. A college education is associated with more liberal sexual attitudes and behavior, but this effect is greater for women than for men. Even more striking is the association between college education and sexual orientation shown in a recent national survey (Laumann, Gagnon, Michael, & Michaels, 1994). Completing college doubled the likelihood that a man identified as gay or bisexual (1.7% among high school graduates vs. 3.3% among college graduates). However, college was associated with a 900% increase in the percentage of women identifying as lesbian or bisexual (0.4% vs. 3.6%).

CONCLUSION AND IMPLICATIONS

Diverse lines of scientific research have identified consistent male-female differences in sexual interest, attitudes toward sex and relationships, the association between sex and aggression, and sexual plasticity. The size of these gender differences tends to be large, particularly in comparison to other male-female differences studied by psychologists. These differences are pervasive, encompassing thoughts, feelings, fantasies, and behavior. Finally, these male-female differences apply not only to heterosexuals but also to lesbians and gay men.

Several limitations of the current research are noteworthy. First, much research is based on White, middle-class American samples. Studies of other populations and cultural groups would be valuable in assessing the generalizability of findings. Second, although research findings on lesbians and gay men are consistent with patterns of male-female difference among heterosexuals, the available empirical database on homosexuals is relatively small. Third, differences between women and men are not absolute but rather a matter of degree. There are many exceptions to the general patterns described. For instance, some women show high levels of sexual interest, and some men seek sex only in committed relationships. Research documenting male-female differences has advanced further than research systematically tracing the origins of these differences. We are only beginning to understand the complex ways in which biology, experience, and culture interact to shape men's and women's sexuality.

These four general differences between women's and men's sexuality can illuminate specific patterns of sexual interaction. For example, in heterosexual couples, it is fairly common for a partner to engage in sex when he or she is not really interested or "in the mood." Although both men and women sometimes consent to such unwanted sexual activity, women are more often the compliant sexual partner (see review by Impett & Peplau, 2003). Each of the gender differences I have described may contribute to this pattern. First, the stage is set by a situation in which partners have differing desires for sex, and the man is more often the partner desiring sex. Second, for compliant sex to occur, the more interested partner must communicate his or her desire. Men typically take the lead in expressing sexual interest. Third, the disinterested partner's reaction is pivotal: Does this partner comply or, instead, ignore or reject the request? If women view sex as a way to show love and caring for a partner, they may be more likely than men to resolve a dilemma about unwanted sex by taking their partner's welfare into account. In abusive relationships, women may fear physical or psychological harm from a male partner if they refuse. Finally, sexual compliance illustrates the potential plasticity of female sexuality. In this case, women are influenced by relationship concerns to engage in a sexual activity that goes against their personal preference at the time.

The existence of basic differences between men's and women's sexuality has implications for the scientific study of sexuality. Specifically, an adequate understanding of human sexuality may require separate analyses of sexuality in women and in men, based on the unique biology and life experiences of each sex. Currently, efforts to reconceptualize sexual issues have focused on women's sexuality. Three examples are illustrative.

Rethinking Women's Sexual Desire

How should we interpret the finding that women appear less interested in sex than men? One possibility is that researchers have inadvertently used male standards (e.g., penile penetration and orgasm) to evaluate women's sexual experiences and consequently ignored activities, such as intimate kissing, cuddling, and touching, that may be uniquely important to women's erotic lives. Researchers such as Wallen (1995) argue that it is necessary to distinguish between sexual desire (an intrinsic motivation to pursue sex) and arousability (the capacity to become sexually aroused in response to situational cues). Because women's sexual desire may vary across the menstrual cycle, it may be more appropriate to describe women's desire as periodic rather than weak or limited. In contrast, women's receptivity to sexual overtures and their capacity for sexual response may depend on situational rather than hormonal cues. Other researchers (e.g., Tolman & Diamond, 2001) argue that more attention must be paid to the impact of hormones that may have special relevance for women, such as the neuropeptide oxytocin, which is linked to both sexuality and affectional bonding.

Rethinking Women's Sexual Orientation

Some researchers have proposed new paradigms for understanding women's sexual orientation (e.g., Peplau & Garnets, 2000). Old models either assumed commonalities among homosexuals, regardless of gender, or hypothesized similarities between lesbians and heterosexual men, both of whom are attracted to women. In contrast, empirical research has documented many similarities in women's sexuality, regardless of their sexual orientation. A new model based on women's experiences might highlight the centrality of relationships to women's sexual orientation, the potential for at least some women to change their sexual orientation over time, and the importance of sociocultural factors in shaping women's sexual orientation.

Rethinking Women's Sexual Problems

Finally, research on women's sexuality has led some scientists to question current systems for classifying sexual dysfunction among women. The widely used *Diagnostic and Statistical Manual of Mental Disorders* (*DSM*) of the American Psychiatric Association categorizes sexual dysfunction on the basis of Masters and Johnson's (1966) model of presumed normal and universal sexual functioning. Critics (e.g., Kaschak & Tiefer, 2001) have challenged the validity of this model, its applicability to women, and its use as a basis for clinical assessment. They have also faulted the *DSM* for ignoring the relationship context of sexuality for women. Kaschak and Tiefer have proposed instead a new "woman-centered" view of women's sexual problems that gives prominence to partner and relationship factors that affect women's sexual experiences, and also to social, cultural, and economic factors that influence the quality of women's sexual lives.

Recommended Reading

Baumeister, R.F., & Tice, D.M. (2001). *The social dimension of sex*. Boston: Allyn and Bacon.
Kaschak, E., & Tiefer, L. (Eds.). (2001). (See References)
Peplau, L.A., & Garnets, L.D. (Eds.). (2000). (See References)
Regan, P.C., & Berscheid, E. (1999). (See References)

Notes

1. Address correspondence to Letitia Anne Peplau, Psychology Department, Franz 1285, University of California, Los Angeles, CA 90095-1563; e-mail: lapeplau@ucla.edu.
2. In a meta-analysis, the findings of multiple studies are analyzed quantitatively to arrive at an overall estimate of the size of a difference between two groups, in this case, between men and women. This effect size (known technically as d) is reported using a common unit of measurement. By convention in psychological research, 0.2 is considered a small effect size, 0.5 is a moderate effect size, and 0.8 is a large effect size.

References

Andersen, B.L., Cyranowski, J.M., & Espindle, D. (1999). Men's sexual self-schema. *Journal of Personality and Social Psychology, 76*, 645–661.
Baumeister, R.F. (2000). Gender differences in erotic plasticity. *Psychological Bulletin, 126*, 347–374.
Baumeister, R.F., Catanese, K.R., & Vohs, K.D. (2001). Is there a gender difference in strength of sex drive? *Personality and Social Psychology Review, 5*, 242–273.
Diamond, L.M. (2003). Was it a phase? Young women's relinquishment of lesbian/bisexual identities over a 5-year period. *Journal of Personality and Social Psychology, 84*, 352–364.
Felson, R.B. (2002). *Violence and gender reexamined*. Washington, DC: American Psychological Association.

Impett, E., & Peplau, L.A. (2003). Sexual compliance: Gender, motivational, and relationship perspectives. *Journal of Sex Research, 40,* 87–100.

Kaschak, E., & Tiefer, L. (Eds.). (2001). *A new view of women's sexual problems.* New York: Haworth Press.

Laumann, E., Gagnon, J., Michael, R., & Michaels, S. (1994). *The social organization of sexuality.* Chicago: University of Chicago Press.

Masters, W.H., & Johnson, V.E. (1966). *Human sexual response.* Boston: Little, Brown, & Co.

Oliver, M.B., & Hyde, J.S. (1993). Gender differences in sexuality: A meta-analysis. *Psychological Bulletin, 114,* 29–51.

Peplau, L.A., Fingerhut, A., & Beals, K. (in press). Sexuality in the relationships of lesbians and gay men. In J. Harvey, A. Wenzel, & S. Sprecher (Eds.), *Handbook of sexuality in close relationships.* Mahwah, NJ: Erlbaum.

Peplau, L.A., & Garnets, L.D. (Eds.). (2000). Women's sexualities: New perspectives on sexual orientation and gender [Special issue]. *Journal of Social Issues, 56*(2).

Regan, P.C., & Berscheid, E. (1999). *Lust: What we know about human sexual desire.* Thousand Oaks, CA: Sage.

Tolman, D.L., & Diamond, L.M. (2001). Desegregating sexuality research: Cultural and biological perspectives on gender and desire. *Annual Review of Sex Research, 12,* 33–74.

Wallen, K. (1995). The evolution of female sexual desire. In P. Abramson & S.D. Pinkerton (Eds.), *Sexual nature/sexual culture* (pp. 57–79). Chicago: University of Chicago Press.

This article has been reprinted as it originally appeared in *Current Directions in Psychological Science*. Citation information for this article as originally published appears above.

Cognitive Biases and Emotional Wisdom in the Evolution of Conflict Between the Sexes

David M. Buss[1]

Department of Psychology, University of Texas, Austin, Texas

Abstract

Two recent theories within evolutionary psychology have produced novel insights into conflict between the sexes. According to *error management theory* (EMT), asymmetries over evolutionary time in the cost-benefit consequences of specific social inferences have produced predictable cognitive biases. Women, for example, appear to underinfer commitment in response to signals of resource display. Men often overinfer a woman's sexual desire when she merely smiles at or casually touches them. These inferential biases, according to EMT, represent functional adaptations rather than markers of irrationality in information processing. According to *strategic interference theory*, certain "negative emotions" function to motivate action to reduce conflict produced by impediments to preferred social strategies. Emotions such as jealousy and anger, rather than reducing rationality, may embody inherited ancestral wisdom functional in dealing with interference inflicted by other individuals. These evolution-based theories have produced novel empirical discoveries and challenge traditional theories anchored in the premise that cognitive biases and negative emotions necessarily lead to irrationality.

Keywords

conflict; cognitive bias; negative emotions; sex differences; sexuality; evolutionary psychology

In mating and sexuality more than in any other domain, women and men have confronted different adaptive challenges over the long course of human evolutionary history. Women have been required to make a 9-month investment to produce a child. Men have not. Because fertilization occurs within women, men have faced the problem of uncertainty that they are the genetic parents. Women have not. It would be astonishing if men and women had not evolved somewhat different mating strategies to grapple with their differing adaptive challenges (Buss & Schmitt, 1993). Predictions generated by evolutionary models about sex differences in mate preferences, sexual desires, and elicitors of romantic jealousy, for example, have all been robustly documented across a variety of cultures (Buss, 1999). What has been less well appreciated is how sex differences in mating strategies produce specific forms of sexual conflict when they are expressed in behavior (see Buss & Malamuth, 1996).

Recent evolutionary work has inspired subtle hypotheses about the ways in which women and men clash, ranging from the erroneous inferences they make about the other sex to the emotions they experience when preferred mating strategies are thwarted. This article highlights two of these evolutionarily inspired research programs, one dealing with cognitive biases and one dealing with emotions as tracking devices.

ERROR MANAGEMENT THEORY: ADAPTIVE COGNITIVE ERRORS AND CONFLICT BETWEEN THE SEXES

Humans live in an uncertain social world. We must make inferences about others' intentions and emotional states. How attracted is he to her? How committed is she to him? Was that bump in the hallway an accident, or does it reveal hostile intentions? Some deeds, such as sexual infidelity and murder, are intentionally concealed, rendering uncertainty greater and inferences more tortuous. We are forced to make inferences about intentions and concealed deeds using a chaos of cues that are only probabilistically related to the deeds' occurrence. An unexplained scent on one's romantic partner, for example, could signal an extramarital affair or innocuous olfactory acquisition from a casual conversation.

Just as there are two types of correct inferences (true positives, true negatives), there are two types of inferential errors. One can falsely infer an intention or deed that is not there. Or one can fail to infer an intention or deed that is there. A spouse might falsely suspect a partner of sexual treachery, for example, or fail to infer an extant infidelity. Both errors cannot simultaneously be minimized. Setting a low threshold for inferring infidelity, for example, minimizes missed detections, but simultaneously increases false accusations. Setting a higher threshold for inferring infidelity minimizes false accusations, but simultaneously increases missed detections.

According to *error management theory* (EMT; Haselton & Buss, 2000), it would be exceedingly unlikely that the cost-benefit consequences of the two types of errors would be identical across their many occurrences. We intuitively understand this in the context of smoke alarms, which are typically set sensitively. The costs of the occasional false alarm are trivial compared with the catastrophic costs of failing to detect a real house fire. EMT extends this logic to cost-benefit consequences in evolutionary fitness.

According to one EMT hypothesis, the recurrent fitness costs of failing to detect spousal infidelities typically would have been greater than the costs of occasional false suspicions (Buss, 2000a). An unknowingly cuckolded man, for example, would have risked investing in a rival's children in the mistaken belief that they were his. An unknowingly betrayed woman would have risked the diversion of her partner's resources and commitments to another woman and her children, producing cascading costs for her own children.

Cognitive Biases

According to EMT, asymmetries in the cost-benefit consequences of social inferences, if they recur over evolutionary time, create selection pressures that produce predictable *cognitive biases*. Just as smoke alarms are biased to produce more false positives than false negatives, EMT predicts that evolved information processing procedures will be biased to produce more of one type of inferential error than another. The direction and degree of bias, of course, greatly depend on such factors as context and gender. Inferences about the sexual intentions of a potential romantic partner, for example, carry a different cost-benefit calculus than inferences about the level of commitment in a current romantic partner. The cost-benefit consequences of particular types of inferential errors differed for men and women, according to EMT, producing different inferential biases in men and women. No prior psychological theory of cognitive biases predicts these sex differences. Nor do prior theories hypothesize different sex-linked inferential biases depending on domain.

Sexual Overperception and Commitment Skepticism

Empirical research has confirmed several hypotheses derived from specific applications of EMT (Haselton & Buss, 2000). It has been used to explain the sex-linked *sexual overperception bias,* whereby men are hypothesized to possess mind-reading biases designed to minimize the costs of missed sexual opportunities. EMT provides a cogent explanation, for example, of why men appear to falsely infer that a woman is sexually interested merely when she smiles or touches a man's arm. Furthermore, this EMT-based hypothesis predicts specific contexts in which the bias will disappear, such as when the target woman is genetically related to the man in question or low in reproductive value.

Another application of EMT has predicted an opposite sort of cognitive bias in women, the *commitment-skepticism bias.* According to this hypothesis, women have evolved an inferential bias designed to underestimate men's actual level of commitment early in courtship in order to minimize the costs of being sexually deceived by men who feign commitment (Haselton & Buss, 2000). If men give flowers or gifts to women, for example, third-party observers infer that the men are signaling greater commitment than do the women who are the recipients of these displays, who show greater skepticism about the depth of the men's feelings.

EMT also predicts cognitive biases linked with sexual jealousy that lead to false inferences of a partner's sexual infidelity (Buss, 2000a). Men and women, in very predictable contexts, sometimes have false beliefs that a partner is unfaithful when he or she has in fact remained loyal. This bias appears to get especially activated in social contexts that historically have tended to be linked with infidelity, even if the target person has never been betrayed. A partner's sexual dissatisfaction, a sudden decline in sexual desire, and an increasing gap in desirability between the two partners, for example, all trigger suspicions of infidelity. Modern humans appear to have inherited ancestral tracking devices that signal circumstances indicating a statistical likelihood of infidelity, even if these procedures produce false positive errors (Buss, 2000a).

EMT offers a fresh perspective on cognitive biases by suggesting that certain types of inferential errors represent adaptive errors rather than design flaws in the psychological machinery (Haselton & Buss, 2000). It has provided new insights into why men and women get into certain types of conflict—for example, men's sexual overperception bias can lead to unwanted sexual overtures. Although extant empirical tests of EMT have borne fruit, only future work can determine whether this theory will provide a more general theory of cognitive biases. Nonetheless, EMT has been a source of inspiration for novel hypotheses about cognitive biases (e.g., commitment-skepticism bias), raised suspicions of some traditional explanations (e.g., that errors necessarily represent design flaws in human cognition), and suggested novel predictions about when biases occur (e.g., contexts in which false accusations of infidelity will occur).

STRATEGIC INTERFERENCE THEORY: "NEGATIVE" EMOTIONS AND CONFLICT BETWEEN THE SEXES

Conflict between the sexes is not produced solely from passionless cognitive biases. *Strategic interference theory* posits that emotions are psychological mechanisms that evolved in part to grapple with particular forms of conflict (Buss, 1989, 2000a). In the scientific history of emotions research, many theorists have contrasted "emotionality" with "rationality" (see Frank, 1988). According to this view, rationality is what causes humans to make sensible decisions. When faced with a problem, we use reason and logic to reach rational solutions. Emotions, according to this view, only get in the way—anger addles the brain; fear distorts reason; jealousy clouds the mind. Emotions are presumed by some theorists to be unfortunate relics from an ancient time in which human ancestors acted more from instinct than from logic. Psychologists have labeled anger, fear, and jealousy the "negative" emotions, presumably because they need to be controlled, reigned in, and subdued so that they do not impede rational action.

Negative Emotions as Functional

According to strategic interference theory, these emotions are adaptively designed to solve problems of strategic interference (Buss, 1989). Strategic interference occurs whenever something or someone impedes or blocks a preferred strategy or set of goal-directed actions. It is hypothesized that the negative emotions have been (and perhaps continue to be) beneficial, serving several related functions. First, they focus attention on the source of strategic interference, temporarily screening out other information less relevant to the adaptive problem. Second, they prompt storage of the relevant information in memory so that it is available for subsequent retrieval under appropriate circumstances. Third, they motivate action designed to eliminate or reduce strategic interference. And fourth, they motivate action designed to avoid future episodes of strategic interference.

Because men and women have evolved somewhat different sexual strategies, the events that cause strategic interference are predicted to differ for the sexes. Therefore, the events that trigger emotions such as anger, jealousy, and subjective distress should differ for the sexes. This theory has heuristic value in guiding researchers to phenomena not predicted by other theories. No other theory of emotions, for example, predicts fundamental sex differences in the events that elicit these emotions.

Strategic interference theory has been tested empirically in several domains. In the domain of sexual strategies, research has shown that the patterns of men's and women's anger correspond precisely to their respective sources of strategic interference (Buss, 1999). Women, far more than men, become angry and upset by individuals who seek sex with them sooner, more frequently, and more persistently than they want. Men, far more than women, become angry and upset by individuals who delay sex or thwart their sexual advances.

Jealousy and Sexual Rivalry

More subtle tests of strategic interference theory have taken place in the domains of jealousy and same-sex rivalry. One series of studies conducted in Korea, Japan, and the United States discovered large and cross-culturally consistent sex differences in whether sexual or emotional betrayal by a partner was more distressing (Buss et al., 1999). These sex-linked emotional reactions were precisely predicted from the premise that sexual infidelity by a man's partner interferes with his strategy of monopolizing her reproductive capacities, producing paternity uncertainty. Emotional infidelity by a woman's partner interferes with her strategy of monopolizing a man's commitments and resources, which could get diverted to a rival woman and her children as a consequence of a man's emotional involvement.

Another domain in which strategic interference theory has been tested pertains to the specific qualities of mating rivals that evoke distress. Because women and men have evolved somewhat different mate preferences, the qualities of intrasexual rivals that will be alluring to one's partner should differ for the sexes (Buss & Schmitt, 1993). Interested rivals inflict strategic interference when they possess these desirable qualities. Partners inflict strategic interference when they are attracted to desirable rivals.

Parallel studies conducted in the Netherlands, the United States, and Korea documented these sex differences (Buss, Shackelford, Choe, Buunk, & Dijkstra, 2000). Dutch, American, and Korean men, more than their female counterparts, reported particular emotional distress when a rival surpassed them on financial prospects, job prospects, and physical strength. Dutch, American, and Korean women, in contrast, reported greater distress when a rival surpassed them on facial attractiveness and body attractiveness. Although the cultures differed in some respects, and the sexes were similarly distressed by rivals who exceeded them on qualities such as kindness and sense of humor, the study demonstrated sex differences in emotional distress precisely for those rival characteristics predicted by strategic interference theory.

The so-called negative emotions, in short, may represent ancestral wisdom, inherited from a long line of successful ancestors who acted to minimize strategic interference. Emotions, far from distorting reason, may alert us to particular ways in which others may be impeding our preferred strategies. Emotions motivate efforts to reduce impedance. Strategic interference theory has inspired several novel hypotheses, raised suspicion of the common view that negative emotions interfere with reason, and led to the discovery of important sex differences in emotional experience that prior approaches had not uncovered.

CONCLUSIONS

Conflict between the sexes and conflict surrounding sex are ubiquitous phenomena in group-living species. The proposal that humans have evolved psychological mechanisms to deal with cross-sex interactions does not imply that what was ancestrally adaptive is necessarily currently functional in modern environments. Nor does it provide a panacea for reducing conflict between the sexes. In fact, it highlights some important obstacles to personal happiness and social harmony— emotions designed to produce subjective distress, inferential biases designed to produce errors, and mechanisms that benefit one person at the expense of others (Buss, 2000b).

Cautious skepticism is appropriate when evaluating new psychological approaches, and many critical issues remain unresolved. Will EMT lead to the discovery of additional cognitive biases beyond those discussed here, such as functional overestimates of other people's homicidal intentions (Buss & Duntley, 2001)? Will EMT prove capable of explaining well-documented cognitive biases, such as the tendency for people to overestimate their likelihood of success at certain tasks? Will EMT furnish a more powerful explanation than traditional treatments of cognitive biases, which typically invoke limited cognitive capacity, simplifying heuristics, and information processing shortcuts?

Similar unresolved issues remain for strategic interference theory. Will it continue to lead to the discovery of new phenomena that must be explained by any comprehensive theory of emotions, such as the connection between specific forms of cross-sex deception and sex-linked anger (Haselton & Buss, 2001) and the difficulty men and women often have in being "just friends" (Bleske & Buss, 2000)? How will strategic interference theory be integrated into a more comprehensive theory that includes both positively and negatively valenced emotions?

Psychology during the past few decades has delighted in demonstrating that humans are irrational information processors—cognitive heuristics produce bias, emotions cloud reason. But what is properly regarded as rational or irrational must be evaluated by the criterion of what problems particular mechanisms are designed to solve. Smoke alarms are biased—they produce many false positives. But they are not "irrational." Humans are designed to solve social adaptive problems. These include grappling with strategic interference. They also include making inferences about the differently constituted minds of the opposite sex. Within these and perhaps other domains, emotions may be rational and cognitive biases functional.

Recommended Reading

Barkow, J., Cosmides, L., & Tooby, J. (Eds.). (1992). *The adapted mind: Evolutionary psychology and the generation of culture*. New York: Oxford University Press.
Buss, D.M. (1999). (See References)
Buss, D.M. (2000a). (See References)
Geary, D. (1999). *Male, female: The evolution of human sex differences*. Washington, DC: American Psychological Association.
Mealy, L. (2000). *Sex differences: Developmental and evolutionary strategies*. New York: Academic Press.

Acknowledgments—I thank Martie Haselton and Art Markman for helpful comments.

Note

1. Address correspondence to David M. Buss, Department of Psychology, University of Texas, Austin, TX 78712; e-mail: dbuss@psy.utexas.edu.

References

Bleske, A., & Buss, D.M. (2000). Can men and women just be friends? *Personal Relationships, 7*, 131–151.
Buss, D.M. (1989). Conflict between the sexes: Strategic interference and the evocation of anger and upset. *Journal of Personality and Social Psychology, 56*, 735–747.

Buss, D.M. (1999). *Evolutionary psychology: The new science of the mind*. Boston: Allyn & Bacon.

Buss, D.M. (2000a). *The dangerous passion: Why jealousy is as necessary as love and sex*. New York: Free Press.

Buss, D.M. (2000b). The evolution of happiness. *American Psychologist, 55*, 15–23.

Buss, D.M., & Duntley, J.D. (2001). *Murder by design: The evolution of homicide*. Manuscript submitted for publication.

Buss, D.M., & Malamuth, N. (1996). *Sex, power, conflict: Evolutionary and feminist perspectives*. New York: Oxford University Press.

Buss, D.M., & Schmitt, D.P. (1993). Sexual Strategies Theory: An evolutionary perspective on human mating. *Psychological Review, 100*, 204–232.

Buss, D.M., Shackelford, T.K., Choe, J., Buunk, B.P., & Dijkstra, P. (2000). Distress about mating rivals. *Personal Relationships, 7*, 235–243.

Buss, D.M., Shackelford, T.K., Kirkpatrick, L.A., Choe, J.C., Lim, H.K., Hasegawa, M., Hasegawa, T., & Bennett, K. (1999). Jealousy and the nature of beliefs about infidelity: Tests of competing hypotheses about sex differences in the United States, Korea, and Japan. *Personal Relationships, 6*, 125–150.

Frank, R. (1988). *Passions within reason*. New York: Norton.

Haselton, M.G., & Buss, D.M. (2000). Error management theory: A new perspective on biases in cross-sex mind reading. *Journal of Personality and Social Psychology, 78*, 81–91.

Haselton, M.G., & Buss, D.M. (2001). *Sex, lies, and strategic interference: The psychology of deception between the sexes*. Manuscript submitted for publication.

This article has been reprinted as it originally appeared in *Current Directions in Psychological Science*. Citation information for this article as originally published appears above.

Men's and Women's Mating Preferences: Distinct Evolutionary Mechanisms?

Lynn Carol Miller,[1] Anila Putcha-Bhagavatula, and William C. Pedersen

Annenberg School for Communication, University of Southern California, Los Angeles, California

Abstract

Have men and women evolved sex-distinct mating preferences for short-term and long-term mating, as postulated by some evolutionary theorists? Direct tests of assumptions, consideration of confounds with gender, and examination of the same variables for both sexes suggest men and women are remarkably similar. Furthermore, cross-species comparisons indicate that humans do not evidence mating mechanisms indicative of short-term mating (e.g., large female sexual skins, large testicles). Understanding human variability in mating preferences is apt to involve more detailed knowledge of the links between these preferences and biological and chemical mechanisms associated with sexual motivation, sexual arousal, and sexual functioning.

Keywords

sex; mating strategies; evolution

For Darwin, evolution via sexual selection occurred when characteristics afforded individuals a reproductive advantage over their rivals, either in competing directly against same-sex competitors (e.g., better weaponry) or in having characteristics that opposite-sex mates preferred (e.g., greater attractiveness). Trivers (1972), in his parental investment theory, argued that an important factor guiding sexual selection is the relative amount of parental investment that males and females devote to offspring. The sex that invests less in offspring (typically males, who minimally invest sperm, compared with females, who minimally invest eggs, gestation, lactation, and other care) should devote proportionately more mating effort to short-term couplings and less to parental investment. The sex that invests less should also be less choosy in its mate-selection criteria and more apt to engage in same-sex competition for mates. Sexual asymmetries in parental investment, according to this approach, should predict sex-differentiated mating preferences and more competition between members of the less-investing sex.

Among psychologists, there are those who have applied parental investment theory to humans (e.g., Buss & Schmitt, 1993; Geary, 2000). Buss and his colleagues, for example, have argued that because men minimally invest sperm, short-term mating is reproductively more advantageous for men than for women. The claim that men and women have evolved sex-distinct sexual strategies (e.g., such that men spend proportionately more of their mating effort in short-term mating than do women) seems to have permeated the popular culture, as well as the professional literature. However, other psychologists dispute these claims, citing evidence from psychology, primatology, cross-cultural analyses, and neuro-biology. In this article, we discuss some recent evidence in this debate.

Part of Buss and Schmitt's (1993) argument is that men and women evolved distinct mechanisms for both short-term and long-term mating. We begin by review-ing relevant evidence from primatology, where similar distinctions between long-term and short-term mating are made.

HUMANS ARE PRIMATES

Are Humans Designed to be Short-Term Maters?

Among primates (Dixson, 1998), there are those with short-term and those with long-term mating systems.[2] Two long-term systems are monogamy (one male mates long term with one female; e.g., gibbon, siamang) and polygyny (one male mates long term with two or more females; e.g., gorilla). In both long-term and short-term mating, males and females attract (and sometimes retain) mates by having desirable characteristics. In addition, characteristics that enhance one's competitive advantage among members of the same gender may afford reproduc-tive advantage. In long-term mating, the male is often able to restrict competitors by maintaining proximity to his female mate (or mates) and by physically defend-ing her (their) territory.

Some evolved mating mechanisms (e.g., large female sexual skins, large tes-ticles) indicate that short-term mating played a significant role in a species' evolved mating strategies. For example, among common chimpanzee and bonobo, large female sexual skins attract so many male competitors when a female is fertile that long-term male defense strategies are inadequate (e.g., to ensure that a given male is the biological father of his mate's offspring). Instead, evolution favors the reproductive success of males who can better compete via mecha-nisms for enhancing the probability that their sperm, and not that of their com-petitors, will impregnate the female. Thus, when females have large sexual skins when fertile, males who have more sperm (i.e., larger testicles) or produce sperm

Table 1. *Mating-system variables: Comparisons of humans and other apes*

	Long-term maters	
Variable	Humans	Gibbons/siamangs (monogamous)
Testicle weight (g)/ body weight (kg)	0.79	0.83–1.00
Copulatory plugs	No	No (4 species)
Sexual skin	No visible swelling or skin (concealed ovulation)	Very small sexual skins (gibbon) (unknown if siamang females have sexual skins)

Note. All data are from Dixson (1998).

plugs (e.g., that might reduce sperm displacement by the next partner) increase their chances of fathering offspring. As indicated in Table 1, chimpanzee females exhibit large sexual skins and chimpanzee males exhibit sperm-competition mechanisms. But humans, and other long-term maters among apes, do not possess such mechanisms.

Researchers suggesting that humans have evolved short-term mating mechanisms have pointed to arguments that there are kamikaze sperm that are designed to kill the sperm of human male competitors. But *in vitro* analyses of spermatozoa from multiple human males (Moore, Martin, & Birk-head, 1999) do not support this claim. Overall, human mating characteristics, discussed here and elsewhere, fit the pattern of primates whose primary or secondary mating systems are long-term and not short-term ones (Dixson, 1998).

Parenting and Mating-System Differences

Primatologists have argued that Trivers's theory does not apply well to primates. One reason may be that "traditional examination of male mating and parental investment has overlooked the wide and costly array of physiological and social mechanisms" that are involved in male primate investment, including the defense of troop members and territory (Fuentes, 2000, p. 602). Including these additional mechanisms in conceptualizations of parental investment would suggest much less sexual asymmetry in investment among primates than among other mammals.

There are many primate species in which males do not typically provide direct care of offspring. Nevertheless, males among some of these species can and will do so. For example, gorilla males, who are polygynous, will assume primary parental caregiving (e.g., nurturing and rearing the infant themselves) when a mate or sister has been killed. That is, the underlying evolved mechanisms for directly providing parental care are present. In any event, with more symmetry in parental investment, the sexes might be expected to have more similar mate preferences.

Long-term maters		Short-term maters
Orangutans (polygynous)	Gorillas (polygynous)	Chimpanzees (promiscuous)
0.33–0.74	0.09–0.18	2.68–2.83
Unknown	Unknown	Yes
No visible swelling or skin (concealed ovulation)	Sexual swelling at midcycle, visible on close inspection; no sexual skin	Very large sexual skins, visible at a considerable distance, that attract multiple males

EVOLVED SEX-DISTINCT MATING PREFERENCES?

Trivers's argument concerning the role of male and female asymmetries in parental investment leads some psychologists (e.g., Buss & Schmitt, 1993) to argue (e.g., sexual strategies theory) for a variety of sex-distinct mating preferences for men and women. Other psychologists, influenced by attachment theory (e.g., Miller & Fishkin, 1997; Miller, Pedersen, & Putcha, 2002) or positing the influence of cultural factors (Eagly & Wood, 1999), argue for relatively few, less pronounced, or no sex-distinct evolved mating preferences in humans. What is the evidence?

Sex Differences in Jealousy

According to Buss and Schmitt (1993), because men need to guard against cuckoldry (investing in nonbiological offspring) and women need to guard against losing a mate's resources, men should focus more on signs of *sexual* infidelity in their partner, whereas women should react more strongly to cues that signal *emotional* infidelity. This prediction was tested and supported by Buss and his colleagues. But both Harris and Christenfeld (1996) and DeSteno and Salovey (1996) suggested that the two types of infidelity are equally upsetting to men and women, and that the sex difference is the result of an artifact (i.e., a sex difference in which type of infidelity more strongly signals the other). They separately found that once this artifact is controlled for, there is not a sex difference.

Sex Differences in Preferences for Mate Resources

Buss and Schmitt (1993) also argued that there are evolved sex differences in men's and women's desire for a mate who has or appears able to procure resources. For example, they argued that in choosing a long-term mate, women—more than men—should value ambition, good earning capacity, professional degrees, and wealth. Across 37 cultures, Buss found that women, more so than men, desired such resource-acquisition cues in long-term mates. But might cultural factors explain these effects? Eagly and Wood (1999) assessed a variety of indicators of women's power, such as access to educational and financial equality, across these 37 cultures. They found that in those cultures where women enjoyed less power, there were stronger sex differences in preferences for these resource cues.

Even in hunter-gatherer societies, women's economic power (e.g., role in hunting and procuring meat and fish) may historically have differentiated cultures where men and women had comparable authority[3] from those where they did not (Boehm, 1999). But in band living, men are equals, meat is shared, and individual hunting ability is obscured. With little if any variability in men's resources within the band, resource cues among males are unlikely to have become the basis for an evolved mating preference in females. With the advent of agriculture less than 10,000 years ago, however, more widespread and larger resource differentials among men were created. Understanding how societal structures and dynamics affect sex-based resource differentials and resultant mating preferences remains an important issue demanding further research.

Testing Theoretical Assumptions

Buss and Schmitt (1993) did not directly test many of sexual strategies theory's assumptions. We consider two examples. First, Buss and Schmitt argued that men should seek more short-term sexual partners than women. But when they asked men and women how many partners they ideally desired over various time periods, they did not ask their participants how many of these were short-term, intermediate-term, or long-term sexual partners. When we (Pedersen, Miller, Putcha-Bhagavatula, & Yang, 2002) directly examined desires for all three types of relationships,[4] we found that virtually all men (98.9%) and all women (99.2%) wanted to eventually settle down in a long-term mutually exclusive sexual relationship, typically within 5 years into the future. Moreover, over this 5-year period, the typical man and woman each desired no short-term partners.

Second, according to sexual strategies theory, "because of a fundamental asymmetry between the sexes in minimum levels of parental investment, men devote a larger proportion of their total mating effort to short-term mating than do women" (Buss & Schmitt, 1993, p. 205). But Buss and Schmitt did not directly test this critical proportional assumption. When we did, we found that men and women did not differ either in the proportion of time or in the proportion of money they expended in short-term mating relative to their total mating effort (Miller et al., 2002).

In addition, Buss and Schmitt (1993) pointed to mean differences between men and women in the desirability of characteristics for a short-term versus a long-term mate as another example of sex-distinct mating mechanisms. But a closer look at the 30 variables (covering 17 of 22 predictions) Buss and Schmitt reported shows that they compared short-term versus long-term preferences on different variables for men than for women (see Table 2). How can one tell if a mean difference in preferences between short-term and long-term contexts among men supports the argument that men and women have distinct mating mechanisms if the same data are not consistently reported for women?

To address this issue, we (Miller et al., 2002) collected new data on nearly all of these preference items for both men and women. With few exceptions, if there was a significant difference between preferences in the short-term and long-term contexts for one gender, there was a significant difference in the same direction for the other gender. In fact, across the data, what men desired most in a mate women also desired most in a mate. What men found most undesirable in a mate women also found most undesirable in a mate. This yielded extraordinarily high correlations between men's and women's ratings for both short-term and long-term sexual partners. Furthermore, we and other researchers have identified a variety of confounds with gender in predicting mating preferences, including age, ethnicity, relationship status, sexual experience, and perceptions of the quality of care provided by one's parents.

Note that typically, in our own work and the work of other scientists, the findings reported by Buss and his colleagues were replicated. By collecting additional data and conducting new analyses of data that went beyond those provided by Buss and his colleagues, however, we and other scientists have been able to develop a fuller and different overall story than that provided by sexual strategies

Table 2. Variables for which Buss and Schmitt (1993) reported means and t tests in their study of college men's and women's preferences for short-term and long-term mates

Preference items provided by Buss and Schmitt (1993)	Means reported				t tests reported			
	Men		Women		Short vs. long term		Men vs. women	
	Short term	Long term	Short term	Long term	Men	Women	Short term	Long term
Already in a relationship	X		X				X	
Promiscuous	X	X	X	X	X		X	
Physically attractive[a]	X	X	X	X	X			
Good looking	X	X	X	X	X			
Physically unattractive	X	X	X	X	X			
Sexually experienced	X	X			X			
Sex appeal	X	X			X			
Prudishness	X	X			X			
Sexual inexperience	X	X			X			
Low sex drive	X	X			X			
Wants a commitment[b]	X	X			X			
Faithfulness	X	X			X			
Sexual loyalty	X	X			X			
Chastity[a,c]	X	X			X			
Unfaithful[c]	X	X			X			
Sleeps around a lot[c]	X	X			X		?	
Spends a lot . . . early on			X	X		X	?	
Gives gifts early on			X	X		X	?	
Has . . . extravagant lifestyle			X	X		X		

Stingy early on	X		X	X
Physical strength		X		?
Good financial prospects[d]	X	X		?
Promising career[d,e]	X	X		?
Likely to succeed . . . [d,e]	X	X		?
Likely to earn . . . [d,e]	X	X		?
Has reliable . . . career[d,e]	X	X		?
Unable to support you . . . [d]	X	X		
Financially poor[c]	X	X	?	?
Lacks ambition[c]	X	X	?	?
Uneducated[c]	X	X	?	?

Note. Xs indicate results that were reported, and ?s indicate that differences were mentioned or implied but not presented. Empty cells indicate no results were mentioned.

[a] Buss and Schmitt (1993) alluded to earlier work in which t-test comparisons between men and women in long-term relationships but not short-term relationships were reported for other (e.g., cross-cultural) samples.

[b] Buss and Schmitt (1993) noted that a "context difference was also found but was not nearly as strong [for women]" (p. 213, material in brackets added). But they provided no t tests for women nor a test of the Context × Sex interaction alluded to. That is, Buss and Schmitt must have collected data on this variable for women as well as for men, but it is not clear from their description if this difference was significant for women and more significant for men than women.

[c] No t tests were provided for men versus women, but Buss and Schmitt (1993) noted in the text that there were significant sex differences for these preferences.

[d] Men and women did not provide personal assessments on these preferences, but made stereotype judgments about men and women (e.g., indicating "how desirable the 'average male' or 'average female' would find each attribute in short-term and long-term mating contexts"; Buss & Schmitt, 1993, p. 223).

[e] Buss and Schmitt (1993) did not provide t tests of sex differences but claimed that they performed the tests and found sex differences.

theory. For example, in contrast to Buss and his colleagues, we did not find overall support for sexual strategies theory when we collected and examined data on the same variables for both genders.

In short, comparative analyses with other primates provide little evidence for biological mechanisms uniquely designed for short-term mating for humans. Emerging reviews and psychological evidence also challenge the claim that there are sex-distinct evolved mating mechanisms involving mating preferences.

FUTURE DIRECTIONS

Understanding evolutionary design, as part of and apart from the effects of cultural diffusion and innovation, is one of the biggest challenges for evolutionary approaches. Social constraint and culture-developing mechanisms are part of the evolutionary design of larger-brained primates. But these mechanisms produce cultural products that can bias mating or sex differences in behavior. For example, alcohol is often used to reduce sexual inhibitions in short-term mating. But alcohol was not produced in the Pleistocene.[5] An important methodological challenge is to not confound cultural products and evolved design, yet understand cultural mechanisms, and adaptation to environmental change, as part of that evolved design. It also behooves researchers to guard against sexual stereotypes and confounds. Even scientists can wear cultural blinders that can bias the collection, presentation, and interpretation of data.

Another challenge is to better specify psychological mechanisms and, where possible, tie them to related brain structures and biological and chemical processes. Researchers also need to better delineate the processes by which these mechanisms predict outcomes (e.g., preferences, decisions, behaviors). For example, primates may provide higher levels of paternal care and investment than most other mammals. Is this related to the greater sex-related plasticity found in primate brains (Dixson, 1998)? In nonprimate mammals, monogamous species have greater overlap in underlying biological and chemical mechanisms for males and females than do promiscuous species, with the former also providing higher levels of paternal care (Insel, 1997). However, in a variety of species, including humans, the brain shows sex differences (e.g., differences in the size of various portions of the brain) that might affect sex-related behaviors. Whether and how these sex differences influence or are influenced by behavior, or might interact with hormones, remains unclear.

Hormonal patterns, however, are more clearly related to some sexual behaviors. For example, hormonal fluctuations throughout the monthly human female cycle seem related to the timing of male and female sexual initiation (proceptivity) or sexual motivation. Such sex differences are similar to those found across many primate species with diverse mating systems, varying from short-term to long-term ones (Dixson, 1998). For example, in all nonsimian primates, unlike other mammals, females are receptive to sex throughout their cycles, but actively seek sex just prior to ovulation, when levels of testosterone and estradiol surge. Because similar sex differences are found across primates with varying mating systems, these sex differences are unlikely to shed much light on differences in mating systems.

But exploring how hormonal fluctuations covary with mating preferences for both men and women might provide exciting insight into variability both within and between individuals. In such investigations, however, scientists should not consider men's and women's preferences and behaviors in isolation. Emerging research, for example, suggests that mutual influence between men and women, hormonally and pheromonally, affects sexual outcomes (Miller & Fishkin, 1997).

Spurred on by the development of Viagra, scientists have undertaken considerable work on humans' sexual dysfunction and sexual arousal. This work suggests that the sexual circuitry system—and the biological and chemical processes affecting sexual functioning and enjoyment—is surprisingly similar in men and women (Goldstein, 2000). The balance of serotonin (which plays a role in inhibiting sexual arousal) to oxytocin (which serves as the sexual-excitation neurotransmitter) is critical to sexual function and affects sexual enjoyment. Psychological factors (e.g., anxiety, anger, comfort, liking, attraction, love), for both men and women, impact the biological and chemical processes affecting inhibition and excitation. Thus, higher levels of emotional bonding are associated with higher levels of sexual enjoyment (Miller & Fishkin, 1997), and anxiety is predictive of reduced sexual enjoyment and functioning. Psychological factors that influence sexual functioning may be key to understanding fluctuations in mating preferences within and between individuals (Miller et al., 2002). Given the observed similarities between men's and women's patterns of mating preferences, sexual circuitry, and sexual enjoyment, however, sex-distinct mating preferences related to sexual arousal and functioning do not seem promising. But, because the wiring of the sexual circuitry system may be species-specific (Insel, 1997), differences across species in these evolved biological, chemical, and psychological systems might shed light on differences in expressed mating preferences and behaviors.

In all this complexity, one thing is clear: Scientists studying mating systems, and sex differences within them, have to more carefully consider the systems of relevant mechanisms (both shared across species and unique to humans) and how these, in combination, interact with environments to affect mating preferences and behaviors.

Recommended Reading

Dixson, A.F. (1998). (See References)
Pedersen, W.C., Miller, L.C., Putcha-Bhagavatula, A.D., & Yang, Y. (2002). (See References)

Notes

1. Address correspondence to Lynn Carol Miller, Annenberg School for Communication, University of Southern California, Los Angeles, CA 90089-0281; e-mail: Lmiller@rcf.usc.edu.

2. Mating systems are not absolute. Rather, each is composed of a set of mechanisms that increase the probability of particular mating outcomes. Primatologists classify primates as having primary, and sometimes secondary, mating systems. Thus, the occurrence of occasional extrapair mating, by itself, does not alter the species' mating classification (e.g., as primarily long-term maters).

3. For example, where females and males hunt boar with dogs (e.g., the Agta of the Philippines), the sexes have economic and political parity (Boehm, 1999).

4. In our study, we employed the same terminology used by Buss and Schmitt (1993) to define these three types of relationships to subjects. Specifically, short-term relationships were defined as "a 1-night stand, brief affair, etc." (p. 210). Intermediate-term relationships were defined as "dating, going steady, brief marriages, or intermediate-length affairs" (p. 204). Long-term mates were defined as "a marriage partner" (p. 210).

5. Mating preferences are fundamental facets of evolutionary processes. Changing them might take tens of thousands of years or more. That is why when scientists search for evolutionary adaptations, they typically consider what humans were like during the Pleistocene era, which ended more than 10,000 years ago. At that point in time, and for most of human evolution, *Homo sapiens* were nomadic hunter-gatherers.

References

Boehm, C. (1999). *Hierarchy in the forest: The evolution of egalitarian behavior.* Cambridge, MA: Harvard University Press.

Buss, D.M., & Schmitt, D.P. (1993). Sexual Strategies Theory: An evolutionary perspective on human mating. *Psychological Review, 100,* 204–232.

DeSteno, D.A., & Salovey, P. (1996). Evolutionary origins of sex differences in jealousy? Questioning the "fitness" of the model. *Psychological Science, 7,* 367–372.

Dixson, A.F. (1998). *Primate sexuality: Comparative studies of the prosimians, monkeys, apes, and human beings.* Oxford, England: Oxford University Press.

Eagly, A.H., & Wood, W. (1999). The origins of sex differences in human behavior: Evolved dispositions versus social roles. *American Psychologist, 54,* 408–423.

Fuentes, A. (2000). Human mating models can benefit from comparative primatology and careful methodology. *Behavioral and Brain Sciences, 23,* 602–603.

Geary, D.C. (2000). Evolution and proximate expression of human paternal investment. *Psychological Bulletin, 126,* 55–77.

Goldstein, I. (2000). Male sexual circuitry. *Scientific American, 283,* 70–75.

Harris, C.R., & Christenfeld, N. (1996). Gender, jealousy, and reason. *Psychological Science, 7,* 364–366.

Insel, T.R. (1997). A neurobiological basis of social attachment. *American Journal of Psychiatry, 154,* 726–735.

Miller, L.C., & Fishkin, S.A. (1997). On the dynamics of human bonding and reproductive success: Seeking "windows" on the "adapted-for" human-environmental interface. In J.A. Simpson & D.T. Kenrick (Eds.), *Evolutionary social psychology* (pp. 197–235). Mahwah, NJ: Erlbaum.

Miller, L.C., Pedersen, W.C., & Putcha, A.D. (2002). *Mating mechanisms for men and women: From smoke, mirrors, and leaps of faith . . . toward a mindful evolutionary dynamics.* Unpublished manuscript, University of Southern California, Los Angeles.

Moore, H.D.M., Martin, M., & Birkhead, T.R. (1999). No evidence for killer sperm or other selective interactions between human spermatozoa in ejaculates of different males in vitro. *Proceedings of the Royal Society of London B, 266,* 2343–2350.

Pedersen, W.C., Miller, L.C., Putcha-Bhagavatula, A.D., & Yang, Y. (2002). Evolved sex differences in the number of partners desired? The long and the short of it. *Psychological Science, 13,* 157–161.

Trivers, R. (1972). Parental investment and sexual selection. In B. Campbell (Ed.), *Sexual selection and the descent of man 1871–1971* (pp. 136–179). Chicago: Aldine-Atherton.

This article has been reprinted as it originally appeared in *Current Directions in Psychological Science*. Citation information for this article as originally published appears above.

Emerging Perspectives on Distinctions Between Romantic Love and Sexual Desire

Lisa M. Diamond[1]
University of Utah

Abstract

Although sexual desire and romantic love are often experienced in concert, they are fundamentally distinct subjective experiences with distinct neurobiological substrates. The basis for these distinctions is the evolutionary origin of each type of experience. The processes underlying sexual desire evolved in the context of sexual mating, whereas the processes underlying romantic love—or pair bonding—originally evolved in the context of infant-caregiver attachment. Consequently, not only can humans experience these feelings separately, but an individual's sexual predisposition for the same sex, the other sex, or both sexes may not circumscribe his or her capacity to fall in love with partners of either gender. Also, the role of oxytocin in both love and desire may contribute to the widely observed phenomenon that women report experiencing greater interconnections between love and desire than do men. Because most research on the neurobiological substrates of sexual desire and affectional bonding has been conducted with animals, a key priority for future research is systematic investigation of the coordinated biological, behavioral, cognitive, and emotional processes that shape experiences of love and desire in humans.

Keywords

attachment; sexual desire; gender; sexual orientation; evolutionary theory

It is a truism that romantic love and sexual desire are not the same thing, but one might be hard pressed to cite empirical evidence to this effect. In recent years, however, researchers in fields ranging from psychology to animal behavior to neurobiology have devoted increasing attention to the experiences, physiological underpinnings, and potential evolutionary origins that distinguish love and desire. The results of these investigations suggest that romantic love and sexual desire are governed by functionally independent social-behavioral systems that evolved for different reasons and that involve different neurochemical substrates. Furthermore, there are gender differences in the interrelationship between love and desire that may have both biological and cultural origins. This emerging body of theory and research has the potential to profoundly reshape the way we conceptualize human sexuality, gender, sexual orientation, and social bonding.

INDEPENDENCE BETWEEN LOVE AND DESIRE

Sexual desire typically denotes a need or drive to seek out sexual objects or to engage in sexual activities, whereas *romantic love* typically denotes the powerful feelings of emotional infatuation and attachment between intimate partners. Furthermore, most researchers acknowledge a distinction between the earlier "passionate" stage of love, sometimes called "limerence" (Tennov, 1979), and the later-developing "companionate" stage of love, called pair bonding or attachment (Fisher, 1998; Hatfield, 1987). Although it may be easy to imagine sexual desire without romantic love, the notion of "pure," "platonic," or "nonsexual" romantic love is somewhat more controversial. Yet empirical evidence indicates that sexual desire is not a prerequisite for romantic love, even in its earliest, passionate stages. Many men and women report having experienced romantic passion in the absence of sexual desire (Tennov, 1979), and even prepubertal children, who have not undergone the hormonal changes responsible for adult levels of sexual motivation, report intense romantic infatuations (Hatfield, Schmitz, Cornelius, & Rapson, 1988).

Furthermore, extensive cross-cultural and historical research shows that individuals often develop feelings of romantic love for partners of the "wrong" gender (i.e., heterosexuals fall in love with same-gender partners and lesbian and gay individuals fall in love with other-gender partners, as reviewed in Diamond, 2003). Although some modern observers have argued that such relationships must involve hidden or suppressed sexual desires, the straightforward written reports of the participants themselves are not consistent with such a blanket characterization. Rather, it seems that individuals are capable of developing intense, enduring, preoccupying affections for one another regardless of either partner's sexual attractiveness or arousal.

MEASURING THE EXPERIENCE AND SUBSTRATES OF LOVE AND DESIRE

Of course, one's interpretation of such data depends on one's confidence in the methods used to assess and contrast love and desire. Whereas sexual arousal can be reliably and validly assessed by monitoring blood flow to the genitals, no definitive test of "true love" exists. Psychologists have, however, identified a constellation of cognitions and behaviors that reliably characterize (and differentiate between) romantic love and passion across different cultures. As summarized by Tennov (1979), passionate love is a temporary state of heightened interest in and preoccupation with a specific individual, characterized by intense desires for proximity and physical contact, resistance to separation, and feelings of excitement and euphoria when receiving the partner's attention. As passionate love transforms into companionate love, desire for proximity and resistance to separation become less urgent, and feelings of security, care, and comfort predominate.

Some of the most provocative and promising research on love and desire focuses on the neurobiological substrates of these distinctive behaviors and cognitions. Although little direct research in this area has been conducted with humans, converging lines of evidence (reviewed by Fisher, 1998) suggest that the marked experiential differences between love and desire may be partially attributable to their distinct neurochemical signatures. Sexual desire, for example, is directly mediated by gonadal estrogens and androgens (see Diamond, 2003; Fisher, 1998), yet these hormones do not mediate the formation of affectional bonds. Rather, animal research indicates that the distinctive feelings and behaviors associated with attachment formation are mediated by the fundamental "reward" circuitry of the mammalian brain, involving the coordinated action of endogenous opioids, catecholamines,[2] and neuropeptides such as oxytocin, which is best known for its role in childbirth and nursing. These neurochemicals regulate a range of emotional, cognitive, behavioral, and biological processes that facilitate social bonding by fostering conditioned associations between specific social partners and intrinsic feelings of reward (reviewed in Carter, 1998).

At the current time, it is not known whether such processes mediate the formation and maintenance of pair bonds between humans, as they have been shown to do in other pair-bonding mammalian species, such as the prairie vole (Carter, 1998). For example, we are only beginning to understand the range of emotional and physical phenomena (other than labor and nursing) that trigger oxytocin release in humans, and whether oxytocin release has consistent effects on subjective experience. Preliminary studies have found fascinating individual differences in the amount of oxytocin released in response to sexual activity, positive emotion, and massage (Carmichael, Warburton, Dixen, & Davidson, 1994; Turner, Altemus, Enos, Cooper, & McGuinness, 1999), and this is a key direction for future research.

Another promising avenue for investigation involves the use of functional magnetic resonance imaging (fMRI) to identify brain regions that are activated during experiences of desire versus infatuation versus attachment. In one preliminary study (Bartels & Zeki, 2000), the brains of individuals who reported being "truly, deeply, and madly in love" were examined under two conditions: while viewing pictures of their beloved and while viewing pictures of other-sex friends. Compared with viewing friends, viewing pictures of loved ones was associated with heightened activation in the middle insula and the anterior cingulate cortex, areas that have been associated in prior research with positive emotion, attention to one's own emotional states, attention to the emotional states of social partners, and even opioid-induced euphoria. Viewing pictures of loved ones was also associated with deactivation in the posterior cingulate gyrus, the amygdala, and the right prefrontal, parietal, and middle temporal cortices, areas that have been associated with sadness, fear, aggression, and depression. Notably, the brain regions that showed distinctive patterns of activity when viewing romantic partners did not overlap with regions typically activated during sexual arousal.

Clearly, much work remains to be done to develop a comprehensive "map" of normative brain activity during both short-term states and longer-term stages of desire, infatuation, and attachment; to examine changes in brain activity as individuals move between these states and stages within specific relationships; and to explore whether inter-individual differences in personality and relationship quality moderate such patterns. Perhaps most important, however, we require a greater understanding of the functional implications of different coordinated patterns of activation and deactivation.

THE EVOLUTIONARY ORIGINS OF LOVE AND DESIRE

Given the accumulating evidence that love and desire are, in fact, functionally independent phenomena with distinct neurobiological substrates, a natural question is, *why*? After all, most individuals end up falling in love with partners to whom they are sexually drawn, and this seems to make good evolutionary sense given that pair bonding with one's sexual partner is a good way to ensure that the resulting offspring have two dedicated parents instead of just one. This view assumes, however, that the basic biobehavioral mechanisms underlying affectional bonding evolved for the purpose of reproductive mating, and this may not be the case. Although these processes would clearly have conferred reproductive benefits on early humans, some researchers have argued that they originally evolved for an altogether different purpose: infant-caregiver attachment.

Bowlby (1982) conceptualized attachment as an evolved behavioral system designed to keep infants in close proximity to caregivers (thereby maximizing infants' chances for survival). Attachment establishes an intense affectional bond between infant and caregiver, such that separation elicits feelings of distress and proximity elicits feelings of comfort and security. Other evolutionary theorists have argued that this system was eventually co-opted for the purpose of keeping reproductive partners together to rear offspring (Hazan & Zeifman, 1999). In other words, adult pair bonding may be an *exaptation*—a system that originally evolved for one reason, but comes to serve another. The fundamental correspondence between infant-caregiver attachment and adult pair bonding is supported by extensive research documenting that these phenomena share the same core emotional and behavioral dynamics: heightened desire for proximity, resistance to separation, and utilization of the partner as a preferred target for comfort and security (Hazan & Zeifman, 1999). Even more powerful evidence is provided by the voluminous animal research documenting that these two types of affectional bonding are mediated by the same opioid- and oxytocin-based neural circuitry (Carter, 1998).

This view helps to explain the independence between love and desire, because sexual desire is obviously irrelevant to the process of infant-caregiver bonding. Yet even if one grants that affectional bonding and sexual mating are fundamentally distinct processes that evolved for distinct purposes, the question still remains: Why do the majority of human adults fall in love only with partners to whom they are sexually attracted? One reason is obviously cultural: Most human societies have strong and well-established norms regarding what types of feelings and behaviors are appropriate for different types of adult relationships, and they actively channel adults into the "right" types of relationships through a variety of social practices. Additionally, however, both human and animal data suggest that attachments are most likely to form between individuals that have extensive proximity to and contact with one another over a prolonged period of time (Hazan & Zeifman, 1999). Sexual desire provides a powerful motive for such extended contact, increasing the likelihood that the average adult becomes attached to sexual partners rather than platonic friends.

IMPLICATIONS REGARDING GENDER AND SEXUAL ORIENTATION

Psychologists have long noted that one of the most robust gender differences regarding human sexuality is that women tend to place greater emphasis on relationships as a context for sexual feelings and behaviors than do men (Peplau, 2003). For example, many lesbian and bisexual women report that they were never aware of same-sex desires until after they fell in love with a particular woman (Diamond, 2003). One potential reason for this gender difference is that women appear more likely than men to have their first experiences of sexual arousal in the context of a heterosexual dating relationship, rather than the solitary context of masturbation. Another potential contributor to this gender difference is that historically women have been socialized to restrict their sexual feelings and behaviors to intimate emotional relationships—ideally, marital ties—whereas males have enjoyed more social license regarding casual sexual relations.

Yet our emerging understanding of the neurochemical substrates of love and desire raises the intriguing possibility that biological factors might also contribute to this gender difference. Specifically, several of the neurochemicals that mediate mammalian bonding processes—most notably, oxytocin, vasopressin, and dopamine—also mediate sexual behavior, and these neurochemicals often show hormone-dependent, gender-specific patterns of functioning. For example, female rats have far more extensive oxytocin brain circuits than do male rats, perhaps to facilitate oxytocin-dependent caregiving behaviors, and oxytocin interacts with estrogen to regulate female rats' sexual receptivity (Panksepp, 1998). Among humans, women show greater oxytocin release during sexual activity than do men, and some women show correlations between oxytocin release and orgasm intensity (Carmichael et al., 1994). Such findings raise the provocative possibility that women's greater emphasis on the relational context of sexuality—that is, their greater experience of links between love and desire—may be influenced by oxytocin's joint, gender-specific role in these processes (in addition to culture and socialization).

Furthermore, the fact that women sometimes develop same-sex desires as a result of falling in love with female friends (a phenomenon rarely documented among men) might be interpreted to indicate that oxytocin-mediated links between love and desire make it possible for a woman's affectionally triggered desires to "override" her general sexual orientation. In other words, whereas the fundamental independence between love and desire means that individuals' sexual orientations do not necessarily circumscribe their capacity for affectional bonding, the biobehavioral links between love and desire may make it possible for either experience to trigger the other (Diamond, 2003). Although this might be true for both sexes, it is perhaps more likely for women because of both gender-specific oxytocin-mediated processes and the greater cultural permission for women to develop strong affectional bonds with members of their own sex (for a similar argument regarding same-sex female bonds and gender-differentiated patterns of stress response, see Taylor et al., 2000).

These notions run counter to the conventional notion that lesbians and gay men fall in love only with same-sex partners and heterosexuals fall in love only with other-sex partners. Yet this conventional notion is also contradicted by cross-cultural, historical, and even animal research. For example, given sufficient cohabitation, both male and female prairie voles have been induced to form nonsexual bonds with same-sex partners (DeVries, Johnson, & Carter, 1997), although these bonds form more quickly and are more robust among females. One fascinating area for future research concerns the conditions under which humans form and maintain sexual and affectional relationships that run counter to their established patterns of desire and affection, the implications of such phenomena for later experience and development, and the specific role played by cognitive, behavioral, emotional, and biological mechanisms in regulating such processes.

Historically, it has been assumed that sexual arousal is a more basic, biologically mediated phenomenon than is romantic love, and therefore is more amenable to scientific study. Yet this assumption is outmoded. Research has demonstrated that the distinct behaviors and intense feelings associated with affectional bonds are governed not only by culture and socialization, but also by evolved, neurochemically mediated processes that are a fundamental legacy of our mammalian heritage. Future research on the nature and functioning of these processes in humans will not only provide researchers with novel tools to investigate age-old debates (can you fall in love with two people at once?), but will also make critical contributions to understanding the basic experience of human intimacy and how it is shaped by gender and sexual orientation over the life course.

Recommended Reading

Carter, C.S. (1998). (See References)
Diamond, L.M. (2003). (See References)
Fisher, H.E. (1998). (See References)
Hazan, C., & Zeifman, D. (1999). (See References)

Notes

1. Address correspondence to Lisa M. Diamond, Department of Psychology, University of Utah, 380 South 1530 East, Room 502, Salt Lake City, UT 84112-0251; e-mail: diamond@psych.utah.edu.

2. The release of catecholamines (most notably, dopamine, epinephrine, and norepinephrine) is associated with a variety of physiological responses that prepare the body to "fight or flee" a stressor (e.g., increased heart rate, blood pressure, and blood glucose levels). In contrast, endogenous opioids are known for their role in diminishing endocrine, cardiovascular, and behavioral stress responses, and are particularly well known for blunting the experience of pain. For this reason, they are often called "the body's own pain killers." These neuropeptides also play a role in the subjective experience of pleasure and reward, and facilitate learning and conditioning.

References

Bartels, A., & Zeki, S. (2000). The neural basis of romantic love. *NeuroReport, 11*, 3829–3834.
Bowlby, J. (1982). *Attachment and loss: Vol. 1: Attachment* (2nd ed.). New York: Basic Books.
Carmichael, M.S., Warburton, V.L., Dixen, J., & Davidson, J.M. (1994). Relationships among cardiovascular, muscular, and oxytocin responses during human sexual activity. *Archives of Sexual Behavior, 23*, 59–79.
Carter, C.S. (1998). Neuroendocrine perspectives on social attachment and love. *Psychoneuroendocrinology, 23*, 779–818.
DeVries, A.C., Johnson, C.L., & Carter, C.S. (1997). Familiarity and gender influence social preferences in prairie voles (*Microtus ochrogaster*). *Canadian Journal of Zoology, 75*, 295–301.
Diamond, L.M. (2003). What does sexual orientation orient? A biobehavioral model distinguishing romantic love and sexual desire. *Psychological Review, 110*, 173–192.
Fisher, H.E. (1998). Lust, attraction, and attachment in mammalian reproduction. *Human Nature, 9*, 23–52.

Hatfield, E. (1987). Passionate and companionate love. In R.J. Sternberg & M.L. Barnes (Eds.), *The psychology of love* (pp. 191–217). New Haven, CT: Yale University Press.

Hatfield, E., Schmitz, E., Cornelius, J., & Rapson, R.L. (1988). Passionate love: How early does it begin? *Journal of Psychology and Human Sexuality, 1,* 35–52.

Hazan, C., & Zeifman, D. (1999). Pair-bonds as attachments: Evaluating the evidence. In J. Cassidy & P.R. Shaver (Eds.), *Handbook of attachment theory and research* (pp. 336–354). New York: Guilford.

Panksepp, J. (1998). *Affective neuroscience: The foundations of human and animal emotions.* New York: Cambridge University Press.

Peplau, L.A. (2003). Human sexuality: How do men and women differ? *Current Directions in Psychological Science, 12,* 37–40.

Taylor, S.E., Klein, L.C., Lewis, B.P., Gruenewald, T.L., Gurung, R.A.R., & Updegraff, J.A. (2000). Biobehavioral responses to stress in females: Tend-and-befriend, not fight-or-flight. *Psychological Review, 107,* 411–429.

Tennov, D. (1979). *Love and limerence: The experience of being in love.* New York: Stein and Day.

Turner, R.A., Altemus, M., Enos, T., Cooper, B., & McGuinness, T. (1999). Preliminary research on plasma oxytocin in normal cycling women: Investigating emotion and interpersonal distress. *Psychiatry, 62,* 97–113.

This article has been reprinted as it originally appeared in *Current Directions in Psychological Science*. Citation information for this article as originally published appears above.

Adaptation to Sperm Competition in Humans

Todd K. Shackelford[1] and Aaron T. Goetz

Florida Atlantic University

Abstract

With the recognition, afforded by recent evolutionary science, that female infidelity was a recurrent feature of modern humans' evolutionary history has come the development of a unique area in the study of human mating: sperm competition. A form of male–male postcopulatory competition, sperm competition occurs when the sperm of two or more males concurrently occupy the reproductive tract of a female and compete to fertilize her ova. Males must compete for mates, but if two or more males have copulated with a female within a sufficiently short period of time, sperm will compete for fertilizations. Psychological, behavioral, physiological, and anatomical evidence indicates that men have evolved solutions to combat the adaptive problem of sperm competition, but research has only just begun to uncover these adaptations.

Keywords

sperm competition; anti-cuckoldry; sexual conflict; female infidelity; evolutionary psychology

Male flour beetles sometimes fertilize females with a rival male's sperm. This "fertilization by proxy" occurs when the mating male's aedeagus (reproductive organ) translocates the sperm of another male into the female's reproductive tract (Haubruge, Arnaud, Mignon, & Gage, 1999). The sperm of a male that a female has copulated with can adhere to a subsequent male's aedeagus because these insects' genitalia have chitinous spines designed to facilitate removal of rival male sperm prior to deposition of self-sperm into a female's reproductive tract. This phenomenon was predicted and observed by researchers who study sperm competition. Although not yet documented empirically, humans also may experience fertilization by proxy (Gallup & Burch, 2004). More generally, a rapidly growing literature indicates that sperm competition has been an important selection pressure during human evolution.

Sperm competition is intrasexual (male–male) competition that occurs after the initiation of copulation. Whereas Darwin and others identified *pre*copulatory adaptations associated with intrasexual competition (e.g., horns on beetles, status seeking in men), researchers studying sperm competition aim to identify *post*copulatory adaptations. Thus, an alternative way of thinking about sexual selection is that there is not only competition between males for mates, but competition between males for fertilizations.

Sperm competition is the inevitable consequence of males competing for fertilizations. If females mate in a way that concurrently places sperm from two or more males in their reproductive tracts, this generates selection pressures on males. If these selection pressures are recurrent throughout a species' evolutionary history, males will evolve tactics to aid their sperm in outcompeting rivals' sperm for fertilizations. These tactics may take the form of anatomical, physiological, and psychological adaptations. Although revolutionary for its time, the first definition of sperm competition, "the competition within a single female between the sperm of two or more males for the fertilization of the ova" (Parker, 1970, p. 527), does not capture the full spectrum of male anatomy, physiology, psychology, and behavior associated with sperm competition.

SPERM COMPETITION AS AN ADAPTIVE PROBLEM IN HUMANS

For species that practice social monogamy—the mating system in which males and females form long-term pair bonds but also pursue extra-pair copulations (i.e., "affairs")—it is the extra-pair copulations by females that creates the primary context for sperm competition. A male whose female partner engages in an extra-pair copulation is at risk of cuckoldry—the unwitting investment of resources into genetically unrelated offspring—and its associated costs, which include loss of the time, effort, and resources the male spent attracting his partner and the misdirection of his current and future resources to a rival's offspring. Consequently, in species with paternal investment in offspring, selection often favors the evolution of adaptations that decrease the likelihood of being cuckolded. Anti-cuckoldry tactics fall into three categories: *preventative tactics,* designed to prevent female infidelity; *sperm competition tactics,* designed to minimize conception risk in the event of female infidelity; and *differential paternal investment,* designed to allocate paternal investment prudently in the event that female infidelity may have resulted in conception.

The extent to which sperm competition occurred in ancestral human populations would have depended largely on rates of female sexual infidelity and cuckoldry. Current estimates of worldwide cuckoldry rates range from 1.7% to 29.8% (Anderson, 2006). Although current estimates of cuckoldry rates provide only a proxy of the occurrence of cuckoldry throughout human evolutionary history, even the most conservative estimates of these rates would have generated sufficient selection pressures on males to avoid the costs of cuckoldry. Moreover, the ubiquity and power of male sexual jealousy provides evidence of an evolutionary history of female infidelity and thus perhaps also of sperm competition. Male sexual jealousy can evolve only if female sexual infidelity was a recurrent feature of human evolutionary history, and female infidelity increases the likelihood that sperm from two or more men occupied concurrently the reproductive tract of a particular woman. This suggests that sexual selection, in the form of sperm competition, has been an important selection pressure during recent human evolution. If this is the case, then specific adaptations to sperm competition may have evolved.

ADAPTATIONS TO SPERM COMPETITION IN HUMANS

In this section, we discuss adaptations men may have evolved in response to an evolutionary history of sperm competition. We limit our discussion of these adaptations to testis size, ejaculate adjustment, semen displacement, sexual arousal, and forced in-pair copulation, as these adaptations have been investigated more rigorously than others.

Testis Size

Across a range of animal species, males have relatively larger testes in species with more intense sperm competition. Because larger testes produce more sperm, a male with larger testes can better compete by inseminating a female with more sperm. Among the great apes, testes size varies predictably with the risk of sperm competition. In gorillas, female promiscuity and sperm competition are rare, and the gorilla's testes are relatively small, making up just 0.03% of their body weight. Chimpanzees, in contrast, are highly promiscuous and, accordingly, males have relatively large testes, making up 0.30% of their body weight. The size of human testes falls between these two extremes at 0.08% of body weight, suggesting intermediate levels of female promiscuity and sperm competition in our evolutionary past (Shackelford & Goetz, 2006).

Ejaculate Adjustment

The number of sperm recruited into a given ejaculate is not constant. Although the physiology is not well understood, there is evidence that sperm number can be adjusted even moments before ejaculation (reviewed in Shackelford, Pound, & Goetz, 2005). A key hypothesis derived from sperm competition theory is that males will adjust the number of sperm they inseminate into a female as a function of the risk that their sperm will encounter competition from the sperm of other males. Baker and Bellis (1993) documented a negative relationship between the proportion of time a couple has spent together since their last copulation and the number of sperm ejaculated at the couple's next copulation. As the proportion of time a couple spends together since their last copulation decreases, there is a predictable increase in the probability that the man's partner has been inseminated by another male. Additional analyses documented that the proportion of time a couple spent together since their last copulation negatively predicts sperm number ejaculated at the couple's next copulation, but not at the man's next masturbation (Baker & Bellis, 1993). Inseminating into a female more sperm following a separation may function to outnumber or "flush out" sperm from rival men that may be present in the reproductive tract of the woman.

Inspired by Baker and Bellis's (1993) demonstration of male physiological adaptations to sperm competition, Shackelford et al. (2002) documented that human male psychology may include psychological adaptations to decrease the likelihood that a rival man's sperm will fertilize a partner's ovum. For example, men who spent a greater proportion of time apart from their partners since the couples' last copulation—and, therefore, face a higher risk of sperm competition— report that their partners are more sexually attractive, have more interest in copulating with their partners, and believe that their partners are more interested in copulating with them, relative to men spent a lesser proportion of time apart from their partners. These effects were independent of relationship satisfaction, total time since last copulation, and total time spent apart, which rules out several alternative explanations (although other plausible alternative mechanisms remain to be evaluated). These perceptual changes may motivate men to copulate as soon as possible with their partners, thereby entering their sperm into competition with any rival sperm that may be present in their partners' reproductive tracts.

Semen Displacement

Features of the penis may have evolved in response to the selective pressures of sperm competition. The penis of the damselfly is equipped with spines that can remove up to 99% of the sperm stored in a female, and the penis of the tree cricket is designed structurally to remove rival sperm prior to insemination of the male's own ejaculate. Spines, ridges, and knobs on the penis of some waterfowl are positioned in a way to displace rival sperm, and these protuberances are larger in species for which the intensity of sperm competition is greater.

The human penis does not have barbs and spines for removing rival sperm, but recent evidence suggests that the human penis may have evolved to function, in part, as a semen-displacement device. Using artificial genitals and simulated semen, Gallup et al. (2003) tested the hypothesis that the human penis is designed to displace semen deposited by other men in the reproductive tract of a woman. The results indicated that artificial phalluses with a glans and coronal ridge that approximated a human penis displaced more simulated semen than did a phallus that did not have such features. When the penis is inserted into the vagina, the frenulum of the coronal ridge makes semen displacement possible by allowing semen to flow back under the penis alongside the frenulum and collect on the anterior of the shaft behind the coronal ridge. Displacement of simulated semen occurred when a phallus was inserted at least 75% of its length into the artificial vagina.

That the penis must reach an adequate depth before semen is displaced suggests that displacing rival semen may require specific copulatory behaviors. Following allegations of female infidelity or separation from their partners (contexts in which the likelihood of rival semen being present is relatively greater), both men and women report that men thrusted the penis more deeply and more quickly into the vagina at the couple's next copulation (Gallup et al., 2003), behaviors likely to increase semen displacement. In an independent study, Goetz et al. (2005) investigated men's copulatory behaviors when under a high risk of sperm competition. Men mated to women who placed them at high risk of sperm competition were more likely to use specific copulatory behaviors arguably designed to displace rival semen (e.g., more frequent thrusts, deeper thrusts) than were men mated to women who did not place them at high risk of sperm competition.

Sexual Arousal

Men's sexual fantasies often involve sex with multiple, anonymous partners—behavior that would have had fitness payoffs in ancestral environments. It has been suggested, however, that although men might desire and seek sexual variety and the absence of competition with other men, cues of sperm competition risk also might be sexually arousing. Because sexual arousal increases the rate of sperm transport in the vas deferens, Pound (2002) argued that ancestral males might have benefited from being aroused to cues of sperm competition. When faced with cues of sperm competition, sexual arousal would have resulted in an increase in sperm transport upon ejaculation, thus enabling men to compete more effectively in such contexts.

Pound hypothesized that men, therefore, will be more aroused by sexually explicit images incorporating cues of sperm competition than by comparable material in which such cues are absent. Content analyses of sexually explicit images on Internet sites and of commercial "adult" video releases revealed that depictions of sexual activity involving a woman and multiple men are more prevalent than those involving a man and multiple women, indicating that the former category may be preferred by men. Additionally, an online survey of self-reported preferences and an online preference study that unobtrusively assessed image selection yielded corroborative results. Pound argued that the most parsimonious explanation for these results is that male sexual arousal in response to visual cues of sperm competition reflects the functioning of psychological mechanisms that would have motivated adaptive patterns of copulatory behavior in ancestral males exposed to evidence of female promiscuity.

Pound's hypothesis recently has been supported by experimental evidence that men viewing images depicting cues to sperm competition produce more competitive ejaculates than men viewing comparable images in which cues to sperm competition are absent (Kilgallon & Simmons, 2005). Kilgallon and Simmons documented that men produce a higher percentage of motile sperm in their ejaculates after viewing sexually explicit images of two men and one woman (sperm competition images) than after viewing sexually explicit images of three women. More generally, these results support the hypothesis that men adjust their ejaculates in accordance with sperm competition theory.

Forced In-Pair Copulation

Noting that instances of forced in-pair copulation (i.e., partner rape) followed extra-pair copulations in waterfowl and anecdotal reports that forced in-pair copulation in humans often followed accusations of female infidelity, Thornhill and Thornhill (1992) hypothesized that sexual coercion in response to cues of a partner's sexual infidelity might function in humans to introduce a man's sperm into his partner's reproductive tract at a time when there is a high risk of extra-pair paternity. Goetz and Shackelford (2006a) found empirical support for this hypothesis. In two studies, Goetz and Shackelford found that men's sexual coercion in the context of an intimate relationship was related positively to his partner's infidelities. According to men's self-reports and women's partner-reports, men who use more sexual coercion in their relationships are mated to women who have been or are likely to be unfaithful. The hypothesis that sexual coercion and forced in-pair copulation may be a sperm competition tactic has been supported directly and indirectly in at least half a dozen studies (reviewed in Goetz & Shackelford, 2006b).

CONCLUSION AND FUTURE DIRECTIONS

Sperm competition was first identified as a form of postcopulatory competition between males by Geoff Parker in the 1970s. Since then, evolutionary biologists and behavioral ecologists have described many anatomical, physiological, and behavioral adaptations to sperm competition in many nonhuman species. The question as to whether sperm competition has been an important selection pressure during human evolution remains somewhat controversial, and further research is needed to establish the extent to which this might be the case. As outlined in this article, however, there is mounting evidence that aspects of men's sexual psychology and behavior, such as their attraction to and sexual interest in their partners, their copulatory behaviors, and sources of sexual arousal, may reflect adaptations to sperm competition.

Although we focused on men's adaptations to sperm competition, women are not passive sperm receptacles. An important avenue for future research is to identify adaptations not only in men but also in women. Sexual conflict between males and females produces a coevolutionary arms race between the sexes, in which an advantage gained by one sex selects for counteradaptations in the other sex. Thus, men's adaptations to sperm competition are likely to be met by counteradaptations in women (e.g., mechanisms that increase retention of sperm inseminated by men with "good genes"; see Shackelford et al., 2005), and the study of such mechanisms is an important direction for future research.

Recommended Reading

Platek, S.M., & Shackelford, T.K. (Eds.). (2006). *Female infidelity and paternal uncertainty*. New York: Cambridge University Press.
Shackelford, T.K., & Goetz, A.T. (2006). (See References)
Shackelford, T.K., & Pound, N. (Eds.). (2006). *Sperm competition in humans*. New York: Springer.
Shackelford, T.K., Pound, N., & Goetz, A.T. (2005). (See References)

Acknowledgments—The authors contributed equally to this article.

Note

1. Address correspondence to Todd K. Shackelford, Florida Atlantic University, Department of Psychology, 2912 College Avenue, Davie, FL 33314; e-mail: tshackel@fau.edu.

References

Anderson, K.G. (2006). How well does paternity confidence match actual paternity? Evidence from worldwide nonpaternity rates. *Current Anthropology, 47*, 513–520.
Baker, R.R., & Bellis, M.A. (1993). Human sperm competition: Ejaculate adjustment by males and the function of masturbation. *Animal Behaviour, 46*, 861–885.
Gallup, G.G., & Burch, R.L. (2004). Semen displacement as a sperm competition strategy in humans. *Evolutionary Psychology, 4*, 12–23.
Gallup, G.G., Burch, R.L., Zappieri, M.L., Parvez, R.A., Stockwell, M.L., & Davis, J.A. (2003). The human penis as a semen displacement device. *Evolution and Human Behavior, 24*, 277–289.

Goetz, A.T., & Shackelford, T.K. (2006a). Sexual coercion and forced in-pair copulation as sperm competition tactics in humans. *Human Nature, 17*, 265–282.

Goetz, A.T., & Shackelford, T.K. (2006b). *Sexual coercion in intimate relationships: A comparative analysis of the effects of women's infidelity and men's dominance and control.* Manuscript submitted for publication.

Goetz, A.T., Shackelford, T.K., Weekes-Shackelford, V.A., Euler, H.A., Hoier, S., Schmitt, D.P., & LaMunyon, C.W. (2005). Mate retention, semen displacement, and human sperm competition: A preliminary investigation of tactics to prevent and correct female infidelity. *Personality and Individual Differences, 38*, 749–763.

Haubruge, E., Arnaud, L., Mignon, J., & Gage, M.J.G. (1999). Fertilization by proxy: Rival sperm removal and translocation in a beetle. *Proceedings of the Royal Society of London B, 266*, 1183–1187.

Kilgallon, S.J., & Simmons, L.W. (2005). Image content influences men's semen quality. *Biology Letters, 1*, 253–255.

Parker, G.A. (1970). Sperm competition and its evolutionary consequences in the insects. *Biological Reviews, 45*, 525–567.

Pound, N. (2002). Male interest in visual cues of sperm competition risk. *Evolution and Human Behavior, 23*, 443–466.

Shackelford, T.K., & Goetz, A.T. (2006). Comparative evolutionary psychology of sperm competition. *Journal of Comparative Psychology, 120*, 139–146.

Shackelford, T.K., LeBlanc, G.J., Weekes-Shackelford, V.A., Bleske-Rechek, A.L., Euler, H.A., & Hoier, S. (2002). Psychological adaptation to human sperm competition. *Evolution and Human Behavior, 23*, 123–138.

Shackelford, T.K., Pound, N., & Goetz, A.T. (2005). Psychological and physiological adaptations to sperm competition in humans. *Review of General Psychology, 9*, 228–248.

Thornhill, R., & Thornhill, N.W. (1992). The evolutionary psychology of men's coercive sexuality. *Behavioral and Brain Sciences, 15*, 363–421.

Section 4: Critical Thinking Questions

1. In both current research and future directions, Peplau discusses factors outside the individual that can affect aspects of sexuality such as sexual desire and malleability in sexuality over time. How do relationship factors underlie gender differences in sexuality? How do cultural factors affect men's and women's sexuality and the differences between them? Why does romantic bonding and sexual desire seem more changeable over time for women than men (Diamond)?

2. Competing points of view about evolutionary pressures on human mating are posited by Buss and Miller and colleagues. Whose perspectives do you find most compelling to you and why?

3. Does Shackelford and Goetz' article about competition among sperm support the views of Buss or Miller and colleagues? Explain.

This article has been reprinted as it originally appeared in *Current Directions in Psychological Science.* Citation information for this article as originally published appears above.

Section 5: Social Context

In the study of moral reasoning, researchers have moved away from broad stage models toward domain-specific models. The examination of intergroup exclusion reflects both knowledge about stereotypes and social conventions on one hand and judgments about fairness, equality, and individual rights on the other. Killen presents a review of developmental research on children's evaluations of intergroup exclusions based on gender and race. Consideration is given to how children and adolescents weigh exclusions based on gender versus race and how types of peer experiences factor into their evaluations.

Sarcasm has received far less attention than other aspects of figurative language. To interpret sarcasm, one must invoke social and cultural factors. As explained by Katz, Blasko, and Kazmerski, gender alone and in interaction with social-cultural factors such as social class affect the use and understanding of sarcastic remarks. Both the gender of the speaker and the listener matter as the text of the spoken message is processed along with gender stereotypes. Katz and colleagues also present new data on event-related potentials (ERPs) as a means of identifying individual differences in whether a statement is comprehended to be sarcastic.

After decades of conducting and reviewing research on gender differences and gender development, Maccoby urges the field to move away from the largely studying of only individual differences in the rate or degree of sex typing and instead, incorporate the level of the group. Boys and girls derive many of their socialization experiences in sex-segregated groups. Group size, and the activities and interactions in these groups, lead to distinctive male and female subcultures. Maccoby offers suggestions for further research on same-sex groups, calls for the integration of individual difference and group process perspectives, and reminds the reader to also understanding that gender is not always salient in group activities and processes.

What is the most accurate way to frame the study of gender? Do males and females differ in more ways than they are similar? Are the gender differences small or large in magnitude? Hyde reviews current scientific research, include meta-analyses, and builds an argument that favors a gender similarities approach. The exceptions to the pattern of gender similarities, she notes, are few, but include sexuality and aggression. Hyde also argues for viewing gender as a social-stimulus variable in addition to its more common use as an individual-difference or person variable. As she defines directions for future research based on a gender similarities hypothesis, Hyde reviews sociocultural influences on gender and lessons gleaned from neuroscience.

Children's Social and Moral Reasoning About Exclusion

Melanie Killen[1]
University of Maryland

Abstract

Developmental research on social and moral reasoning about exclusion has utilized a social-domain theory, in contrast to a global stage theory, to investigate children's evaluations of gender- and race-based peer exclusion. The social-domain model postulates that moral, social-conventional, and personal reasoning coexist in children's evaluations of inclusion and exclusion, and that the priority given to these forms of judgments varies by the age of the child, the context, and the target of exclusion. Findings from developmental intergroup research studies disconfirm a general-stage-model approach to morality in the child, and provide empirical data on the developmental origins and emergence of intergroup attitudes regarding prejudice, bias, and exclusion.

Keywords

social reasoning; exclusion; intergroup attitudes; moral judgment

How early do individuals become capable of moral reasoning? What is the evidence for morality in the child? Over the past two decades, research on children's moral judgment has changed dramatically, providing new theories and methods for analysis. In brief, the change has been away from a global stage model toward domain-specific models of development. According to Kohlberg's foundational stage model of moral development (Kohlberg, 1984), which followed Piaget's research on moral judgment (Piaget, 1932), children justify acts as right or wrong first on the basis of consequences to the self (preconventional), then in terms of group norms (conventional), and finally in terms of a justice perspective in which individual principles of how to treat one another are understood (postconventional). This approach involved assessing an individual's general scheme (organizing principle) for evaluating social problems and dilemmas across a range of contexts.

By the mid-1980s, however, studies of contextual variation in judgments provided extensive evidence contesting broad stages (Smetana, 2006; Turiel, 1998). For example, young children's evaluations of transgressions and social events reflect considerations of the self, the group, and justice; these considerations do not emerge hierarchically (respectively) but simultaneously in development, each with its own separate developmental trajectory (e.g., self-knowledge, group knowledge, and moral knowledge). Thus, multiple forms of reasoning are applied to the evaluations of social dilemmas and interactions. Social judgments do not reflect one broad template or stage, such as Kohlberg's preconventional stage to characterize childhood morality. Instead, children use different forms of reasoning, moral, conventional, and psychological, simultaneously when evaluating transgressions and social events.

One area of recent empirical inquiry pertains to social and moral evaluations of decisions to exclude others, particularly on the basis of group membership (such as gender, race, or ethnicity), referred to as *intergroup exclusion*. What makes this form of exclusion a particularly compelling topic for investigation from a moral viewpoint is that it reflects, on the one hand, prejudice, discrimination, stereotyping, and bias about groups, and, on the other hand, judgments about fairness, equality, and rights (Killen, Lee-Kim, McGlothlin, & Stangor, 2002). Conceptually, these judgments are diametrically opposed; prejudice violates moral principles of fairness, discrimination violates equality, and stereotyping restricts individual rights. Do both forms of reasoning exist within the child? What do children do when confronted with an exclusion decision that involves moral considerations of fairness and equal treatment, on the one hand, and stereotypic and social-conventional expectations, on the other?

A social-domain model proposes that morality includes fairness, justice, rights, and others' welfare (e.g., when a victim is involved; "It wouldn't be fair to exclude him from the game"); social-conventional concerns involve conventions, etiquette, and customs that promote effective group functioning (e.g., when disorder in the group occurs; "If you let someone new in the group they won't know how it works or what it's about and it will be disruptive"); and psychological issues pertain to autonomy, individual prerogatives, and identity (e.g., acts that are not regulated but affect only the self; "It's her decision who she wants to be friends with"). Social-domain-theory approaches to moral reasoning, along with social-psychological theories about intergroup attitudes, provide a new approach to understanding social exclusion.

Social exclusion is a pervasive aspect of social life, ranging from everyday events (e.g., exclusion from birthday parties, sports teams, social organizations) to large-scale social tragedies (e.g., exclusion based on religion and ethnicity resulting in genocide). These forms of interindividual and intergroup exclusion create conflict, tension, and, in extreme cases, chronic suffering. In the child's world, exclusion has been studied most often in the context of interindividual, rather than intergroup, conflict. Research on peer rejection and victimization, for example, has focused on individual differences and the social deficits that contribute to being a bully (lack of social competence) or a victim (wariness, shyness, fearfulness; Rubin, Bukowski, & Parker, 1998). The findings indicate that the long-term consequences for children and adults who experience pervasive exclusion are negative, resulting in depression, anxiety, and loneliness.

DEVELOPMENTAL APPROACHES

Recently, developmental researchers have investigated children's evaluations of intergroup exclusion (e.g., "You're an X and we don't want Xs in our group"). Decisions to exclude others involve a range of reasons, from group norms and stereotypic expectations to moral assessments about the fairness of exclusion. Much of what is known about group norms has been documented by social psychologists, who have conducted extensive studies on intergroup relationships. The findings indicate that social categorization frequently leads to intergroup bias and that explicit and implicit attitudes about others based on group membership contribute to prejudicial and discriminatory attitudes and behavior (Dovidio, Glick, & Rudman, 2005). Few researchers, however, have examined the developmental trajectory of exclusion from a moral-reasoning perspective.

Social-domain theory has provided a taxonomy for examining the forms of reasoning—moral, social-conventional, and psychological—that are brought to bear on intergroup exclusion decisions. One way that a social-domain model differs from the traditional stage model of moral reasoning, as formulated by Kohlberg in the late 1960s, is that the former provides a theory and a methodology for examining how individuals use different forms of reasons when evaluating everyday phenomena.

SOCIAL REASONING ABOUT EXCLUSION

One of the goals of social-domain research is to identify the conditions under which children give priority to different forms of reasons when evaluating social decisions, events, and interactions. What are the major empirical findings on intergroup exclusion decisions by children? Most centrally, children do not use one scheme ("stage") to evaluate all morally relevant intergroup problems and scenarios; moreover, although some types of decisions are age related, others are not. In a study with children in the 1st, 4th, and 7th grades, the vast majority of students (95%) judged it wrong to exclude a peer from a group solely because of gender or race (e.g., a ballet club excludes a boy because he's a boy; a baseball club excludes a girl because she's a girl), and based their judgment on moral reasons, such as that such exclusion would be unfair and discriminatory (Killen & Stangor, 2001); there were no age-related differences, contrary to what a stage-model approach would predict.

Introducing complexity, however, revealed variation in judgments and justifications. As shown in Figure 1, in an equal-qualifications condition ("What if there was only room for one more to join the club, and a girl and a boy both were equally qualified, who should the group pick?"), most children used moral reasons ("You should pick the person who doesn't usually get a chance to be in the club because they're both equally good at it"); but in an unequal-qualification condition ("What if X was more qualified, who should the group pick?"), age-related increases in the use of social-conventional reasons ("The group won't work well if you pick the person who is not very good at it") were found. Young adolescents weighed individual merits and considered the functioning of the club or team. Qualifications (e.g., good at ballet or baseball) were considered to be more salient considerations than preserving the "equal opportunity" dimensions (e.g., picking a girl for baseball who has not had a chance to play).

In fact, how children interpret their group's ingroup and outgroup norms (conventions) appears to be related to prejudice and bias (moral transgressions; Abrams, Rutland, Cameron, & Ferrell, in press). Abrams et al. (in press) showed that children's view of whether exclusion is legitimate or wrong was contingent on whether they viewed an individual as supporting or rejecting an ingroup-identity norm. In other related developmental intergroup research, children's lay theories (conventional knowledge) about what it means to work in a group, and whether effort or intrinsic ability is what counts, have been shown to be significantly

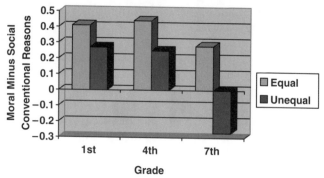

Fig. 1. Proportion of moral minus social-conventional reasons given by 1st, 4th, and 7th graders for peer-exclusion judgments based on gender or race. In one condition (equal), participants stated which of two children should be excluded from an after-school club with only one available opening when a stereotypical and nonstereotypical applicant both were equally qualified. In the other (unequal) condition, participants stated which child should be excluded if the child who fit the stereotype for that activity was also more qualified. After-school clubs were baseball/ballet and basketball/math, reflecting gender- and race-associated stereotypes, respectively. Reprinted from Killen & Stangor (2001).

related to whether they view the denial of allocation of resources as fair or unfair (moral decision making); focusing on intrinsic ability in contrast to effort results in condoning prejudicial treatment (Levy, Chiu, & Hong, 2006). Moreover, adolescents' perceptions of the social status of membership in peer cliques (conventional knowledge) determine whether they view exclusion (e.g., excluding a "goth" from the cheerleading squad) as fair or legitimate (Horn, 2003). These findings demonstrate the nuanced ways in which children make judgments about groups and how group knowledge and group norms bear directly on moral judgments about exclusion and inclusion.

Research on intergroup contact in childhood provides information regarding how social experience influences the manifestation of children's stereotypes and conventional reasoning to justify exclusion. Intergroup-contact theory states that under certain conditions, contact with members of outgroups decreases prejudice (Pettigrew & Tropp, 2005). In a developmental study with participants enrolled in 13 public schools ($N = 685$) of varying ethnic diversity (see Fig. 2), European American students enrolled in heterogeneous schools were more likely to use explicit stereotypes to explain why interracial interactions make their peers uncomfortable, and were less likely to use moral reasons to evaluate peer exclusion, than were European Americans enrolled in homogeneous schools (Killen, Richardson, Kelly, Crystal, & Ruck, 2006). Children's positive experiences with students who are different from themselves, under certain conditions, facilitate moral reasoning about intergroup exclusion and suppress stereotypic expectations as a reason for an exclusion decision.

These findings support a domain-model view of social and moral judgment and challenge stage theory, which proposes that children are limited in their ability to make moral judgments by a general-processing scheme for assimilating information (their "stage"). From a stage view, one would expect children to use

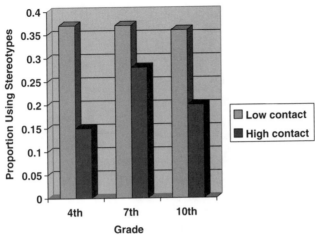

Fig. 2. Proportion of European American students who explicitly used stereotypes to explain what it is about interracial interactions that makes their peers uncomfortable, as a function of positive intergroup contact. Positive intergroup contact included cross-race friendship in classrooms, schools, and neighborhoods (based on data reported in Killen et al., 2006).

conventional or stereotypic (group-expectations) reasons, and expect older children to use moral reasons. Instead, researchers now find that children's reasoning varies by the context and a balance of priorities.

Context has many variables, and determining it involves investigating the role of the target of exclusion as well as participant variables (age, gender, race/ethnicity) on exclusion decisions. Regarding the target of exclusion, a series of findings reveals that gender exclusion is viewed as more legitimate than exclusion based on ethnicity, with more social-conventional reasons and stereotypic expectations used to support the former than the latter (Killen et al., 2002). As shown in Figure 3, children used fewer moral reasons to evaluate exclusion in a peer-group music context with a gender target ("What if the boys' music club will not let a girl join?") than with a race target ("What if the white students in a music club will not let a black student join?"). A significant proportion of students used social-conventional reasons, such as: "A girl/black student likes different music, so she/he won't fit in with the group." Not surprisingly, though, European American females, and minority participants (both males and females), were more likely to reject these forms of exclusion and to use moral reasons than were European American males. This inclusive orientation may be due to the perspective, empathy, and reciprocity that result from experiencing prior exclusion. Thus, these findings support social-domain-theory propositions that the target of exclusion is influential on evaluations of exclusion, and that specific types of peer experiences may contribute to judgments that exclusion is wrong.

Children reject atypical peers based on stigmatized group identity (Nesdale & Brown, 2004). This finding further indicates that peer experience with exclusion is an important variable for investigation. Nesdale and Brown propose that children who experience extensive exclusion may be at risk for demonstrating prejudicial

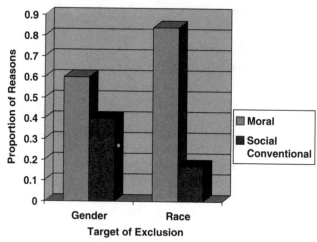

Fig. 3. Proportion of moral and social-conventional reasons for gender and racial targets of exclusion in peer-group contexts. Peer-group contexts referred to after-school music clubs that excluded a target child from joining the club due to his or her gender or race. Reasons were moral (unfairness) or social-conventional (group functioning; based on data from Killen, Lee-Kim, McGlothlin, & Stangor, 2002).

behavior toward others, and for perpetuating a cycle of negative intergroup attitudes. At the same time, however, adolescents are cognizant of the wrongfulness of discrimination regarding stigmatized peers (Verkuyten & Thijs, 2002).

Although stereotypes and conventions are powerful forces that legitimize exclusion, there is also extensive evidence of how adolescents explain the wrongfulness of discrimination in terms of social justice. Social-reasoning categories provide evidence for the types of norms that children use to justify or reject exclusion decisions and for the conditions that promote children's change from a priority on morality to group functioning, which may, at times, occur at the expense of fairness.

NEW DIRECTIONS

Adults frequently use traditions and customs to justify exclusion. Tiger Woods' initial response to playing at the Augusta (Georgia) National Golf Club (host of the legendary Masters Tournament), which excludes women, was "That's just the way it is" (Brown, 2002)—categorized as social-conventional reasoning. More recently, Woods has stated, "Is it unfair? Yes. Do I want to see a female member? Yes" ("Woods Thinks Masters Debate Deserves a Private Meeting," 2005)—categorized as moral reasoning. Yet, he refuses to give up his participation in the event: "They're asking me to give up an opportunity to win the Masters three straight years" (Smith, 2003)—personal priority over the wrongfulness of exclusion. These quotes, which do not reflect coded responses from an in-depth systematic interview, nonetheless, reveal how an individual can give different priorities to exclusion decisions and how these priorities change depending on the context (Killen, Sinno, & Margie, in press). Social-conventional or personal reasons do not necessarily reflect a developmentally "primitive" response (as put forth by stage theory).

Are children moral? Yes, children demonstrate spontaneous and elaborated reasons for why it is wrong to exclude others based on group membership, referring to fairness, equality, and rights. Do children have stereotypes about others? Yes; how these stereotypes enter into moral decision making requires an in-depth analysis of how children weigh competing considerations, such as group functioning, traditions, customs, and cultural norms, when evaluating exclusion. What changes as children age is how these considerations are weighed, the contexts that become salient for children and adolescents, and the ability to determine when morality should take priority in a given situation.

What is not well known is how children's intergroup biases (those that are not explicit) influence their judgments about exclusion; what it is about intergroup contact that contributes to children's variation in reliance on stereotypes to evaluate exclusion; and how early intergroup attitudes influence children's awareness of justice, fairness, and equality. Given that stereotypes are very hard to change in adulthood, interventions need to be conducted in childhood. Understanding when children resort to stereotypic expectations is crucial information for creating effective interventions. Developmental findings on social reasoning about exclusion provide a new approach for addressing these complex issues in childhood and adulthood and for creating programs to reduce prejudice.

Recommended Reading

Aboud, F.E., & Amato, M. (2001). Developmental and socialization influences on intergroup bias. In R. Brown & S. Gaertner (Eds.), *Blackwell handbook of social psychology: Intergroup relations* (pp. 65–85). Oxford, England: Blackwell.

Gaertner, S.L., & Dovidio, J.F. (2000). *Reducing intergroup bias: The common ingroup identity model.* New York: Psychology Press.

Killen, M., Margie, N.G., & Sinno, S. (2006). Morality in the context of intergroup relationships. In M. Killen & J. Smetana (Eds.), *Handbook of moral development* (pp. 155–183). Mahwah, NJ: LEA.

Rutland, A. (2004). The development and self-regulation of intergroup attitudes in children. In M. Bennett & F. Sani (Eds.), *The development of the social self* (pp. 247–265). East Sussex, England: Psychology Press.

Turiel, E. (2002). *Culture and morality.* Cambridge, England: Cambridge University Press.

Acknowledgments—The author would like to thank Judith G. Smetana, Stefanie Sinno, and Cameron Richardson, for helpful comments on earlier drafts of this manuscript, and the graduate students in the Social and Moral Development Laboratory for collaborative and insightful contributions to the research reported in this paper. The research described in this manuscript was supported, in part, by Grants from the National Institute of Child Health and Human Development (1R01HD04121-01) and the National Science Foundation (#BCS0346717).

Note

1. Address correspondence to Melanie Killen, 3304 Benjamin Building, Department of Human Development, University of Maryland, College Park, MD 20742-1131; e-mail: mkillen@umd.edu.

References

Abrams, D., Rutland, A., Cameron, L., & Ferrell, A. (in press). Older but wilier: Ingroup accountability and the development of subjective group dynamics. *Developmental Psychology.*

Brown, J. (2002, August 16). Should Woods carry the black man's burden? *The Christian Science Monitor* [electronic version]. Retrieved January 5, 2007, from http://www.csmonitor.com/2002/0816/p01s01-ussc.html

Dovidio, J.F., Glick, P., & Rudman, L. (Eds.). (2005). *Reflecting on the nature of prejudice: Fifty years after Allport.* Malden, MA: Blackwell.

Horn, S. (2003). Adolescents' reasoning about exclusion from social groups. *Developmental Psychology, 39,* 11–84.

Killen, M., Lee-Kim, J., McGlothlin, H., & Stangor, C. (2002). How children and adolescents evaluate gender and racial exclusion. *Monographs for the Society for Research in Child Development* (Serial No. 271, Vol. 67, No. 4). Oxford, England: Blackwell.

Killen, M., Richardson, C., Kelly, M.C., Crystal, D., & Ruck, M. (2006, May). *European-American students' evaluations of interracial social exchanges in relation to the ethnic diversity of school environments.* Paper presented at the annual convention of the Association for Psychological Science, New York City.

Killen, M., Sinno, S., & Margie, N. (in press). Children's experiences and judgments about group exclusion and inclusion. In R. Kail (Ed.), *Advances in child psychology.* New York: Elsevier.

Killen, M., & Stangor, C. (2001). Children's social reasoning about inclusion and exclusion in gender and race peer group contexts. *Child Development, 72,* 174–186.

Kohlberg, L. (1984). *Essays on moral development: Vol. 2. The psychology of moral development—The nature and validity of moral stages.* San Francisco: Harper & Row.

Levy, S.R., Chiu, C.Y., & Hong, Y.Y. (2006). Lay theories and intergroup relations. *Group Processes and Intergroup Relations, 9,* 5–24.

Nesdale, D., & Brown, K. (2004). Children's attitudes towards an atypical member of an ethnic ingroup. *International Journal of Behavioral Development, 28,* 328–335.

Pettigrew, T.F., & Tropp, L.R. (2005). Allport's intergroup contact hypothesis: Its history and influence. In J.F. Dovidio, P. Glick, & L. Rudman (Eds.), *Reflecting on the nature of prejudice: Fifty years after Allport* (pp. 262–277). Malden, MA: Blackwell.

Piaget, J. (1932). *The moral judgment of the child.* New York: Free Press.

Rubin, K.H., Bukowski, W., & Parker, J. (1998). Peer interactions, relationships and groups. In W. Damon (Ed.), *Handbook of child psychology: Vol. 3. Social, emotional, and personality development* (5th ed., pp. 619–700). New York: Wiley.

Smetana, J.G. (2006). Social domain theory: Consistencies and variations in children's moral and social judgments. In M. Killen & J.G. Smetana (Eds.), *Handbook of moral development* (pp. 119–154). Mahwah, NJ: Erlbaum.

Smith, T. (2003, February 20). A Master's challenge. *Online NewsHour.* Retrieved July 16, 2006, from http://www.pbs.org/newshour/bb/sports/jan-june03/golf_2-20.html

Turiel, E. (1998). The development of morality. In W. Damon (Ed.), *Handbook of child psychology: Vol. 3. Social, emotional, and personality development* (5th ed., pp. 863–932). New York: Wiley.

Verkuyten, M., & Thijs, J. (2002). Racist victimization among children in the Netherlands: The effect of ethnic group and school. *Ethnic and Racial Studies, 25,* 310–331.

Woods thinks Masters debate deserves a private meeting. (2005, February 14). *USA Today* [electronic version]. Retrieved January 10, 2007, from http://www.usatoday.com/sports/golf/2002-10-16-woods-masters_x.htm

This article has been reprinted as it originally appeared in *Current Directions in Psychological Science*. Citation information for this article as originally published appears above.

Saying What You Don't Mean: Social Influences on Sarcastic Language Processing

Albert N. Katz[1]
University of Western Ontario, London, Ontario, Canada

Dawn G. Blasko and Victoria A. Kazmerski
Pennsylvania State University at Erie

Abstract

In recent years, an increasingly large body of research has examined the common situation in which one thing is said in order to express another. Although research has examined the understanding of figurative language such as metaphor in some depth, sarcasm has been less studied. Understanding sarcasm requires considering social and cultural factors, which are often ignored in models of language. We report diverse experiments that point to the same conclusions: Sarcastic interpretation occurs early in processing, with gender and social-cultural factors associated with class playing an important role. These data support interactive models of nonliteral language processing, in which social and cultural factors serve as early-acting constraints on interpretation.

Keywords

figurative language; sarcasm; social-cultural factors; ERPs

Consider a statement such as "all men are animals." The intent and meaning of this simple statement is quite different if its author is a professor teaching logic, a biologist speaking on human evolution, or a woman, being sarcastic, telling her friend about her passive and boring boyfriend. But in the latter case, how would the listener recover the sarcastic intent from any of the plausible alternatives?

Although computational models of language processing have begun to address the basic question of how a language comprehender can understand the nonliteral sense of a statement, they have yet to be extended to the processing of sarcasm, nor have they acknowledged the important role of social factors in language comprehension. We argue here that in order to fully understand the processes of language processing, it is critical to consider the nature of the person who makes a statement, the nature of the person who receives it, and the context in which this social interaction occurs.

SARCASM AND ITS RELATION TO OTHER FORMS OF NONLITERAL LANGUAGE

Although figurative usage is ubiquitous in natural language, most theories focus only on literal language. In recent years, cognitive scientists have begun to focus on metaphor, simile, and idioms, but there has been much less work on sarcasm and irony. This neglect is unfortunate because, relative to metaphor and idioms, sarcasm is especially dependent on both the discourse and the social contexts in which it is embedded. Irony is typically understood as conveying the opposite meaning from that expressed. Sarcasm, a variant of irony, has a caustic element in its usage and is, unlike irony in general, directed at a specific victim (Lee & Katz, 1998). Indeed, Winner (1988) made the developmental claim that whereas understanding of metaphor is usually present by about age 4, a child's understanding of irony is not manifested until a few years later because irony, unlike metaphor, cannot be understood from the words alone, but depends on an understanding of social factors that does not develop until later in life.

There is a long but nonexperimental tradition that makes the human actor and the social context central to the act of irony in general, and to sarcastic irony specifically. About 2000 years ago, Quintilian (trans. 1920) wrote that "[irony] is made evident to the understanding either by the delivery, the character of the speaker, or the nature of the subject. For if any one of these three is out of keeping with the words, it at once becomes clear that the intention of the speaker is other than what he actually says" (p. 333). Or, as Hutcheon (1994) put it,

> It seems to me that it is precisely the mutual contexts that an existing community creates that set the scene for the very use and comprehension of irony. . . . I want to define these "discursive communities" in general by the complex configuration of shared knowledge, beliefs, values, and communicative strategies. (p. 91)

Although there has been some examination of these communities in the sociolinguistic tradition, these studies have been largely naturalistic observations regarding the frequency, type, or perceived function of language use in different communities.

In contrast, we present here experimental approaches to the study of sarcasm. The studies described typically used short passages ("textoids") describing the interactions of two or more people in a common social situation, such as moving to a new house or going to the beach. In each passage, one character makes an everyday statement, such as "You are sure a good friend." We have gained insight into how sarcasm is understood by comparing reactions to these statements when they are produced under different conditions that make them more or less likely to be understood as literally true. For example, we have varied factors such as the context preceding the critical statement, the nature of the person making the statement (for instance, designating the speaker as John or Jane), and the nature of the person to whom the statement is directed.

USING AND UNDERSTANDING SARCASM

Figurative language plays an important role in conveying emotion and modulating emotional intensity (Gibbs, Leggitt, & Turner, 2002). The emotional effects can be different for the speaker and the listener, and a sarcastic comment is seen as more caustic and less funny by the victim than by the speaker. In reading tasks, people perceive characters who use a statement sarcastically as more verbally aggressive, and yet more humorous, than characters who use the same statement literally (Toplak & Katz, 2000). A sarcastic message is also perceived as more insincere, impolite, noninstructional, and ambiguous than a literal statement.

The classic theoretical position holds that sarcastic language (and other forms of nonliteral language) is processed by obligatory processes during the initial stages of language comprehension, and that contextual and pragmatic effects come into play only later. For instance, Searle (1979) claimed that one must initially process the literal sense of a trope and only when that fails, find a plausible (and nonliteral) interpretation. These classic models suggest that nonliteral language processing should be optional if a literal interpretation is possible and that nonliteral understanding should take more time than literal understanding, because additional processing is needed. In contrast, several more recent models suggest that, with appropriate contextual support, the nonliteral (sarcastic) meaning of a statement is made available as rapidly as the literal sense and that accessing the nonliteral interpretation is not dependent on a failure to achieve a plausible literal interpretation. Both classes of models have been asocial inasmuch as social factors, such as the nature of the speaker or audience, have not been considered. Moreover, both classes of models have lumped sarcasm in with other forms of nonliteral language.

The majority of psychological studies of language comprehension have employed off-line procedures. In comparison with on-line studies, in which investigators attempt to assess language during comprehension, off-line studies involve inferring what occurs in the mind during comprehension by analyzing readers' interpretations or ratings of an utterance some time after they first encounter it. Such off-line studies have identified some of the social and cultural factors important in producing a sarcastic reading. For example, the effect of a verbal barb is perceived differently depending on the closeness and social status of the speaker and listener. Participants are particularly likely to remember statements that are incongruous with social status, such as when a low-status person talks in an impolite manner to a high-status person. Moreover, perception of a statement as being ironic varies as a function of audience privilege; an interpretation of irony is especially salient when the listener not only perceived a speaker to be making an incongruent statement (perceived the speaker as rejecting its truth value), but also recognizes that someone else in the conversation (the non-privileged listener) was unaware that the speaker was not, in fact, endorsing the position he or she just espoused.

In addition to contextual constraints engendered by the degree of relatedness and shared knowledge of the participants in a conversation, there are contextual constraints engendered by social stereotypes, such as those associated with gender or socioeconomic class. For instance, in everyday usage, males make sarcastic remarks almost twice as often as do females. Consequently, when the gender of the speaker is manipulated in a textoid, the same comment is rated as more sarcastic when made by a male than when made by a female.

One marker of social class, occupation, has been shown to serve as a contextual marker of ironic and sarcastic language. Members of certain occupations (e.g., clergy and teachers) are perceived stereotypically as likely to use metaphor, whereas members of other occupations (e.g., comedians and factory workers) are perceived as more likely to use irony. Statements such as "that child is a precious gem" are seen as being more sarcastic when made by speakers in high-irony occupations than when made by speakers in high-metaphor occupations (and are also more likely to be recalled correctly). The effect of the speaker's occupation on creating a sarcastic reading depends on the discourse context and the salience of the statement itself, indicating that multiple sources of information are weighed conjointly when a listener attempts to understand the possibly sarcastic intent behind a given statement.

When participants are asked to read textoids one word at a time, we find evidence for the emergence of sarcasm at a very early stage of processing—by the last word of a target, potentially sarcastic, statement. This effect is produced by having a character in the textoid make a statement incongruent with events unfolding in the story. We have now demonstrated that the information that this statement is made by a comedian (rather than a priest, for instance) further predisposes people to a sarcastic interpretation while they read it. The evidence is based on a convergence of reading-time data with ratings of the subjective sense produced by reading the text. With respect to reading time, we find that when the discourse context is congruent with a sarcastic interpretation, the target sentence is read more rapidly if it is made by a person from a high-irony occupation rather than a person from a low-irony occupation; in addition, if the statement is made by a person from a high-irony occupation, there is no slowdown in reading the first words of the next sentence in the textoid, indicating that the target statement's meaning is integrated very shortly after the statement is read. However, when there is an incongruity created by having a high-irony speaker make a comment in a context that invites a nonsarcastic interpretation, this incongruity is noted by the beginning of the next sentence, as evidenced by a spike in reading times. In addition, we find that ratings of the degree to which the statement seems sarcastic are correlated reliably with differences in how long it takes to read the last word of the target sentence. Thus, a sense of sarcasm, which is associated with the time taken to read the potentially sarcastic sentence, is present by the last word of the sentence.

There is also emerging data suggesting on-line influences of the speaker's gender: Participants are slower reading the last words of a sarcastic statement when it is made by a female character than when it is made by a male character, an effect that is particularly marked when the comment is directed at a female. Because sarcasm is more likely to be associated with males than females, comprehension of noncanonical usage is delayed as people attempt to integrate the text they are reading with their stored "knowledge" (stereotypes) of men and women.

These results have implications for theoretical models of language comprehension. Models that posit obligatory processing of the literal or expressed sense of statements predict that evidence for the processing of sarcasm should not, on average, occur until some time after a critical statement is encountered. More interactive, context-driven models predict that the evidence for processing of sarcasm should occur very early, during the initial processing of the critical statement. Our evidence favors the latter class of theories and indicates that context involves stored social-cultural stereotypes, such as those relating to gender and class.

We have recently begun investigating these same theoretical questions with event-related potentials (ERPs), which are electrical recordings of the ongoing electrical activity of the brain that are directly linked in time to the onset of the presentation of a specific stimulus or event. ERPs provide a true on-line measure of the brain's processing of specific information and are recorded with millisecond accuracy. ERP waveforms have series of positive and negative peaks, relative to a baseline, that are correlated with sensory, motor, and cognitive processes. Although often used to study literal language processing, ERPs have seldom been employed for the study of non-literal language processing. We have shown that ERPs are a sensitive means of identifying individual differences in automatic activation of metaphorical meaning (Kazmerski, Blasko, & Dessalegn, 2003) and have now expanded this methodology to the examination of how sarcasm is comprehended.

Our first goal was to examine whether the ERPs in response to a given statement (e.g., "Bob, you're a really good driver") would differ depending on whether the preceding context biased toward a literal or sarcastic interpretation. Figure 1 shows the ERPs, from a central scalp site, evoked by the final word of a critical utterance. The ERPs for the sarcastic context, compared with those for the literal context, showed a greater negativity beginning at 500 ms and peaking at 650 ms, followed by a larger positivity at 900 ms (P900). Figure 2 shows activation across all 64 scalp sites at 650 and 900 ms after the initial presentation of the final word of a critical utterance. It is clear that the difference between the conditions is broadly distributed across the scalp.

A negative peak at 400 ms (N400) is often associated with sentence-level semantic integration. The greater negativity for our sarcastic than for our literal stimuli may reflect a greater difficulty in integrating the critical utterance with the ongoing mental representation of the discourse; that is, this integration process may be more resource intensive for the sarcastic than for the literal condition. Alternatively, we know that ERP amplitude has been correlated with emotional intensity (Carretie, Mercado, Tapia, & Hinojosa, 2001), and so the difference between the two sentence types may reflect greater emotional processing associated with sarcastic than literal sentences. Finally, the late P900 we found is

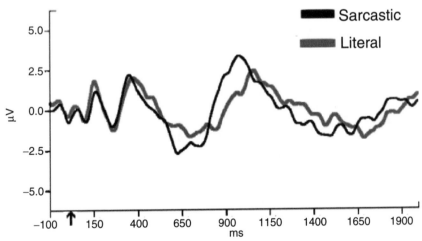

Fig. 1. Event-related potentials (ERPs) evoked by the last word of a key statement, in both literal and sarcastic contexts. These tracings show activity at a central parietal scalp site, Pz. Onset of the last word is indicated by an arrow.

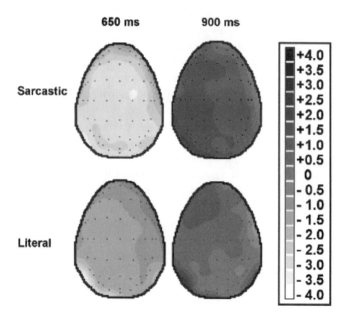

650 ms   **900 ms**

Sarcastic

Literal

+4.0
+3.5
+3.0
+2.5
+2.0
+1.5
+1.0
+0.5
0
- 0.5
- 1.0
- 1.5
- 2.0
- 2.5
- 3.0
- 3.5
- 4.0

Fig. 2. Scalp distribution of the mean amplitude of event-related potentials (ERPs) 650 and 900 ms after presentation of the last word of a key statement. ERPs were recorded in both sarcastic (top) and literal (bottom) contexts.

somewhat novel but may be related to the processing of humor (Coulson, 2001). Recall that humor is highly associated with the use of sarcasm and, indeed, in an earlier study, we found that people rated our sarcastic passages as more humorous than the literal passages.

CONCLUSIONS

The data presented here support the following conclusions. First, the nature of the person who makes a statement and the context in which he or she makes it play a role in influencing whether the statement is interpreted as sarcastic. The fact that social and cultural factors influence the processing of sarcasm opens the door for a wide range of studies identifying processing similarities and differences cross-culturally. Such studies might compare sarcasm with other forms of verbal aggression, such as ridicule, or with other forms of nonliteral language. Second, it is the combination of social, cultural, and other factors that determines the likelihood that a statement is interpreted as sarcastic. Gender, occupation, familiarity of the statement, and whether the discourse invites a literal, metaphoric, or sarcastic reading of the statement have all been shown to play a role in producing a sense of sarcasm. In principle, other factors, such as whether there is a victim targeted in the statement, may also prove to be effective. Third, there are implications for the roles of humor and emotion in the ERP data that must be pursued. Finally, the on-line data indicate that at least some of these sources of information come into play very early in the comprehension process, and this time course is inconsistent with the theoretical models positing initial obligatory processing of the literal sense of the expressed meaning. The reading-time data indicate effects that occur by the time the last word of a statement is read, though we have reason to believe that a more sensitive methodology may isolate processing differences between literal and nonliteral readings even earlier. The ERP data may provide clues to when these differences emerge. By analyzing the ERPs occurring prior to the last word of key sentences, we may be able to discover the exact point in the sentences where the brain responses begin to diverge.

How can we integrate the early processing of sarcasm with the fact that a number of factors interactively influence the likelihood that a statement will be perceived as sarcastic? We propose that a constraint-satisfaction approach is a viable option to pursue. In this type of model, different sources of information (i.e., constraints) provide immediate probabilistic support for competing interpretations (e.g., literal vs. nonliteral or metaphoric vs. ironic interpretations). These constraints operate in parallel over time. In general, the duration of the competition between interpretations (and thus reading time) is itself a function of the strength of the various alternatives; competition is resolved rapidly if the constraints all point to the same interpretation, whereas settling on an interpretation is delayed if support for different alternatives is nearly equal. This type of model can explain many of the seeming contradictions in the literature on nonliteral language processing, such as the fact that some studies have found that literal meaning is assessed more rapidly than nonliteral meaning, whereas other studies have found either that there are no differences in processing or that the nonliteral sense is processed more rapidly. Aspects of the constraint-satisfaction explanation of this discrepancy have been supported experimentally for proverbs, an instance of nonliteral language (Katz & Ferretti, 2003).

For this model to be successful, it must also be linked to neurological evidence. We are only now beginning to explore how sarcasm is processed in the brain. Now that we have validated the use of ERPs as a sensitive tool for investigating the processing of sarcastic language, we are ready to begin using this tool to investigate the many social factors that may influence sarcastic understanding.

Recommended Reading

Colston, H., & Katz, A. (Eds.). (in press). *Figurative language comprehension: Social and cultural influences*. Mahwah, NJ: Erlbaum.

Giora, R. (2003). *On our mind: Salience, context and figurative language*. New York: Oxford University Press.

Kutas, M., Federmeier, K., Coulson, S., King, J., & Munte, T. (2000). Language. In J. Cacioppo, L. Tassinary, & G. Berntson (Eds.), *Handbook of psychophysiology* (2nd ed., pp. 576–601). New York: Cambridge University Press.

Note

1. Address correspondence to Albert Katz, Psychology Department, University of Western Ontario, London, Ontario, Canada N6A 5C2; e-mail: katz@uwo.ca.

References

Carretie, L., Mercado, F., Tapia, M., & Hinojosa, J. (2001). Emotion, attention and the "negativity bias", studied through event-related potentials. *International Journal of Psychophysiology, 41*, 75–85.

Coulson, S. (2001). *Semantic leaps*. New York: Cambridge University Press.

Gibbs, R., Jr., Leggitt, J., & Turner, E. (2002). What's special about figurative language in emotional communication? In S.R. Fussell (Ed.), *The verbal communication of emotions* (pp. 125–149). Mahwah, NJ: Erlbaum.

Hutcheon, L. (1994). *Irony's edge: The theory and politics of irony*. London: Routledge.

Katz, A., & Ferretti, T. (2003). Reading proverbs in context: The role of explicit markers. *Discourse Processes, 36*, 19–46.

Kazmerski, V., Blasko, D., & Dessalegn, B. (2003). ERP and behavioral evidence of individual differences in metaphor comprehension. *Memory & Cognition, 31*, 673–689.

Lee, C., & Katz, A. (1998). The differential role of ridicule in sarcasm and irony. *Metaphor and Symbol, 13*, 1–15.

Quintilian. (1920). *The Institutio Oratoria of Quintilian, Vol. 3* (H.E. Butler, Trans.). London: William Heinemann.

Searle, J. (1979). Metaphor. In A. Ortony (Ed.), *Metaphor and thought* (pp. 92–123). New York: Cambridge University Press.

Toplak, M., & Katz, A. (2000). On the uses of sarcastic irony. *Journal of Pragmatics, 32*, 1467–1488.

Winner, E. (1988). *The point of words: Children's understanding of metaphor and irony*. Cambridge, MA: Harvard University Press.

Gender and Group Process:
A Developmental Perspective

Eleanor E. Maccoby[1]
*Department of Psychology, Stanford University,
Stanford, California*

Abstract

Until recently, the study of gender development has focused mainly on sex typing as an attribute of the individual. Although this perspective continues to be enlightening, recent work has focused increasingly on children's tendency to congregate in same-sex groups. This self-segregation of the two sexes implies that much of childhood gender enactment occurs in the context of same-sex dyads or larger groups. There are emergent properties of such groups, so that certain sex-distinctive qualities occur at the level of the group rather than at the level of the individual. There is increasing research interest in the distinctive nature of the group structures, activities, and interactions that typify all-male as compared with all-female groups, and in the socialization that occurs within these groups. Next steps in research will surely call for the integration of the individual and group perspectives.

Keywords

sex; gender; groups; socialization

Among researchers who study the psychology of gender, a central viewpoint has always been that individuals progressively acquire a set of behaviors, interests, personality traits, and cognitive biases that are more typical of their own sex than of the other sex. And the individual's sense of being either a male or a female person (*gender identity*) is thought to be a core element in the developing sense of self. The acquisition of these sex-distinctive characteristics has been called *sex typing*, and much research has focused on how and why the processes of sex typing occur. A favorite strategy has been to examine differences among individuals in how sex typed they are at a given age, searching for factors associated with a person's becoming more or less "masculine" or more or less "feminine" than other individuals. In early work, there was a heavy emphasis on the family as the major context in which sex typing was believed to take place. Socialization pressures from parents were thought to shape the child toward "sex-appropriate" behaviors, personality, and interests and a firm gender identity.

On the whole, the efforts to understand gender development by studying individual differences in rate or degree of sex typing, and the connections of these differences to presumed antecedent factors, have not been very successful. The various manifestations of sex typing in childhood—toy and activity preferences, knowledge of gender stereotypes, personality traits—do not cohere together to form a cluster that clearly represents a degree of sex typing in a given child. And whether or not a given child behaves in a gender-typical way seems to vary greatly from one situation to another, depending on the social context and other conditions that make an individual's gender salient at a given moment. Only weak and inconsistent connections have been found between within-family socialization practices and children's sex-typed behavior (Ruble & Martin, 1998). And so far, the study of individual variations in sex typing has not helped us to understand the most robust manifestation of gender during childhood: namely, children's strong tendency to segregate themselves into same-sex social groups. Although work on gender development in individual children continues and shows renewed vigor, a relatively new direction of interest is in children's groups. This current research and theorizing considers how gender is implicated in the formation, interaction processes, and socialization functions of childhood social groupings.

In some of this work, the dyad or larger group, rather than the individual child, is taken as the unit of analysis. Through the history of theoretical writings by sociologists and social psychologists, there have been claims that groups have emergent properties, and that their functioning cannot be understood in terms of the characteristics of their individual members (Levine & Moreland, 1998). Accumulating evidence from recent work suggests that in certain gender configurations, pairs or groups of children elicit certain behaviors from each other that are not characteristic of either of the participants when alone or in other social contexts (Martin & Fabes, 2001). Another possibility is that the group context amplifies what are only weak tendencies in the individual participants. For example, in their article "It Takes Two to Fight," Coie and his colleagues (1999) found that the probability of a fight occurring depended not only on the aggressive predispositions of the two individual boys involved, but also on the unique properties of the dyad itself. Other phenomena, such as social approach to another child, depend on the sex of the approacher and the approachee taken jointly, not on the sex of either child, when children's sociability is analyzed at the level of the individual (summarized in Maccoby, 1998). It is important, then, to describe and analyze children's dyads or larger groups as such, to see how gender is implicated in their characteristics and functioning.

GENDER COMPOSITION OF CHILDREN'S GROUPS

Beginning at about age 3, children increasingly choose same-sex playmates when in settings where their social groupings are not managed by adults. In preschools, children may play in loose configurations of several children, and reciprocated affiliation between same-sex pairs of children is common while such reciprocation between pairs of opposite sex is rare (Strayer, 1980; Vaughan, Colvin, Azria, Caya, & Krzysik, 2001). On school playgrounds, children sometimes play in mixed-sex groups, but increasingly, as they move from age 4 to about age 12, they spend a large majority of their free play time exclusively with others of their own sex, rarely playing in a mixed-sex dyad or in a larger group in which no other child of their own sex is involved. Best friendships in middle childhood and well into adolescence are very heavily weighted toward same-sex choices. These strong tendencies toward same-sex social preferences are seen in the other cultures around the world where gender composition of children's groups has been studied, and are also found among young nonhuman primates (reviewed in Maccoby, 1998).

GROUP SIZE

Naturally occurring face-to-face groups whose members interact with one another continuously over time tend to be small—typically having only two or three members, and seldom having more than five or six members. Some gender effects on group size can be seen. Both boys and girls commonly form same-sex dyadic friendships, and sometimes triadic ones as well. But from about the age of 5 onward, boys more often associate together in larger clusters. Boys are more often involved in organized group games, and in their groups, occupy more space on school playgrounds. In an experimental situation in which same-sex groups of six children were allowed to utilize play and construction materials in any way they wished, girls tended to split into dyads or triads, whereas boys not only interacted in larger groups but were much more likely to undertake some kind of joint project, and organize and carry out coordinated activities aimed at achieving a group goal (Benenson, Apostolaris, & Parnass, 1997). Of course, children's small groups—whether dyads or clusters of four, five, or six children—are nested within still larger group structures, such as cliques or "crowds."

Group size matters. Recent studies indicate that the interactions in groups of four or more are different from what typically occurs in dyads. In larger groups, there is more conflict and more competition, particularly in all-male groups; in dyads, individuals of both sexes are more responsive to their partners, and a partner's needs and perspectives are more often taken into account than when individuals interact with several others at once (Benenson, Nicholson, Waite, Roy, & Simpson, 2001; Levine & Moreland, 1998). The question of course arises: To what extent are certain "male" characteristics, such as greater competitiveness, a function of the fact that boys typically interact in larger groups than girls do? At present, this question is one of active debate and study. So far, there are indications that group size does indeed mediate sex differences to some degree, but not entirely nor consistently.

INTERACTION IN SAME-SEX GROUPS

From about age 3 to age 8 or 9, when children congregate together in activities not structured by adults, they are mostly engaged in some form of play. Playtime interactions among boys, more often than among girls, involve rough-and-tumble play, competition, conflict, ego displays, risk taking, and striving to achieve or maintain dominance, with occasional (but actually quite rare) displays of direct aggression. Girls, by contrast, are more often engaged in what is called collaborative discourse, in which they talk and act reciprocally, each responding to what the other has just said or done, while at the same time trying to get her own initiatives across. This does not imply that girls' interactions are conflict free, but rather that girls pursue their individual goals in the context of also striving to maintain group harmony (summary in Maccoby, 1998).

The themes that appear in boys' fantasies, the stories they invent, the scenarios they enact when playing with other boys, and the fictional fare they prefer (books, television) involve danger, conflict, destruction, heroic actions by male heroes, and trials of physical strength, considerably more often than is the case for girls. Girls' fantasies and play themes tend to be oriented around domestic or romantic scripts, portraying characters who are involved in social relationships and depicting the maintenance or restoration of order and safety.

Girls' and boys' close friendships are qualitatively different in some respects. Girls' friendships are more intimate, in the sense that girl friends share information about the details of their lives and concerns. Boys typically know less about their friends' lives, and base their friendship on shared activities.

Boys' groups larger than dyads are in some respects more cohesive than girls' groups. Boys in groups seek and achieve more autonomy from adults than girls do, and explicitly exclude girls from their activities more commonly than girls exclude boys. Boys more often engage in joint risky activities, and close ranks to protect a group member from adult detection and censure. And friendships among boys are more interconnected; that is, friends of a given boy are more likely to be friends with each other than is the case for several girls who are all friends of a given girl (Markovitz, Benenson, & Dolenszky, 2001). The fact that boys' friendships are more interconnected does not mean that they are closer in the sense of intimacy. Rather, it may imply that male friends are more accustomed to functioning as a unit, perhaps having a clearer group identity.

HOW SEX-DISTINCTIVE SUBCULTURES ARE FORMED

In a few instances, researchers have observed the process of group formation from the first meeting of a group over several subsequent meetings. An up-close view of the formation of gendered subcultures among young children has been provided by Nicolopoulou (1994). She followed classrooms of preschool children through a school year, beginning at the time they first entered the school. Every day, any child could tell a story to a teacher, who recorded the story as the child told it. At the end of the day, the teacher read aloud to the class the stories that were recorded that day, and the child author of each story was invited to act it out with the help of other children whom the child selected to act out different parts. At the beginning of the year, stories could be quite rudimentary (e.g., "There was a boy. And a girl. And a wedding."). By the end of the year, stories became greatly elaborated, and different members of the class produced stories related to themes previously introduced by others. In other words, a corpus of shared knowledge, meanings, and scripts grew up, unique to the children in a given classroom and reflecting their shared experiences.

More important for our present purposes, there was a progressive divergence between the stories told by girls and those told by boys. Gender differences were present initially, and the thematic content differed more and more sharply as time went on, with boys increasingly focusing on themes of conflict, danger, heroism, and "winning," while girls' stories increasingly depicted family, nonviolent themes. At the beginning of the year, children might call upon others of both sexes to act in their stories, but by the end of the year, they almost exclusively called upon children of their own sex to enact the roles in their stories. Thus, although all the children in the class were exposed to the stories told by both sexes, the girls picked up on one set of themes and the boys on another, and two distinct subcultures emerged.

Can this scenario serve as a prototype for the formation of distinctive male and female "subcultures" among children? Yes, in the sense that the essence of these cultures is a set of socially shared cognitions, including common knowledge and mutually congruent expectations, and common interests in specific themes and scripts that distinguish the two sexes. These communalities can be augmented in a set of children coming together for the first time, since by age 5 or 6, most will already have participated in several same-sex groups, or observed them in operation on TV, so they are primed for building gender-distinct subcultures in any new group of children they enter. Were we to ask, "Is gender socially constructed?" the answer would surely be "yes." At the same time, there may well be a biological contribution to the nature of the subculture each sex chooses to construct.

SOCIALIZATION WITHIN SAME-SEX GROUPS

There has long been evidence that pairs of friends—mostly same-sex friends—influence one another (see Dishion, Spracklen, & Patterson, 1996, for a recent example). However, only recently has research focused on the effects of the amount of time young children spend playing with other children of their own sex. Martin and Fabes (2001) observed a group of preschoolers over a 6-month period, to obtain stable scores for how much time they spent with same-sex playmates (as distinct from their time spent in mixed-sex or other-sex play). They examined the changes that occurred, over the 6 months of observation, in the degree of sex typing in children's play activities. Martin and Fabes reported that the more time boys spent playing with other boys, the greater the increases in their activity level, rough-and-tumble play, and sex-typed choices of toys and games, and the less time they spent near adults. For girls, by contrast, large amounts of time spent with other girls was associated with increasing time spent near adults, and with decreasing aggression, decreasing activity level, and increasing choices of girl-type play materials and activities. This new work points to a powerful role for same-sex peers in shaping one another's sex-typed behavior, values, and interests.

WHAT COMES NEXT?

The recent focus on children's same-sex groups has revitalized developmental social psychology, and promising avenues for the next phases of research on gender development have appeared. What now needs to be done?

1. Investigators need to study both the variations and the similarities among same-sex groups in their agendas and interactive processes. The extent of generality across groups remains largely unexplored. The way gender is enacted in groups undoubtedly changes with age. And observations in other cultures indicate that play in same-sex children's groups reflects what

different cultures offer in the way of materials, play contexts, and belief systems. Still, it seems likely that there are certain sex-distinctive themes that appear in a variety of cultural contexts.

2. Studies of individual differences need to be integrated with the studies of group process. Within each sex, some children are only marginally involved in same-sex groups or dyads, whereas others are involved during much of their free time. And same-sex groups are internally differentiated, so that some children are popular or dominant while others consistently occupy subordinate roles or may even be frequently harassed by others. We need to know more about the individual characteristics that underlie these variations, and about their consequences.

3. Children spend a great deal of their free time in activities that are not gender differentiated at all. We need to understand more fully the conditions under which gender is salient in group process and the conditions under which it is not.

Recommended Reading

Benenson, J.F., Apostolaris, N.H., & Parnass, J. (1997). (See References)
Maccoby, E.E. (1998). (See References)
Martin, C.L., & Fabes, R.A. (2001). (See References)

Note

1. Address correspondence to Eleanor E. Maccoby, Department of Psychology, Stanford University, Stanford, CA 94305-2130.

References

Benenson, J.F., Apostolaris, N.H., & Parnass, J. (1997). Age and sex differences in dyadic and group interaction. *Developmental Psychology, 33,* 538–543.

Benenson, J.F., Nicholson, C., Waite, A., Roy, R., & Simpson, A. (2001). The influence of group size on children's competitive behavior. *Child Development, 72,* 921–928.

Cole, J.D., Dodge, K.A., Schwartz, D., Cillessen, A.H.N., Hubbard, J.A., & Lemerise, E.A. (1999). It takes two to fight: A test of relational factors, and a method for assessing aggressive dyads. *Developmental Psychology, 36,* 1179–1188.

Dishion, T.J., Spracklen, K.M., & Patterson, G.R. (1996). Deviancy training in male adolescent friendships. *Behavior Therapy, 27,* 373–390.

Levine, J.M., & Moreland, R.L. (1998). Small groups. In D.T. Gilbert, S.T. Fiske, & G. Lindzey (Eds.), *Handbook of social psychology* (Vol. 2, pp. 415–469). Boston: McGraw-Hill.

Maccoby, E.E. (1998). *The two sexes: Growing up apart, coming together.* Cambridge, MA: Harvard University Press.

Markovitz, H., Benenson, J.F., & Dolenszky, E. (2001). Evidence that children and adolescents have internal models of peer interaction that are gender differentiated. *Child Development, 72,* 879–886.

Martin, C.L., & Fabes, R.A. (2001). The stability and consequences of young children's same-sex peer interactions. *Developmental Psychology, 37,* 431–446.

Nicolopoulou, A. (1997). Worldmaking and identity formation in children's narrative play-acting. In B. Cox & C. Lightfoot (Eds.), *Sociogenic perspectives in internalization* (pp. 157–187). Hillsdale, NJ: Erlbaum.

Ruble, D.N., & Martin, C.L. (1998). Gender development. In W. Damon & N. Eisenberg (Eds.), *Handbook of child psychology* (5th ed., Vol. 3, pp. 933–1016). New York: John Wiley & Sons.

Strayer, F.F. (1980). Social ecology of the preschool peer group. In W.A. Collins (Ed.), *Minnesota Symposium on Child Psychology: Vol. 13. Development of cognitions, affect and social relations* (pp. 165–196). Hillsdale, NJ: Erlbaum.

Vaughn, B.E., Colvin, T.N., Azria, M.R., Caya, L., & Krzysik, L. (2001). Dyadic analyses of friendship in a sample of preschool-aged children attending Headstart. *Child Development, 72,* 862–878.

This article has been reprinted as it originally appeared in *Current Directions in Psychological Science*. Citation information for this article as originally published appears above.

New Directions in the Study of Gender Similarities and Differences

Janet Shibley Hyde[1]
University of Wisconsin–Madison

Abstract

I review new trends in research on the psychology of gender. The gender similarities hypothesis holds that males and females are similar on most, but not all, psychological variables. Gender is not only an individual-difference or person variable but also a stimulus variable. Emerging approaches to cross-national measurement of constructs such as gender equality provide new insights into patterns of gender differences and similarities across cultures. Current neuroscience approaches emphasize neural plasticity and provide the opportunity to study neural correlates of males' and females' differential experiences.

Keywords

gender differences; meta-analysis; cultural influence; brain plasticity

For at least the last century, psychological scientists, as well as members of the general public, have been convinced that human males and females differ psychologically in important and substantial ways. Psychological scientists, basing their ideas on key reviews such as Maccoby and Jacklin's (1974), have thought and taught that there are reliable gender differences in verbal ability (females scoring higher), mathematical and spatial abilities (males scoring higher on both), aggressiveness (males higher), and activity level (males higher). Members of the general public, influenced by bestsellers such as John Gray's *Men Are from Mars, Women Are from Venus* and Deborah Tannen's *You Just Don't Understand: Men and Women in Conversation,* believe that men and women are fundamentally different (Prentice & Miller, 2006). Here I review current scientific evidence on psychological gender differences and similarities, as well as current and future directions to advance this area of research.

GENDER SIMILARITIES AND DIFFERENCES

Gender-differences research is an extremely active area; often 50 or more studies can be found on a single aspect of gender differences. *Meta-analysis* has emerged as an excellent method for assessing these large research literatures to determine which findings are reliable. Meta-analysis is a statistical method that allows the researcher to synthesize the statistical findings from numerous studies of the same question—for example, "Are there gender differences in aggression?" An important statistic in meta-analysis is the *effect size,* which measures the magnitude of the gender difference:

$$d = \frac{M_M - M_F}{S_W}$$

where d is the effect size, M_M is the mean score for males, M_F is the mean score for females, and s_w is the pooled within-gender standard deviation. Positive values indicate that males scored higher and negative values indicate that females scored higher; d measures how far apart the average male and female scores are, in standard-deviation units.

In a recent review, I was able to identify 46 different meta-analyses that assessed psychological gender differences (Hyde, 2005). They spanned a wide range of domains, including cognitive abilities, communication, social behavior and personality, psychological well-being, and other miscellaneous areas. A sample of these meta-analyses and the associated effect sizes is shown in Table 1.

I extracted the effect sizes from the meta-analyses and analyzed them for patterns. Which are the large gender differences? Which are the small ones? Cohen (1988) provided guidelines for interpreting the magnitude of effect sizes based on the d statistic: .20 is a small effect, .50 is a moderate effect, and .80 is large. I therefore grouped effect sizes into those that fell in the small range ($0.11 \leq d \leq 0.35$), the moderate range ($0.36 \leq d \leq 0.65$), and the large range ($d = 0.66$ to 1.00). I added two categories: differences that are near zero or trivial ($0 \leq d \leq .10$) and differences that are very large ($d > 1.0$).

The surprising result was that 48% of the effect sizes were in the small range and an additional 30% were near zero. That is, fully 78% of the effect sizes for gender differences were small or close to zero. Stated another way, within-gender variability is typically much larger than between-gender variability.

Table 1. *A sample of effect sizes extracted from 46 meta-analyses of research on psychological gender differences*

Variable	No. of reports	Effect size (d)
Cognitive variables		
Mathematics problem solving (Hyde, Fennema, & Lamon, 1990)	48	+0.08
Mathematics (Hedges & Nowell, 1995)	6*	+0.16
Reading comprehension (Hedges & Nowell, 1995)	5*	−0.09
Mental rotation (Voyer, Voyer, & Bryden, 1995)	78	+0.56
Communication		
Self-disclosure (Dindia & Allen, 1992)	205	−0.18
Smiling (La France, Hecht, & Paluck, 2003)	418	−0.40
Social and personality variables		
Physical aggression (Archer, 2004)	111	+0.33 to +0.84
Verbal aggression (Archer, 2004)	68	+0.09 to +0.55
Helping behavior (Eagly & Crowley, 1986)	99	+0.13
Leadership effectiveness (Eagly, Karau, & Makhijani, 1995)	76	−0.02
Self-esteem (Kling, Hyde, Showers, & Buswell, 1999)	216	+0.21
Depression symptoms (Twenge & Nolen-Hoeksema, 2002)	49	−0.16
Attitudes about casual sex (Oliver & Hyde, 1993)	10	+0.81
Miscellaneous		
Throwing velocity (Thomas & French, 1985)	12	+2.18
Moral reasoning: Justice orientation (Jaffee & Hyde, 2000)	95	+0.19

Source: Hyde (2005).
Asterisks indicate that data were from major, national samples.

These findings led me to propose the Gender Similarities Hypothesis (Hyde, 2005), which states that males and females are similar on most, but not all, psychological variables. This view is strikingly different from the prevailing assumptions of difference found among the general public and even among researchers.

Exceptions to the pattern of gender similarities do exist, but they are few in number. The largest gender differences were in the domain of motor performance, for behaviors such as throwing velocity ($d = 2.18$; Thomas & French, 1985). Large gender differences were found in some—but not all—aspects of sexuality, including incidence of masturbation and attitudes about sex in a casual, uncommitted relationship (Oliver & Hyde, 1993). Across several meta-analyses, aggression showed a moderate gender difference ($d = 0.50$), with males being more aggressive (e.g., Archer, 2004).

Meta-analyses also provide abundant evidence that effect sizes in a given domain are heterogeneous and that not only the magnitude but even the direction of gender differences depends on the context in which behavior is measured. A classic example comes from Eagly and Crowley's (1986) meta-analysis of research on gender differences in helping behavior. Averaged over all studies, $d = 0.34$, indicating that men helped more. However, for studies in which onlookers were present and participants were aware of it, $d = 0.74$, and when no onlookers were present, $d = -0.02$. These findings were consistent with Eagly and Crowley's predictions based on social-role theory; chivalrous and heroic helping is part of the male role and is facilitated when onlookers are present, resulting in a large gender difference.

I argue that gender similarities are, scientifically, as interesting as gender differences. Future researchers, whether they are gender researchers or researchers who have conducted casual tests for gender differences in research focused on another question, should report both differences and similarities so that we have a balanced view of the two.

GENDER AS A STIMULUS

In the preponderance of psychological research, gender is considered to be an individual-difference or person variable. An alternative approach recognizes that gender is a social-stimulus variable as well. Here I review two lines of research that support this view: research on gender bias in evaluations of leaders, and the Baby X studies.

In experimental research on gender and the evaluation of leaders, evaluators receive information about a leader, typically as a written vignette but sometimes as a videotape or live scenario by a person trained to engage in a standard set of behaviors. The gender of the leader is manipulated while all other factors are held constant. Thus any differences in ratings of male and female leaders must be due to gender and not to other confounding factors.

Eagly and colleagues meta-analyzed this research literature, locating 61 relevant studies (Eagly, Makhijani, & Klonsky, 1992). Overall, there was little evidence of gender bias in the evaluation of leaders ($d = 0.06$). In certain circumstances, however, gender bias was larger. For example, female leaders portrayed as using an autocratic style were evaluated less favorably than comparable male leaders ($d = 0.30$).

A second example comes from a classic experiment by Condry and Condry (1976). Participants viewed a videotape of a baby's emotional responses to a jack-in-the-box popping open. The baby stared and then cried. Half the adult viewers were told that the baby was a boy and half were told it was a girl. Those who thought the baby was a boy labeled the emotions "anger"; the other half called the "girl's" emotions "fear." In short, the adults read the emotions differently depending on the baby's gender. Numerous studies using this Baby X paradigm have replicated the finding that adults respond differently to an infant depending on whether they think the child is a boy or a girl (Stern & Karraker, 1989).

The broader implication here is that, both in laboratory experiments and in real life, an individual's gender acts as a stimulus that influences people's responses to the person. This principle deserves more theoretical, empirical, and methodological attention. Methodologically, for example, participants' behavior may be substantially influenced by the gender of the experimenter, but researchers rarely test this effect.

SOCIOCULTURAL INFLUENCES ON GENDER DIFFERENCES

Some of the most exciting research and theory on sociocultural influences on psychological gender differences is coming from cross-national research and research on gender and ethnicity in the United States.

Cross-National Research

The availability of major databases such as the United Nations data on gender equality (or lack thereof) in nations around the world (http://hdr.undp.org/hdr2006/statistics/indicators/229.html) has contributed to important developments in the ability of psychological scientists to test hypotheses about links between sociocultural factors and gender differences and similarities in behavior. These advances in research capabilities have been accompanied by advances in theory.

Eagly and Wood (1999) proposed social-structural theory as an explanation for the origins of gender differences in human behavior. According to social-structural theory, a society's division of labor by gender drives all other gender differences in behavior. That is, gender differences in behavior are created by social structures, and particularly by the different roles that women and men occupy. Psychological gender differences result from individuals' adaptations to the particular restrictions on or opportunities for their gender in their society. Eagly and Wood acknowledged biological differences between women and men, such as differences in size and strength and women's capacity to bear and nurse children, but they argued that these physical differences are important mainly because they are amplified by cultural beliefs and roles. Men's greater size and strength have led them to pursue activities such as warfare that in turn gave them greater status and power than women. Once men were in these roles, their behavior became more dominant and women's behavior accommodated and became more subordinate. The division of labor by gender, in which women were responsible for home and family, led women to acquire role-related skills such as cooking and caring for children. In this way, women acquired nurturing behaviors and a facility for relationships.

Eagly and Wood (1999) reanalyzed Buss's 37-cultures data (Buss, 1989), which are widely believed to support evolutionary-psychology theories, to examine variations in patterns of mate preferences across cultures, making use of the U.N. database on gender equality across nations. Their hypothesis was that the greater the gender gap in status in a culture, the greater would be the psychological gender differences. Societies characterized by gender equality should show far less psychological gender differentiation. Consistent with predictions, correlations were high between societies' gender inequality and the magnitude of the difference between women and men in that society on psychological measures of mate preferences. Studies such as this represent an important future direction for gender research.

Gender and Ethnicity in the United States

Scholars in women's studies have long urged the study of the intersection of gender and ethnicity. Translated to the language of psychological science, this is equivalent to a hypothesis of an interaction of gender by ethnicity. That is, gender differences—or gender phenomena more generally—are expected to differ across ethnic groups. Because so much research is based on samples of college students and because the great majority of them are White, most of what we know about gender differences and similarities is actually about gender differences and similarities among Whites. Clearly, investigations of gender phenomena in different U.S. ethnic groups are an important new direction for research.

One example comes from a meta-analysis of studies of gender differences in self-esteem, based on 216 effect sizes (Kling, Hyde, Showers, & Buswell, 1999). It is widely believed that girls and women have lower self-esteem than men and boys do, particularly beginning in adolescence. The meta-analysis found, in contrast, that the effect size was small ($d = 0.21$). The important point here, though, is that the effect size for White samples was $d = 0.20$, whereas the effect size for Black samples was $d = -0.04$ (insufficient numbers of studies of other ethnic groups were available to permit computation of average effect sizes). That is, the much-touted gender gap in self-esteem is small in Whites and nonexistent in Blacks. This illustrates the extent to which psychology has been a psychology of Whites and, in particular, gender psychology has been a psychology of White women and men. An important new direction in research will be to examine whether "well established" gender phenomena are similar or different across ethnic groups.

NEUROSCIENCE AND GENDER DIFFERENCES

Although members of the general public tend to believe that any pattern of behavior that is rooted in the brain is "hard wired," immutable, or something one is "born with," contemporary neuroscientists are in fact immersed in the study of brain *plasticity* (e.g., Cohen-Cory, 2002; Kolb, Gibb, & Robinson, 2003;

Tang et al., 2006): the capacity of the nervous system to change its organization and function over time. As the brain develops, certain synapses form and stabilize, whereas others are pruned and removed. Brain plasticity can be affected by many factors including experience, drugs, hormones, maturation, and stress. For example, a repeated experience that results in the activation of a particular set of synapses can lead to long-term potentiation (or alternately, depression) of the activity of those synapses.

In the era of functional magnetic resonance imaging research, it is common to see reports of studies finding that different brain regions are activated in males compared with females during activities such as solving difficult mathematics problems. It is easy to assume that these differences are "hard wired" and that they explain gender differences in performance, but an equally viable interpretation is that males and females have different experiences related to mathematics as they grow up, and that these different experiences have, on average, enhanced synaptic connections in some regions for males and in other regions for females. Moreover, gender similarities in performance can be associated with activation of different brain regions in males and females, and gender differences in performance can be found when similar brain regions are activated in males and females (Bell, Willson, Wilman, Dave, & Silverstone, 2006). Certainly the study of gender-related brain plasticity will be an important direction for new research.

CONCLUSIONS

I have identified four current and future directions for gender research: the gender similarities hypothesis, analysis of gender as a stimulus variable, studies of sociocultural variations in gender differences, and the recognition of brain plasticity. These ideas lead to four suggestions for future research. First, researchers should strive for balanced reporting of both gender differences and gender similarities. Second, although the tradition in psychological research has been to view gender as an individual-difference or person variable, gender can also be a potent stimulus variable. Research and theory analyzing ways and situations in which gender acts as a stimulus are important directions for the future. This approach could effect a major change in the way in which we conceptualize gender in psychology. Third, cultural psychology is a rapidly expanding area, providing researchers with new tools to measure and understand sociocultural influences on women's and men's behavior. I envision far more ambitious studies of gender roles cross-nationally, as well as more dedicated attention to patterns of gender differences and similarities across ethnic groups in the United States. Fourth, the nervous system is characterized by great plasticity. Future neuroscience research can profitably seek to discover linkages between gender-differentiated experiences on the one hand and gender differences in brain structure and function on the other.

Recommended Reading

Eagly, A.H., & Wood, W. (1999). (See References)
Hyde, J.S. (2005). (See References)

Hyde, J.S., & Linn, M.C. (2006). Gender similarities in mathematics and science. *Science, 314,* 599–600.

Kling, K.C., Hyde, J.S., Showers, C., & Buswell, B. (1999). (See References)

Acknowledgments—Research reported here was supported by NSF REC 0635444. I thank Sara Lindberg for comments on an earlier draft.

Note

1. Address correspondence to Janet Shibley Hyde, Department of Psychology, University of Wisconsin, 1202 W. Johnson St., Madison, WI 53706; e-mail: jshyde@wisc.edu.

References

Archer, J. (2004). Sex differences in aggression in real-world settings: A meta-analytic review. *Review of General Psychology, 8,* 291–322.

Bell, E.C., Willson, M.C., Wilman, A.H., Dave, S., & Silverstone, P.H. (2006). Males and females differ in brain activation during cognitive tasks. *NeuroImage, 30,* 529–538.

Buss, D.M. (1989). Sex differences in human mate preferences: Evolutionary hypotheses tested in 37 cultures. *Behavioral and Brain Sciences, 12,* 1–14.

Cohen, J. (1988). *Statistical power analysis for the behavioral sciences* (2nd ed.). Hillsdale, NJ: Erlbaum.

Cohen-Cory, S. (2002). The developing synapse: Construction and modulation of synaptic structures and circuits. *Science, 298,* 770–776.

Condry, J.C., & Condry, S. (1976). Sex differences: A study of the eye of the beholder. *Child Development, 47,* 812–819.

Dindia, K., & Allen, M. (1992). Sex differences in self-disclosure: A meta-analysis. *Psychological Bulletin, 112,* 106–124.

Eagly, A.H., & Crowley, M. (1986). Gender and helping behavior: A meta-analytic review of the social psychological literature. *Psychological Bulletin, 100,* 283–308.

Eagly, A.H., Karau, S.J., & Makhijani, M.G. (1995). Gender and the effectiveness of leaders: A meta-analysis. *Psychological Bulletin, 117,* 125–145.

Eagly, A.H., Makhijani, M.G., & Klonsky, B.G. (1992). Gender and the evaluation of leaders: A meta-analysis. *Psychological Bulletin, 111,* 3–22.

Eagly, A.H., & Wood, W. (1999). The origins of sex differences in human behavior: Evolved dispositions versus social roles. *American Psychologist, 54,* 408–423.

Hedges, L.V., & Nowell, A. (1995). Sex differences in mental test scores, variability, and numbers of high-scoring individuals. *Science, 269,* 41–45.

Hyde, J.S. (2005). The gender similarities hypothesis. *American Psychologist, 60,* 581–592.

Hyde, J.S., Fennema, E., & Lamon, S. (1990). Gender differences in mathematics performance. A meta-analysis. *Psychological Bulletin, 107,* 139–155.

Jaffee, S., & Hyde, J.S. (2000). Gender differences in moral orientation: A meta-analysis. *Psychological Bulletin, 126,* 703–726.

Kling, K.C., Hyde, J.S., Showers, C.J., & Buswell, B.N. (1999). Gender differences in self-esteem: A meta-analysis. *Psychological Bulletin, 125,* 470–500.

Kolb, B., Gibb, R., & Robinson, T.E. (2003). Brain plasticity and behavior. *Current Directions in Psychological Science, 12,* 1–5.

LaFrance, M., Hecht, M.A., & Paluck, E.L. (2003). The contingent smile: A meta-analysis of sex differences in smiling. *Psychological Bulletin, 129,* 305–334.

Maccoby, E.E., & Jacklin, C.N. (1974). *The psychology of sex differences.* Stanford: Stanford University Press.

Oliver, M.B., & Hyde, J.S. (1993). Gender differences in sexuality: A meta-analysis. *Psychological Bulletin, 114,* 29–51.

Prentice, D.A., & Miller, D.T. (2006). Essentializing differences between women and men. *Psychological Science, 17,* 129–135.

Stern, M., & Karraker, K.H. (1989). Sex stereotyping of infants: A review of gender labeling studies. *Sex Roles, 20,* 501–522.

Tang, Y., Zhang, W., Chen, K., Feng, S., Ji, Y., Shen, J., et al. (2006). Arithmetic processing in the brain shaped by cultures. *Proceedings of the National Academy of Sciences, USA, 103,* 10775–10780.

Thomas, J.R., & French, K.E. (1985). Gender differences across age in motor performance: A meta-analysis. *Psychological Bulletin, 98,* 260–282.

Twenge, J.M., & Nolen-Hoeksema, S. (2002). Age, gender, race, socioeconomic status, and birth cohort differences on the Children's Depression Inventory: A meta-analysis. *Journal of Abnormal Psychology, 111,* 578–588.

Voyer, D., Voyer, S., & Bryden, M.P. (1995). Magnitude of sex differences in spatial abilities: A meta-analysis and consideration of critical variables. *Psychological Bulletin, 117,* 250–270.

Section 5: Critical Thinking Questions

1. How do experiences in the peer group shape children's likelihood of excluding peers based on their gender (Killen)? How do experiences with same-sex and other-sex peers affect children's use and understanding of sarcasm (Katz and colleagues)?

2. Both Maccoby and Hyde have conducted research on gender for years and offer insightful directions for future work in this area. Is Maccoby's emphasis on sex-segregated socialization compatible with Hyde's argument for a gender similarities approach to the study of gender? Explain.

This article has been reprinted as it originally appeared in *Current Directions in Psychological Science*. Citation information for this article as originally published appears above.